EUROPE
by
BIKE

"To be able to feel a storm in the air when the sky is perfectly blue...
to spend days in the rain and realize that you can survive...to sense
your body becoming stronger and your mind more self-sufficient and,
of course...to experience what you otherwise would have missed —
this is bicycle touring.

"Sitting on the seat of a bicycle slows down your world to a pace
where you can't avoid your surroundings. You begin to share other
people's lives by peddling slowly into them, rather than speeding by.
When you take up bicycle touring, you will be surprised by how much
you've missed in life. Even so, taking that first big step into the
unknown is always kind of scary. To make that step a little easier,
Karen and Terry Whitehill have written a guide to help you plan your
own adventure. So good luck...you are about to experience life in the
slow lane!"

— by Larry Savage, whose unforgettable
round-the-world bicycle adventure with his
late wife, Barbara, is told in her best-selling
book Miles from Nowhere

the
MOUNTAINEERS

EUROPE
by
BIKE

Karen & Terry Whitehill

THE MOUNTAINEERS: Organized 1906
*"... to explore, study, preserve, and enjoy the
natural beauty of the Northwest."*

© 1987 by The Mountaineers
All rights reserved

Published by The Mountaineers
306 2nd Avenue West, Seattle, Washington 98119

Published simultaneously in Canada by Douglas & McIntyre, Ltd.
1615 Venables Street, Vancouver, British Columbia V5L 2H1

Cover design by Elizabeth Watson
Book design by Bridget Culligan
Photos by the authors
Maps by Newell Cartographics

Manufactured in the United States of America

Cover photo: Cobblestones and windmills in southern Holland
Title photo: Bouncing down a cobblestone street in Beilstein, West Germany

Library of Congress Cataloging in Publication Data

Whitehill, Karen, 1957-
    Europe by bike.

    Includes index.
        1. Bicycle touring — Europe — Guide-books.   2. Europe —
Description and travel — 1971-   — Guide-books.
I. Whitehill, Terry, 1954-   . II. Title.
GV1046.E85W55   1987   914   86-28579
ISBN 0-89886-119-5 (pbk.)

0   9   8   7

5   4   3   2

CONTENTS

Preface 9

Part I — EUROPE BY BIKE

Why by bicycle? 12
Planning your trip 13
Buying and outfitting a bike 17

What to take 21
Survival skills 26

Part II — 18 TOURS GEARED FOR DISCOVERY

Tour No. 1: A National Trust
  Tour of England —
  Canterbury to York,
  England 35

Tour No. 2: Waffles, Champagne,
  and Châteaux — *Brussels,*
  Belgium, to Angers,
  France 55

Tour No. 3: Say Cheese —
  Rotterdam, Holland, to the
  Ijsselmeer 71

Tour No. 4: Biking with the
  Vikings — *Stockholm,*
  Sweden, to Copenhagen,
  Denmark 77

Tour No. 5: Ferry Tales in
  Denmark — *Copenhagen,*
  Denmark, to Kiel, West
  Germany 87

Tour No. 6: A Hill-Studded Ride
  to the Rhine — *Kiel to Köln,*
  West Germany 97

The harbor ferry in Amsterdam carries scores of cyclists.

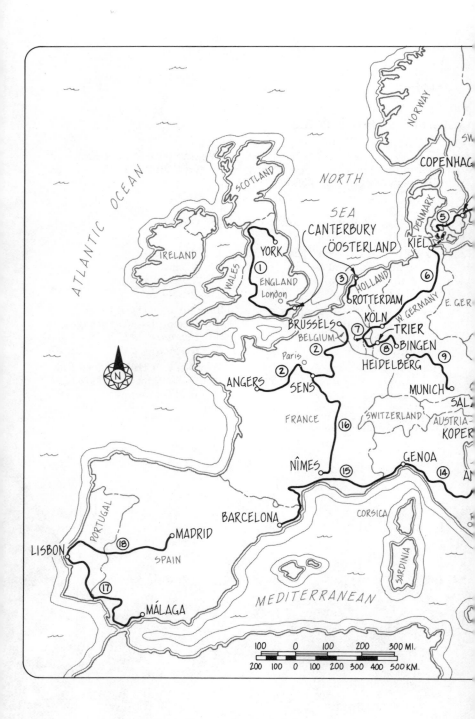

Tour No. 7: To Belgium,
    Luxembourg, and Back —
    *Köln to Trier, West
    Germany* 109

Tour No. 8: Rhine, Wine, and
    Tourists — *Trier to Bingen,
    West Germany* 117

Tour No. 9: Romantic Roaming
    — *Heidelberg to Munich,
    West Germany* 123

Tour No. 10: In Tune with the
    Danube — *Salzburg to
    Vienna, Austria* 135

Tour No. 11: Tip-to-Tip along a
    Stunning Coast — *Koper to
    Bar, Yugoslavia* 145

Tour No. 12: Pedaling on the
    Peloponnese — *Patras to
    Athens, Greece* 161

Tour No. 13: Visions of the
    Ancients — *Iraklion to
    Patras, Greece* 175

Tour No. 14: Touring Tuscany —
    Ancona to Genoa, Italy 185

Tour No. 15: Rolling along the
    Rivieras — *Genoa, Italy, to
    Barcelona, Spain* 197

Tour No. 16: All in Good Taste —
    Nîmes to Sens, France 211

Tour No. 17: Coasting the Sol —
    *Málaga, Spain, to Lisbon,
    Portugal* 221

Tour No. 18: Corks, Storks, and
    Conquistadores — *Lisbon,
    Portugal, to Madrid,
    Spain* 233

Index 243

Amsterdam gives the green light to cyclists in big-city style.

PREFACE

On a grey, drizzly night in early April, 1984, we wheeled our pack-laden touring bicycles through the outer doors of Brussels' Zaventem Airport and out into the rapidly darkening Belgian evening. We were exhausted and tense from an 18-hour ordeal of plane hopping and baggage hunting, and we were still blushing from the mass hilarity that swept through the airport crowd when, helmeted in sturdy white plastic, we pushed our ridiculously loaded mounts out through the swinging doors of customs. Weary, worried, and embarrassed, we had one more challenge left to face. How would we find an unseen, unfamiliar campground hiding somewhere beyond the city limits before total darkness or complete panic left us unable to ride another kilometer?

Ninety minutes later, after a misdirected sortie down a Brussels highway and a friendly admonition from two Belgian motor police who politely guided us onto a safer and more legal route, we were settled into a large, muddy campground, thinking wistfully of home while the icy spring rain beat against the walls of our tent.

Thus began a European adventure that would take us 11,000 miles (17,600 kilometers), introduce us to 14 countries and 13 languages, and enrich our lives with dozens of memorable encounters and a score of cherished friendships that warm our hearts to this day.

During the course of our one-year trek, we gained steadily in conditioning and experience, learned from our mistakes as well as from conversations shared with other bicyclers, and hungrily gathered tidbits of information from a 12-month "picnic" of delicious tastes, spectacular sights, and unforgettable experiences.

Europe by Bike: 18 Tours Geared for Discovery is the result of that year of discovery and exploration. We needed this book at hundreds of road junctions; we needed this book in the downtown tangles of cities without number; we needed this book that first cold and rainy night in Brussels when home seemed very far away.

Part I, "Europe by Bike," tells you how to prepare for your European cycling trip: route planning, packing, paperwork, equipment, and so forth. You should study it well in advance of your departure day, so that you'll have all the time you need to get ready.

Part II, "18 Tours Geared for Discovery," consists of 18 detailed, point-to-point tours. Each tour describes a ride within a single country or in two or three adjacent countries, and individual tours can be combined to give the specific cycling blend you want.

The introductory portion of each tour description offers useful information about the area you'll be riding in—shopping tips, points of interest, notes on culture and language, and suggestions about road maps and tourist literature. The descriptions of each tour include simple maps to aid in visualizing the route, detailed narrations of turns and terrain, and recommendations on camping and rooms. (To make these sections easier to use, turns, road names, and prominent landmarks are printed in boldface type.)

Use Part I to help you get yourself and your gear to Europe. Use Part II to help you discover Europe by bike. And, if you feel as we did after 12 never-to-be-forgotten months of pedaling, use the blank page inside the back cover to begin your list of tours for next year!

A NOTE ON SAFETY

The authors have provided important tips on bicycle safety in the introduction to this book. In addition, they and the publisher have taken all reasonable measures to ensure the accuracy of the route descriptions contained herein. Even so, bicycling on roads and highways entails certain unavoidable risks, and routes may have changed after this book was written. Current political conditions also may add to the risks of travel in Europe in ways that this book cannot predict. For these reasons, the descriptions in this book are not representations that a particular trip will be safe for you or your party. When you take a trip, you assume responsibility for your own safety. Keeping informed about current road conditions, weather changes, and political developments, combined with common sense, are the keys to a safe, enjoyable tour.

The Mountaineers

PART I

EUROPE BY BIKE

*Cycling the
Yugoslav Coast.*

11

Why by bicycle?

Antonio Ramos de Figueiredo is a storekeeper in a small city in Portugal. We rode into his town one rainy Sunday afternoon, shivering from the February chill, and found ourselves a hotel room. Or rather, Antonio found it for us. As was so often the case when we pedaled into the out-of-the-way towns in Europe — the little places that train and bus travelers seldom see and rarely take time to appreciate — the townspeople were drawn to us, their curiosity aroused by our unconventional mode of travel. Antonio was no different.

When he saw us standing in the rain in front of the only hotel in the city's downtown plaza and heard us speaking English, he graciously offered to act as our interpreter while we made arrangements for a room. This short, soft-spoken groceryman became a cherished friend that drizzly afternoon. He took us for a terrifying and unforgettable auto tour of the area at a minimum speed of 70 mph (that was before we broke free of the city limits); he treated us to coffee and pastries at his favorite cafe; and he invited us to his home for conversation and glasses of dark port wine that evening.

Like so many of our new European friends, Antonio was reluctant to see us go when it was time for us to ride on, and he urged us to return for another visit someday. "But next time," he assured us with a wink, "you'll come in a normal way." We smiled politely, as we'd done so many times before, then

A well-marked junction in France provides a good spot for a midday break.

looked at each other and shrugged. For we both knew that bicycling had spoiled us for life as "normal" European travelers, and never would we rely on planes or trains or tour buses to show us the delights that this amazing continent has to offer.

With planes and trains and tour buses, we could still have seen Europe's awesome cathedrals, luxurious palaces, and history-rich castles, but without our bicycles, we would never have met Antonio the storekeeper. Nor would we have met Alexsey the Russian scientist, André the French dairy farmer, Gunnar the Danish oil painter, Lauric the Yugoslav musician, or Mike the British fisheries inspector.

Perhaps we would have seen a few more fortresses without our bicycles. Certainly we would have covered more ground. But we wouldn't have heard the cows tearing up mouthfuls of grass on a hot August day in Luxembourg, and we wouldn't have breathed in the fragrance of fresh-washed sheets beside a farmhouse in Normandy. We wouldn't have felt such sorrow at leaving good friends behind us when we climbed aboard our plane for home after a year of cycling, nor would we have returned to the United States with so many invitations for future visits — in a more "normal" way.

So — that's why by bicycle.

Planning your trip

Begin with a good general book on European travel. *Let's Go: Europe* by Harvard Student Agencies and *Europe Through the Back Door* by Rick Steves are two of the books we studied. They'll provide you with more of the information pertinent to general European travel than this book has room for. Just to get you started, here's a brief summary of the most important things to do.

PASSPORTS AND VISAS. If you don't have a passport for international travel, you should apply for one two or three months in advance of your departure date. At peak times, the application process can take several weeks. Go to a passport agency or U.S. Post Office. Once you get your passport, record the number, the date of issue, and the issuing office — twice. Leave one copy at home with someone you can contact from Europe, and take one copy with you, stored separately from your passport. This will facilitate quick replacement if the passport is lost or stolen.

You'll also need to apply in advance for visas to certain Eastern European countries. Check with the passport office to be sure. None of the countries covered in this book requires an advance visa.

CAMPING PERMITS. A document we pulled out almost as often as our passports during the trip was our International Camping Carnet. If you're planning to camp as you cycle, this is a handy document to have. You'll be required to use it for camping in Denmark (although you can buy a Danish camping pass instead), and it's good for discounts in some other campgrounds in Western Europe. We found our carnet to be an excellent piece of identification to hand over at camping offices or hotels when we didn't want to part with our passports — for instance, when we needed them for banking or mail pickup during the day. (Tourist registration practices vary from country to country. Some managers will require that you turn over your passport until they can complete endless paperwork; others will settle for the carnet, and others will ask only for your first name.)

If you buy the carnet before you go, you'll need to purchase it through the National Campers and Hikers Association, 7172 Transit Road, Buffalo, New York 14221. The Canadian address is 51 West 22nd, Hamilton, Ontario, Canada L9C 4N5. The cost of about $20 includes a mandatory membership in the NCHA, with associated privileges (organization magazine, accidental death insurance, and equipment discounts).

The European campground system is extensive, well organized, and inexpensive, so take advantage of the campgrounds whenever possible. You'll meet the Europeans at their best — when they're on vacation, having fun, and eager to talk to others.

Camping outside of organized campgrounds is acceptable provided you obtain the landowner's permission (note the exception for Yugoslavia, Tour No. 11). We met a host of fascinating people this way — from dairy farmers to auto salesmen to olive growers. Sweden also allows freelance camping on unfenced land (Tour No. 4), but most other European countries frown on the practice. Make it a policy to always get an okay before you stay.

HEALTH INSURANCE. If you're taking a brief vacation from work or school to travel, you'll probably have health insurance already. But if you're giving up "normal" life, as we were, with goodbyes to job, apartment, car, and related insurance policies, you may want to give serious thought to investing in special medical insurance for travelers.

Ask your travel agent about a policy that covers medical and hospital expenses, medical evacuation, and repatriation of remains, baggage, and trip cancellation.

Also, write to the International Association for Medical Assistance to Travelers, 736 Center Street, Lewiston, New York 14092, or 188 Nicklin Road, Guelph, Ontario, Canada N1H 7L5. A free membership (donations are eagerly accepted) in this non-profit organization will provide you with the names of English-speaking physicians in more than 400 cities throughout the world. Associated doctors have agreed to serve English-speaking patients on a set fee system.

HOSTELS. If you're thinking of using hostels as one of your accommodation options along the way, you'll need to get an International Youth Hostel Federation card. Non-members can stay, but must pay more, in hostels in Israel, Sweden, and Yugoslavia. (Some Greek hostels don't require cards at all.)

As a married couple, we did our best to avoid the segregated lodgings and noisy surroundings common to hostels, but there were a few times when, stuck without a campground or an affordable hotel, we wished we'd had a card. Check your city telephone directory under "American Youth Hostels" to find a local office where you can purchase your card, or write to American Youth Hostels, P.O. Box 37613, Washington, D.C. 20013-7613, or the Canadian Hostelling Association, Place Vanier, Tower A, 333 River Road, Vanier City, Ottawa, Ontario, Canada K1L 8H9. Ask for information and an application form.

RESEARCH. Another worthwhile task to spend time and postage on

Greeting the morning with a toothbrush in a Greek olive grove.

before you begin your trip is contacting the national tourist offices of the European countries you're planning to visit. We wrote to each country's office, telling them of our trip and requesting free maps and general information. Any good city maps you can get in advance will be a blessing later, as there's nothing worse than riding into a large city without an adequate map. We also asked for specific information on cycling and camping. Holland, Denmark, and Ireland are especially helpful in providing detailed information for cycle tourists.

We've included tourist office addresses with the tours in Part II. Once you've written your letters and sent them off, it will be exciting to discover what the mailbox holds for you each day, and you can spend your evenings dreaming over brochures and maps and beginning to plan your sightseeing itinerary.

We used tourist-office literature, along with travel books checked out from the library, to help us make our choices about what to see, composing our cycling routes in a connect-the-dots game that was both challenging and exciting. The tours in Part II reflect our hours of research, and you'll find that each of the 18 routes includes a number of major tourist destinations.

A Swiss cyclist plans his route to Athens.

Undoubtedly, you'll want to learn more about the history and specific features of the areas you'll visit than this book can tell you, so get to know the travel shelves of your local library before you go.

You may want to carry a favorite travel guide with you on your trip. We waited to buy our guides until we arrived in each new area, thus cutting down on weight and expense, but if you're visiting only one or two countries on your ride, it will be easier to make your purchases in advance. The names of available guidebooks are noted with each tour route.

MAPS. Rather than spend an incredible amount of money buying detailed maps of each country at home, we used the free maps provided by the tourist offices to do our rough figuring of routes, times, and distances, then bought 1:200,000 or 1:300,000 maps within each country when we arrived. Maps are considerably less expensive in Europe than in bookstores at home. Again, if you'll be covering only a small area on your trip, you may want to go ahead and buy your maps in advance. Do take along a good map of the area you'll be arriving in. That way, you'll at least be able to get out of the airport and on your way without difficulty.

MAIL. We completed one more task during our pretrip planning that brought us a day of excitement and joy every three weeks for the next year. As we worked out our cycling routes, we compiled a list of cities, addresses, and tentative dates, choosing the best times and places to pick up mail from home. We distributed this list to families and friends, instructing them how to address the letters correctly and warning them to mail at least two weeks in advance of our pickup dates (three weeks in Yugoslavia, Greece, Spain, and Portugal).

For pickup at post offices, use the following address style: *WHITEHILL,* Terry, c/o *Poste Restante,* Brussels, Belgium. *Poste Restante* (general delivery) mail is sent to the main post office in cities with more than one post office. For American Express pickups (free if you have their travelers' checks), use this address style: *WHITEHILL,* Terry, Client Mail Service, American Express, 2 Place Louise, Brussels, Belgium. You can get a list of American Express office addresses when you buy your checks.

CONDITIONING. One more thing you should begin working on well in advance of your departure date is you! Too many cyclists spend the first weeks of their already short vacations wishing they had replacement sets of muscles and extra cardiovascular systems. Start working on your physical conditioning several months before your trip if you want to get the most enjoyment from those early weeks in the saddle.

If winter weather won't allow you to do much preparatory riding for a spring tour, any strenuous physical activity will help. Try jogging, racquetball, swimming, or rapid walking — anything that gets your heart rate up and your muscles pumping. Of course, cycling is the best way to toughen up the muscles you'll need. Try making friends with a stationary bicycle at the local gym. The fact that you haven't been "sitting around" before your trip will help you toughen up the beginning tourer's constant foe — the tender rear end.

If you haven't done cycle touring before, go out on at least one realistic trial run before your trip. If you'll be camping in Europe, it's a good idea to ride and camp at home first. If you're going to stay in hotels or hostels, then simply go out with loaded packs, preferably overnight, to get a feel for handling your bicycle and to find out what a daily riding regimen is like.

We rode a one-week, 400-mile loop around our home state about a month before our flight, and besides the conditioning benefit, we discovered a few things that helped us farther down the line. When a patch kit we were carrying suddenly refused to patch 10 miles from the nearest town, we learned the importance of having spare tubes, and when a logging truck nearly put us in a ditch, we gained a memory that made the European courtesy to come an even sweeter treat.

Buying and outfitting a bike

If you'll be buying a touring bike especially for your trip, and your knowledge of what to look for is limited, do what we did. Find two or three bike shops that specialize in touring, acquaint yourself with some knowledgeable employees, and begin asking questions. You'll probably get different opinions on which brand is best from every person you talk to, but if you keep listening, eventually you'll be able to make a good decision based on the information you've collected.

Another good way to find out more about touring bicycles, equipment, and maintenance is to read a general book on the sport of bicycle touring. *The Bicycle Touring Book* by Tim and Glenda Wilhelm or *Living on Two Wheels* by Dennis Coello are both good resources.

Important things to look for in touring bikes are the following:

- A sturdy frame, strong enough to carry heavy loads.
- Correct fit for the rider. It's too big if you can't straddle the frame with both feet flat on the ground and have an inch of clearance between you and the bar.
- Superior-quality wheels and touring tires (we recommend "clinchers" with Kevlar reinforcing) to provide you with a stable and durable ride. We chose the narrower 1-1/8-in tires because we didn't plan to do much rough-road riding, but if you want to explore lots of back roads, especially in Portugal, Spain, Yugoslavia, or Greece, you may want to opt for the 1-1/4-in width. (Mountain bikes are essentially an overkill for the majority of European roads, and you'll pay dearly in daily mileage and ease of ride if you choose to use one.)
- A high-quality, dependable braking system. If you haven't toured before, you'll be surprised at how much longer it takes to stop a loaded bicycle than an unloaded one. "Side-pull" brakes are easier to adjust than "center-pull," and we prefer them for that reason.
- Gearing that provides from 10 to 18 speeds, with the most important factor being the low-range capability. If you're new to touring, ask a bike shop employee to explain the complexities of gears and sprockets to you. Hills seem much steeper with a loaded bicycle, and you'll need the "granny" gears a good touring bike offers more often than you might expect.

Price is an important factor to consider when making your purchase, too. We went for middle-of-the-line Japanese bikes and equipped them with low-riding front racks and with rear racks. Because we knew we would be traveling together, we selected identical bikes (except for frame size) for ease of maintenance. Each bike cost about $425, and each carried its rider several thousand miles without a major breakdown.

"Extras" we consider to be essentials include frame-mounted water bottles, front and rear fenders, a rearview mirror, and a bell. European cyclists live and die by their bells, and in West Germany you'll be dinged right off the road by friendly tourers if you can't say hello with a bell. Other extras you'll need for your bike are toe clips, padded handlebars (or padded riding gloves), and a comfortable bike seat.

Get to know your bike seat before you go. Some hardcore cyclists might tell you that discomfort is just one of the penalties of the sport, that the seat must be rock hard to ensure freedom of movement, or some other crazy thing. Don't listen to them. You and your bike seat are going to be spending a lot of hours together. Make sure you're not incompatible before you go. If you just can't get comfortable on any seat, try out a sheepskin cover or one of the new gel covers on the market.

You'll need to choose touring bags for your bike, as well. If you'll be staying in hotels or hostels and you're a light packer, you might be able to get along with a handlebar bag and two rear saddlebags. If you're camping out or going for the long haul, you'll probably need the works — two front bags, two rear bags, and a handlebar bag.

Important things to look for in touring bags are quality of construction, ease of attachment to the racks, and strength of zippers and fasteners. We

A beaten bike bag tells a tale of many miles.

selected low-priced bags of bright, durable material instead of spending 35 to 50 percent more on top-of-the-line bags. Again, this will be a choice dictated by budget as well as personal preference. We used our bags for one year, day in and day out, and didn't have a broken zipper or snapped cord during the entire trip.

We talked to other cyclists who had spent twice as much on their touring bags, and all agreed on one thing. No matter how expensive the bags, they didn't keep their contents dry in major downpours. All of us relied on simple plastic grocery or garbage sacks to keep our belongings dry within the bags. But check on the latest developments before you make your purchase. Perhaps some innovative manufacturer has finally mastered the trick of keeping water out of bags that are repeatedly subjected to driving rainstorms, gallons of road spray, and occasional tidal waves from passing trucks.

Select your bags with their purposes in mind — a handlebar bag for valuables, delicate items, and things you want quick access to (camera, sunglasses, chocolate bars), two back bags to carry heavy or bulky items, and low-riding front bags (always a source of amazement to Europeans, as they're still quite rare among European tourers) to catch the extras.

You'll need to do some experimenting with loading to minimize wobble and weave. It's particularly important to load the front bags evenly in regard to weight and bulk. We were surprised to discover what seemingly insignificant things affected our wobble rates. As a result, we became positively superstitious about packing, driving each other crazy with our quirks and arguing about who got the bottle of vitamins or where an extra package of dry soup should go.

One trick for riders who have identical bags or for a single rider who has trouble staying organized is to number bike bags or differentiate them in some way and try to pack the same items in the same bag each day. Our packs started out with numbers, then they gained identities from the cloth souvenir patches we sewed on them. These patches, showing cities or tourist sights, also make excellent conversation starters with the local citizens.

Finally, you'll need to put together a maintenance kit for your bicycle, including such items as the following:

- Adjustable wrench — 6 in
- Allen wrenches
- Bike maintenance handbook — something lightweight for reference
- Brake pads
- Cables — one replacement each for gears and brakes
- Chain link removal tool
- Foldup tire
- Freewheel tool
- Helmet
- Locks — we carried both a metal shackle and a cable lock
- Lubricant
- Phillips and/or regular screwdriver
- Pliers
- Pump with pressure gauge
- Spokes — at least three or four

- Spoke wrench
- Tire irons
- Tubes — one or two for irreparable punctures or quick changes

We also mailed complete tire changes to a friend we planned to visit five months into our trip. Good-quality 27-in tires are difficult to find in many parts of Europe. If you're planning a trip of more than 4,000 miles, particularly in southern Europe, this is a good precaution. Otherwise, one emergency foldup tire should suffice.

What to take

The items you'll require as a "normal" European traveler are listed in most general travel books — passport, camping carnet, hostel card, and money. We've already dealt with most of these, but here are some things you should know about money, security, and equipment.

MONEY. Travelers' checks are one of the safest and most convenient ways to go. Purchasing travelers' checks usually involves paying a commission charge, but members of some organizations and holders of certain types of bank accounts can avoid those extra fees. Even if you do have to pay a commission charge, the security of knowing your travelers' checks will be replaced if lost or stolen is well worth the effort and cost of getting them.

If you'll be staying in Europe for several months, you may want to consider having part of your funds sent over later, but this can be quite an inconvenience — and expense. We chose to live with plump money pouches for a few months instead.

While you're doing your banking chores, it's also a good idea to pick up $30 or $40 worth of the currency of the country you'll be arriving in. Many large banks in the United States offer such international currency exchange. That way, you'll be sure you don't get caught "penniless" when you get off your plane in Europe.

SECURITY. Three essential pieces of personal equipment you'll want to take along on your trip are an under-clothing money pouch, a sturdy bicycle lock, and your common sense.

Money pouches come in many styles (shoulder, neck, or belt), but their purpose is always the same — to help you avoid the pickpockets and purse snatchers who prowl the streets of tourist areas, looking for anyone foolish enough to carry an exposed wallet or handbag. For comfort, we stowed our pouches in our handlebar bags when we were riding, but we always put them on immediately when we entered a large city or if we left our bikes even for a moment. Don't make the mistake of one California cyclist we talked to. He put down his handlebar bag "just for a minute" while waiting for a train in Rome. The next time he looked, the bag was gone, complete with passport, travelers' checks, and his visa for a trip to India.

Simple good fortune and the efforts of the guardian angel who rode 11,000 bumpy miles on our handlebars may be responsible for the fact that we never had a single item stolen during an entire year of travel. Certainly, we were often forced into vulnerable positions simply because of the nature of our transportation and accommodations. But, throughout our trip, we also un-

failingly followed some common-sense rules that helped us emerge un-
scathed when those around us were not so lucky:

- We always wore our money pouches inside our clothing when we were in
  a large city or mingling with a crowd.
- We always removed our valuables from our bicycles when we left them
  unattended.
- We always locked our bikes securely if we were leaving them for even a
  moment in a large city, or for several minutes in a small one.

Most of the crime that victimizes tourists in Europe takes place in big
cities or high-density tourist areas, so be especially careful there. But the
great thing about bicycle touring is that you'll be in between these places as
much as you'll be in them. We were continually delighted by the honesty of
the Europeans we encountered. Despite our disadvantage as linguistically
ignorant foreigners, we experienced very few attempts to overcharge us or
steal from us. Still, it never hurts to be careful.

PLANE TICKETS. Another essential thing you'll be taking with you to
Europe is your plane ticket. You'll want to shop around for the package that's
best for you. Because we were planning to stay in Europe for several months
but didn't have a specific return date set, we bought an "open-ended" ticket.
This allowed us to select our return date any time within one year after our
departure. However, it limited us as to the cities we could choose for our
arrival and departure, eventually forcing us into a snowy ride to Brussels to
catch a late-March plane flight home.

You'll have more freedom if you buy a one-way ticket to Europe and
purchase your return flight there, but this option is usually more expensive,
and it requires responsible money management on your part.

One other thing you should consider when you buy your plane ticket is your
arrival time in Europe. A midday or morning landing time will help you
avoid the frustrations we faced — a frenzied assembly and loading job in the
airport lobby and a twilight sortie into an unfamiliar city on arrival day.

BICYCLES AND RELATED GEAR. What about your bicycle? Can you
bring it with you? Yes. Getting it to Europe can be a bit of a headache, but it's
well worth it. The Europeans love bicycles — for racing. As a result, finding a
good touring bike there can be quite a chore. In some areas, it's almost
impossible. The majority of European tourers we met had bicycles and
equipment that were inferior to ours in quality, sophistication, and value for
the money. The few superior touring setups we did see were custom built to
the riders' specifications. You certainly won't have time for that on a three-
week visit!

Bike rental is common and inexpensive in Europe. Northern countries
have an overwhelming number of rental shops, with outlets in train stations,
tourist offices, and youth hostels. However, despite the quantity, the quality is
limited.

So if you already have a touring bike, bring it with you. If you're thinking
of buying one for the trip, save yourself a lot of time and effort — buy it at
home.

Most major airlines will accept your bike at no extra charge as one of your
two allotted pieces of checked luggage. Charter flights may be more stingy.

Regulations will vary as to whether your bike must be boxed, bagged, or simply wheeled aboard. The majority of carriers require you to at least loosen the handlebars and turn them sideways and remove the pedals, so that the bike takes up less space.

We recommend you also detach your rear derailleur and remove any loose items such as water bottles and handlebar-bag rack if you're not putting your bike in a carton. Also, if you have a bike computer, remove the wiring and mounting. We met one American cyclist whose computer setup was destroyed by the time he got his bike to Europe. He found himself with an expensive portable mileage meter and nothing to hook it up to.

We carefully dismantled our bikes, removing handlebars, pedals, and front wheels. Then we put them inside sturdy bike cartons provided by a local bike shop, padding them with excess baggage such as sleeping bags and clothing. We closed the boxes securely with a strong filament tape, and we wrote names, passport numbers, and flight numbers on the boxes and all other pieces of luggage.

You'll probably sweat and squirm when you relinquish your bike to a burly baggage handler, and you'll probably worry about it during the entire flight. We did! But if you're careful in your packing job, the odds are good that you and your bicycle will roll happily out of the airport and onto European soil several hours later.

CLOTHING. Once you've got your bicycle and bags, what are you going to carry? This will vary, depending upon the length of your trip. Don't overdo it on clothes, as you'll undoubtedly want to buy souvenirs, and you can put them to use right away if you leave an extra T-shirt or pair of shorts behind.

A good rain jacket is crucial. Rain pants are limited in their effectiveness for the cyclist, however. They tend to get you wet from the inside if the rain doesn't get you from without. We opted for polypropylene long underwear instead, wearing this under gym shorts when the weather was wet or cold. It provided needed warmth, and it dried quickly when the rain finally stopped (or when we did). Also, a pair of sweat pants is a great thing to have when you enter a city to look for a room or when you're setting up your tent in a campground and don't want to freeze before you have a place to change.

We didn't use cycling shoes, mainly because we did so much walking when we weren't pedaling. Two sturdy pairs of tennis shoes apiece got us through the year, despite some hot — and fragrant — July evenings in Denmark, when they were banished to the outside of the tent. Invest in a pair of rubberized biking booties to avoid the discomfort of cold and soggy feet in inclement weather. The booties are light and compact, and they help prevent frozen toes when you get off your bike after a cold day. Warm, waterproof gloves are also a wonderful luxury in nasty weather.

CAMPING GEAR. If you're camping, your baggage weight will increase markedly, but we found the extra pounds to be worth the payoff in campground friendships and reduced costs. In fact, after several months on the road, we still preferred the familiar walls of our tent to the constantly changing and often drab surroundings of hotel rooms.

If you'll be camping in Europe, you're probably an experienced camper at home. You'll need the same equipment — tent and rainfly, sleeping bag,

A Danish cyclist enjoys a biking holiday with his two-year-old son.

groundsheet, a plastic tarp for covering your bike (good for security, as well), stove and fuel, matches, potholder, cookset, and an all-purpose rope to use as a clothesline. We also carried two flashlights and let them double as emergency bike lights rather than equipping our bicycles for night riding we didn't intend to do. A flashlight also can come in handy if you hit an unexpected or unlit tunnel.

Choose your tent carefully. Make sure it's roomy enough to allow you to bring in your bags for security and protection from the weather, tough enough to withstand European downpours, and light enough to allow you to navigate the hills without hiring a sag wagon to carry your gear. European campgrounds are usually set up for car and trailer use, and this often means less-than-ideal surfaces for sleeping. A good lightweight sleeping pad is a welcome pleasure for tired muscles at the end of a tough riding day.

You won't be able to build fires in European campgrounds, and you shouldn't plan on any freelance wiener roasts, either. We carried a Gaz cookstove that did morning coffee duty and evening dinner duty for one year without giving us a problem. Unlike white gas, the small blue fuel cartridges the stove uses are easy to obtain in Europe. They grace the shelves of grocery stores and gas stations, are often sold at campgrounds, and are almost always available in hardware stores. Watch for small blue Camping Gaz signs in store windows as you ride through towns.

Water is always a concern when you're on the road and exercising hard, and a cloth-covered plastic water sack can come in handy. We never had anyone refuse us a "fillup" when we asked. In fact, this was often a good lead-in to the more important question — "Can we camp on your land?" Alternatively, if we had already obtained permission to camp on private land or planned to ask later in the day, we would usually stop at a store in late afternoon and buy a couple of the 1-1/2-liter plastic bottles of mineral water that abound in Europe. That way, we were sure we'd have water for our evening soup, our morning coffee, and our toothbrushes.

You'll need to be careful about food shopping if you're camping and cooking, as well. Regardless of our day's destination, we always carried one night's emergency rations (a couple of packages of dry soup) so that if we stumbled on a lovely campspot or got caught between towns, we could sleep and eat without having to ride to a restaurant or store.

MISCELLANEOUS GEAR. Here's an alphabetical list of other general items we took along:

- Address book — for sending postcards
- Aspirin
- Camera and film; also a blower brush for cleaning and a photo log
- Cards — for late-night cribbage games
- First-aid kit
- Gifts — something lightweight for new European friends; we carried small leather footbags.
- Glasses or contacts — second pair for emergency replacement
- Guidebooks
- Maps — for arrival area and any good city maps
- Mirror
- Needle and thread
- Phrase book
- Pictures — family snapshots to share with Europeans
- Prescriptions
- Shampoo and soap
- Toilet paper — a definite requirement if you're camping, as European campgrounds often neglect this item; when faced with a desperate situation, an unused section of our phrase book proved to be an invaluable reference.
- Towel
- Vitamins
- Watch

Survival skills

At last, after all the planning, the preparation, the purchases, and the planes, you'll arrive. You'll watch as your bike carton comes tumbling down the baggage chute, and you'll claim it with trembling hands. You'll unpack, assemble, repack, and load, then make your way through customs to officially set foot on European soil. Now what? Enjoy!

All the preparation you've done should ensure a pleasurable trip, but here are a few additional tips, gathered from our year of "learning by doing," that will help you avoid the potholes and find the smoother roads ahead.

SECURITY AGAIN. We've already mentioned the importance of keeping your valuables in an under-clothing money pouch and of locking your bicycle when you leave it unattended. Security is always a concern when you leave your bags and bike to enter the tourist flow on foot—for example, when you're visiting a large city while staying in a hotel or campground. When we stayed in rooms, we always asked the proprietors to provide us with a place to lock our bicycles (off the street) and they generally complied quite graciously. If a hotelkeeper won't accommodate your bicycle and there are other rooms available, try again.

Our bikes claimed the other bed in a tiny room in Vienna where we celebrated our fourth wedding anniversary; they spent Christmas with us in our room above Las Ramblas in Barcelona; they had a spot beneath the television set in our hotel lobby in Nafplion; and they crowded into a corner on a back patio in Florence.

In campgrounds, we used a tree or post to lean and lock our bikes, then covered them with a sheet of plastic to protect them from the weather and provide a noisy alarm if anyone got too close. We zipped our bags and gear in the tent when we left to sightsee, and we took our cameras and other valuables with us. A zipper and a bit of fabric won't do much to deter a thief, so strike up conversations with your campground neighbors before you leave. That way, those around you know what body goes with what tent, and they'll usually keep an eye on things while you're away.

SAFETY AND HEALTH. Besides taking care of your passport, money, and possessions, what are some ways you can take care of yourself?

For riding safety, keep to secondary roads whenever possible. If you follow the tour routes we've described, you'll be on quiet roads most of the time. We made a point of sacrificing short riding days whenever we had to decide between main road "straight shots" and circuitous secondary routes. In countries like France and Denmark, you'll hardly have to sacrifice at all, as the small roads are often the most direct. In other countries, the extra kilometers are well worth the effort for the solitude, safety, and scenery they'll provide.

Try to make your helmet a habit. It's easy to remember to reach for the plastic "brain bucket" when you're forced to cycle heavily traveled routes, busy city streets, or dangerous terrain (steep downhills, for example), but the unexpected tumbles on ordinary roads can be every bit as dangerous — more so when your helmet is tucked inside a bike bag instead of cinched beneath your chin. So, if you can discipline yourself to lash on your helmet every morning, and you don't mind arousing a bit of European mirth along your way (helmets are not yet standard equipment among European cyclists), do your head a favor and make your helmet a habit.

Another key element of safety is bicycle maintenance. If you get into a daily checkup routine, you'll avoid unnecessary breakdowns and accidents. Check tire pressure, brake pads, cables, spokes, and wheels on a daily basis. One

A bicycle maintenance book provides advice on dealing with a grumbling freewheel.

tedious task that will save you time in the long run is a daily "sliver search." Examine your tires regularly for tiny shards of glass imbedded in the tread and dig them out gently with the tip of a pocketknife blade to prevent them from working into the tube and giving you those hated flats. Don't forget to lubricate your chain and derailleur at least once a week, more often if you're riding through rain.

Of course, you'll want to keep your body in good working condition, too. Eat enough food to replace the calories you're burning each day. This won't be a difficult task, especially with the endless selection of European delicacies tempting you from every store window you'll cycle past. But choose your fuel with care. We shared part of our ride in Spain with an English tourer whose daily breakfast and lunch consisted of three giant chocolate bars — tasty and calorie packed, but not exactly a nutritionist's ideal.

It's also important to leave your American "7-11" mentality behind when you enter Europe. Once you're away from the 24-hour shopping options in the United States, you'll find that having a dollar, a *franc*, or a *dinar* in your pocket doesn't mean you'll always be able to find a place to spend it. Familiarize yourself with the shopping hours of the countries you'll visit, and take those opening and closing times seriously. Ignore them, and you may go hungry. We've listed general shopping hours in the introductory sections of the tours.

INFORMATION, PLEASE. You'll find additional information on shopping, holidays, culture, and courtesy in the companion travel guides you buy for your routes. *Michelin Green Guides* have helpful sections that cover these subjects, as do *Baedeker's Guides, Rand McNally Blue Guides,* and the *Let's Go* series. A guidebook's cost and weight is well worth the increased understanding and appreciation you'll gain from it, and the small city maps that accompany the text can come in handy in a pinch.

Of course, the thousands of tourist offices scattered throughout Europe serve a similar function, and they have the added advantage of providing most materials free. Relying entirely on the tourist offices does have its drawbacks, though. You'll have to battle lunch-hour closures and occasional inconvenient locations, and some tourist office brochures are full of superficial "fluff" designed to convince all comers that their town is the gem of Europe.

ROUTE FINDING. One important rule to remember as a bicycle tourer is this — "Pride goeth before a wrong turn." We learned this lesson the hard way, after too many dead ends and extra miles. When you're confused, ask for help. Europeans will be delighted to come to your rescue. They won't ridicule your ignorance or laugh at your despair. So what, if the husband and wife you question argue for 15 minutes before agreeing on which road to point you toward? In most cases, the people you seek out will know a lot more about the area than you do, and their friendly aid will save you from a host of wrong turns. And occasionally, these roadside conversations will result in dinner invitations, impromptu picnics, refreshments at local cafes, and delightful new friendships, as well.

Of course, your main information sources as you ride will be the maps fastened atop your handlebar bag, the tours you're tracing from Part II of this book, and the road signs you'll constantly be searching for. Make a point of getting acquainted with the shapes and colors of the signs for the country you're riding in. They follow definite patterns, and knowing them can help you with your route-finding chores. Often, signs indicating motorway routes are one color, signs for primary roads are another, and signs for secondary roads are yet another. Think of yourself as a detective with several sets of clues to piece together. Use them all, and you'll arrive at your destination with a minimum of difficulty.

We've included a page of international road signs you'll encounter frequently in Europe, with explanations from a cyclist's point of view.

Circular Signs — Give Orders

White bar on red background. No entry for vehicles. (One-way traffic coming at you!)

Red ring around motorcycle and automobile. No motor vehicles. (OK for non-motorized you!)

Red ring around bicycle. No cycling. (Tunnel, freeway or bike-eating dog ahead!)

White bicycle on blue background. Pedal cyclists only. (Sometimes obligatory. Follow local custom.)

Rectangular Signs — Give Information

Black letter "i" on blue field. Tourist information. (Where am i?)

Tourist information

White bar with red tip on blue. No through road. (So much for the shortcut!)

Triangular Signs — Give Warnings

Black bump
in red border.
Uneven road.
(Look out for
potholes!)

Black gate
in red border.
Railroad crossing
with barrier.
(Slow down for
tracks or trains!)

Black train
in red border.
Unguarded crossing.
(Slow down for
tracks and look
for trains!)

Parallel lines
bending closer.
Road narrows.
(So long, shoulder!)

Black hill
in red border.
Steep downhill.
(Yahoo!)

Black hill
in red border.
Steep uphill.
(Could be a
"pusher"!)

To help with the daily task of route finding, we suggest you take a few minutes each morning to study your map, your guidebook, and the tour you're following from Part II of this book. Use a yellow highlighter to draw the day's intended route on your map. This will help you make quick decisions at junctions, and you can refer to our detailed route descriptions whenever you get stumped.

We've used kilometers as the distance unit in all tours except Tour No. 1, A National Trust Tour of England. This way, you'll be operating in the units employed by the country you're in. A simple formula for kilometer-to-mile conversion is 8 km = 5 mi. So, an 80-km day amounts to a 50-miler, the basic distance we aimed for as we planned our cycling days. When there's a

A budget hotel in France provides an interesting window on the world.

lot to see or tough terrain to ride through, you'll shorten your rides accordingly. No single distance is "right" or "respectable." Find the pace that works for you, and go from there.

MEMORIES. Each day of your tour will bring you a host of new sights and sounds, and you may start to find the castles and cathedrals, forests and fields, honks and hellos blending together in a happy blur. Try to slow down long enough each day to open up a notebook and scribble a few lines about your experiences — a face, a place, a taste, or a feeling. The time you spend recording those moments will be a small investment for the future, and you'll go home at the end of your tour with a treasure of experiences that fading memories and jumbled recollections can never erase.

PART II

18 TOURS
GEARED FOR DISCOVERY

*Ancient door on a
Swedish church.*

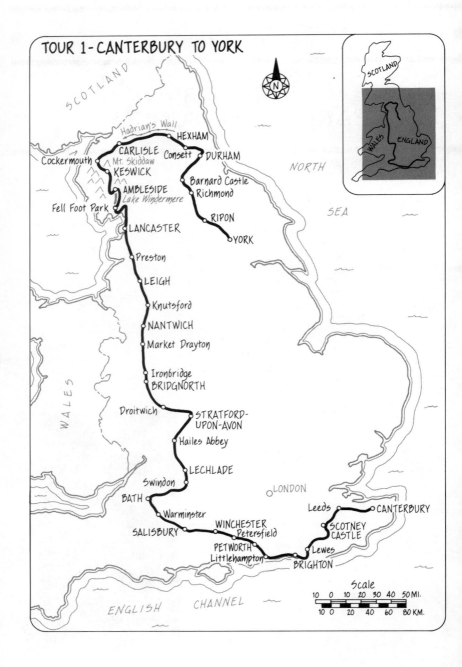

TOUR 1-CANTERBURY TO YORK

SCOTLAND

N

SCOTLAND

WALES ENGLAND

Hadrian's Wall HEXHAM
CARLISLE Consett DURHAM
Cockermouth Mt. Skiddaw
KESWICK Barnard Castle
AMBLESIDE Richmond
Lake Windermere
Fell Foot Park RIPON
LANCASTER YORK

NORTH

SEA

Preston
LEIGH
Knutsford
NANTWICH
Market Drayton
Ironbridge
BRIDGNORTH
Droitwich STRATFORD-
UPON-AVON
Hailes Abbey
LECHLADE
Swindon
BATH oLONDON
Warminster Leeds CANTERBURY
WINCHESTER SCOTNEY
SALISBURY Petersfield CASTLE
PETWORTH Lewes
Littlehampton BRIGHTON

WALES

ENGLISH   CHANNEL

Scale
10 0   10 20 30 40 50 MI.
10 0   20   40   60   80 KM.

TOUR NO. 1

A NATIONAL TRUST TOUR OF ENGLAND
Canterbury to York, England

Distance: 806 miles (1,297 kilometers)
Estimated time: 19 riding days
Best time to go: Late May to mid-September
Terrain: Gruesomely steep hills; narrow, shoulderless roads; some of the most beautiful pastoral scenery in Europe
Connecting tours: Tours No. 2 and 3

Keep left! Keep left! Now, with that critical detail out of the way, what should you know about cycling in England? Well, it's rewarding, stimulating, and challenging. You'll be surprised by the toughness of the English hills and delighted by the countryside you'll pedal through.

Seriously, though, remembering to keep to the left may be a problem. Even after a month of cycling in England, it took great mental effort for us to head to the left side of the road after a lunch stop or sightseeing break. Turning into correct lanes, negotiating roundabouts, and dealing with merging traffic presented new challenges. And the shock of seeing cars pass each other on the right or approach us from the "wrong" side of blind curves had us grabbing for our brakes more than once.

English roads have lots of traffic and English drivers are the worst we encountered in Europe, so use your helmet and stay on secondary routes whenever possible. More cautious than their Continental counterparts, English drivers are unwilling to swing wide to pass a bicycle, and they'll crowd you on the narrow roads. (Their caution on the road may drive you crazy, but their courtesy in shops and towns will more than make up for it.)

Route finding in England can be a challenge, too. Many of the rural signposts were taken down during World War II, when the threat of an invasion by Germany was powerful. As a result, the small roads in England are often poorly marked. You'll have to watch your map carefully to keep track of your location. Don't hesitate to take advantage of that wonderful English courtesy — ask the locals for help if you get confused.

CONNECTIONS. If you fly into London or arrive by ferry from the Continent, you can take the train or cycle to Canterbury to begin the tour. We managed to hook up with the tour by continuing on from Tour No. 2, taking a ferry from Dieppe, on France's northern coast, to Newhaven,

England. Then we cycled through Eastbourne, Battle, and Rye to reach Canterbury and the start of Tour No. 1. When you've completed this tour, you can continue cycling from York to the start of Tour No. 3 by pedaling south to Lincoln and Cambridge, then east to Harwich and the ferry to Holland. If you're heading back to London for a plane flight home, you can easily make train connections in York.

INFORMATION. There's always an abundance of printed literature available in England. The tourist offices are good sources of reading material, once you're in the country. To request information before you go, write to the British Tourist Authority, 680 Fifth Avenue, New York, New York 10019. Ask for free city maps, information on cycling and camping, or lists of accommodations. To do additional advance planning, write to the Cyclists' Touring Club, Cotterell House, 69 Meadrow, Godalming, Surrey GU7 3HS, England, to request information on club membership and bicycle touring in England.

Baedeker's Great Britain, Let's Go: Britain and Ireland, and Michelin's *Green Guide England the West Country* or Rand McNally's *Blue Guide England* are just a few of the many commercial guidebook choices you'll have for your trip.

One reason you'll enjoy cycling in England is included in the title of this tour — the National Trust. This historic-preservation group owns and maintains more than 240 properties in England, Wales, and Northern Ireland, from parks to manor houses to flower gardens. If you join the National Trust for your ride, you'll be able to visit the Trust properties listed in this tour free of charge. It will be a worthwhile investment for your trip, as entry fees in England are steep, and the Trust properties are delightful. Imagine cheerful English guides enthusiastically explaining the complexities of Chippendale furniture, the writings of Beatrix Potter, or the lifespan of the red deer, and you'll get an idea of the wonderful visits you'll enjoy almost daily on your ride.

Americans can purchase a one-year membership in the Royal Oak Foundation — the U.S. affiliate of the National Trust — for approximately $25 for the first member and $15 for all additional family members. Write to the Royal Oak Foundation, Inc., 41 East 72nd Street, New York, New York 10021, for details. Or you can wait to join until you get to England — simply inquire at the first National Trust property you visit.

MAPS. The English are great map lovers, so your selection will be enormous. Michelin covers the country in two 1:400,000 maps, but you'll need better detail to cope with the often unmarked secondary roads. A 1:250,000 map series published by Estate Publications and available at most tourist offices has the road detail you'll want. These maps also show campgrounds, castles, abbeys, parks — even rugby grounds. (Be forewarned, though — not all the campgrounds shown on the maps actually exist.)

Another excellent route-finding choice is the *Ordnance Survey Routemaster Series* at 1:250,000. These maps provide helpful contour lines, but they are limited on tourist information.

ACCOMMODATIONS. The falling pound and the rising dollar have combined in recent years to make England an affordable stop for budget tourists, but the country is still in the high to middle range as far as European prices go. Lodgings in hotels can be expensive. Bed-and-breakfast opportunities abound, however, and these rooms in private homes are more economical and infinitely more interesting than drab hotels. Plan on paying at least $10 in even the cheapest B&B. You'll have to shop around if you're on a strict budget.

Campgrounds in England are generally clean, well maintained, and pleasant. Prices are reasonable, too. Unfortunately, the British are avid "caravanners," and you'll have to share your sites with fleets of metal camping trailers, complete with "tellies," lawn chairs, and teapots. Some campgrounds are licensed only for trailers and will not accept tents. If you'll be camping exclusively, the Michelin camping guide, *Camping and Caravanning in Britain,* is nice to have along.

SUPPLIES: Stores are closed Sundays, and grocers in small towns usually take a Wednesday or Thursday afternoon off every week. General hours Monday through Saturday are 9:00 a.m. to 5:30 p.m.

For picnicking, be sure to sample the delightful variety of English cheeses. They vary widely from county to county, and each region is proud of its specialty. Add slices of flavorful corned beef to hunks of grainy brown bread, throw in a handful of sinfully greasy English "crisps," and you'll have the makings of a delicious lunch. The sweet, bubbly English cider makes a cheery picnic beverage, but watch out for "Scrumpy," a home-brewed cider that packs a mighty punch.

Pay your respects, too, to British institutions like fish and chips, Cornish pasties, Yorkshire pudding, afternoon tea with the ever-present "biscuits," and English food will win a warm place in your heart.

If you find time to cycle between all those meals, remember that bicycle touring is very popular in England, so you should find replacement parts without difficulty.

Canterbury to Scotney Castle: 45 miles

Canterbury Cathedral, famed as the site of the martyrdom of Thomas Becket and venerated by English Christians for hundreds of years, is the highlight of any pilgrim's visit. In addition to its historical associations, the cathedral is an architectural shrine as well. Wander the vast interior, and marvel at the high, vaulted ceiling, the endless rows of pillars, and the exquisite stained glass.

To escape the disconcerting neon signs of Kentucky Fried Chicken and Big M Burger, seek out the emerald lawns and beds of scarlet tulips in the beautiful creekside garden near Canterbury's west gate. And visit the city's tourist office at 22 St. Peters Street for information on the town and its accommodations. We passed on Canterbury's B&Bs and youth hostel and cycled 1¼ mi to an excellent city campground. It's up a steep hill east of town, on **Road A257** toward **Sandwich,** and offers hot showers and pleasant, grassy surroundings.

Leave Canterbury on the narrow and busy **Road A28,** which heads southwest to **Chilham.** Ride through town, turn right onto a smaller road for

Shottenden, climb a steep hill, and ride through lovely apple orchards. They're stunning in May. From Shottenden, follow signs for **Charing,** turn right onto **Road A252** after about 5½ mi, then take the first right **off A252,** following signs for **Warren Street** and the village of **Lenham.** Stay on the secondary road through Lenham, an attractive town just off **Road A20,** then **join A20** for about 4 mi before turning left onto **Road B2163** for Leeds. You can get a good look at **Leeds Castle** from the small road pulloff above the Leeds golf course. But you'll have to pay the admission fee to get a closer view of this beautifully situated building, as it's not a National Trust property.

From Leeds, continue on B2163 and **cross Road A274.** After crossing, ride past one turnoff to the left, then take the **second left off B2163** for **Cross-at-Hand.** Continue toward Cross-at-Hand, where you'll gain **Road A229** for **Staplehurst.** If you'd like to visit **Sissinghurst Castle Gardens,** one of the Trust's mansion/garden properties, stay **on A229** and follow the signs.

We opted for a visit to another Trust spot instead, taking the first right **off A229** after Cross-at-Hand, turning onto a small road for **Curtisden Green** and **Goudhurst.** Endure a series of short, steep hills as you pass Curtisden Green, then join **Road B2079** for **Goudhurst.** Stay on B2079 through Goudhurst, then turn right for **Kilndown,** climbing a very steep hill just before town. Pass through Kilndown and turn right on **Road A21.** National Trust markers will lead you to **Scotney Castle Garden,** where a scenic moated castle is tucked into a quiet, forested dale.

There's a small, private campground next to bed-and-breakfast facilities on Road A21, within a mile of Scotney Castle. From the castle, turn left on **A21** toward **Hurst Green** and **Hawkhurst.** The campground and B&B are on the right.

Scotney Castle to Brighton: 52 miles

Continue south on **Road A21.** In **Flimwell,** go left onto **Road A268** for **Hawkhurst.** Take a right 1½ mi later to bypass the congestion of Hawkhurst, cycling a secondary road to **Road A265,** where you'll go left for **The Moor.**

When you reach a junction with **Road A229** about 1 mi later, turn right onto A229. This is a hilly stretch of road with moderate traffic. Look for signs for **Bodiam Castle** soon after you gain A229, and turn left to descend a long hill to the Trust property.

Bodiam Castle, built in 1385, is a true classic for castle lovers. Its grey turrets reflect in the still surface of a forbidding moat, and the gutted interior evokes visions of the past. Arrive at the 10:00 a.m. opening time, and you might even have the cold stones to yourself for awhile.

Return to **A229** and continue straight across it, following signs for **Hurst Green.** Go right on **Road A21** to reach Hurst Green, then turn left in town onto **Road A265** for **Lewes.**

If you're a Rudyard Kipling fan, don't skip a visit to **Bateman's,** Kipling's country home. You can stroll through the study where he wrote some of his most famous stories, admire his 1928 Rolls Royce, or wander his extensive gardens, all for a flash of your National Trust card. To make the short detour to Bateman's, take the first left in **Burwash** as you cycle along **A265.** You'll descend a short hill and be confronted with a sign for Bateman's that points right back up the incline. Ignore it and go right instead, avoiding the indirect car routing, but be sure to watch out for oncoming vehicles on the narrow road.

From Bateman's, return to **A265** and continue southwest toward **Heathfield** and **Lewes.** In Heathfield, you'll gain **Road B2102** and follow signs for **Lewes.** This road can have heavy traffic, especially on weekends, so ride cautiously. You'll enjoy vistas of rolling green fields sprinkled with grazing clumps of shaggy wool as you cycle along the ridge.

The bypass road around Lewes goes through a **"no bikes" tunnel,** so you'll need to turn right just before the tunnel and cycle through the interesting town, overlooked by its guardian castle. Soon after entering Lewes, you'll reach an **intersection** with a sign pointing right for the **city center.** Turn left here to regain the bypass road and **Road A27** for **Brighton.**

If you want a closer look at **Lewes's Castle,** follow the **city center** sign to the right and climb up through town before joining **A27** on the outskirts of the city.

You'll add 10 mi to your ride to Brighton, but gain a quiet, rolling route along the Ouse River, by turning south at the sign for **Newhaven** in Lewes. The scenery is pure England — vibrant green fields, fat sheep, and rounded hillsides.

Enter Newhaven and turn right on **A259** for **Brighton.** Follow the flat coast road west, sharing the stunning vistas of sparkling blue-green water with heavy tourist traffic along the way.

There's a huge hillside campground east of Brighton, just beyond the city golf course. Follow the well-signed route to the right off the main road to find your tent spot for the night. True tourist town that it is, Brighton also offers hotels, B&Bs, and a youth hostel (4 mi north of town in Patcham) for those in search of a softer bed.

Continue into Brighton on A259, staring at dozens of tourist information signs, cotton candy stands, and go-cart tracks along the way. Turn into the city streets to escape the coastal road, and pedal to the Royal Pavilion — a bizarre building that looks right at home in the carnival atmosphere of this seaside city.

Brighton to Petworth: 39 miles

Leave Brighton by continuing along **A259** for **Worthing.** Resign yourself to the traffic and feast your eyes on one coastal town after another — endless rows of tidy houses and scores of boat-filled marinas. Cycle through Worthing, and follow signs to **Littlehampton.** Then turn right onto **Road A284** for **Arundel,** leaving the coast behind.

Although it's not a National Trust property, **Arundel Castle** is well worth a visit and an entry fee. The grounds are especially stunning in spring. Lush green grass and blossom-heavy trees provide a picturesque setting for the handsome castle of the Dukes of Norfolk. And the tour of the interior overwhelms the visitor with an avalanche of finely crafted furniture, delicate porcelain, royal paintings, and leather-bound books.

From Arundel, climb a long hill as you continue north on **Road A284** and **A29.** Turn left off the busy A29 about 2 mi after joining it, to ride for **Bignor Roman Villa.** Cycle through **Bignor** and **Sutton,** following signs for **Petworth.** The ride is hilly, with steep ascents and descents, and you'll grumble about English road engineers more than once along the way.

In Petworth, follow signs to **Petworth House,** a Trust spot surrounded by a 700-acre park full of deer, sheep, and exotic farm animals. The house boasts a magnificent painted staircase and holds a treasure of paintings and sculpture.

If it's late in your cycling day, you may want to seek a room in Petworth or the larger town of **Midhurst,** 7 mi west on **Road A272.**

Petworth to Winchester: 37 miles

Leave Petworth on **A272** for **Easebourne** and **Midhurst.** Pass golf courses, polo fields, and parks on your way into the busy Easebourne/ Midhurst sprawl, then continue on **A272** for **Petersfield.** The route to Petersfield is very hilly, with moderate traffic. As you pass through Petersfield, stay on **A272** for **Winchester** and enjoy a bit of flat riding before regaining roller coaster terrain. You'll have a long, steady hill before Winchester, but there's a striking view from the top.

Descend into the city and follow signs for the **city center** and tourist information office (in the Guildhall on Broadway).

The short riding day should allow you lots of time to explore Winchester's massive cathedral and the 13th-century Great Hall with King Arthur's famed Round Table (if you can believe the tourist literature). Take a walk in the quiet park along the River Itchen, or stroll the picturesque High Street to get to know the city better.

Winchester offers a centrally located hostel in an 18th-century watermill (a National Trust property). There's also a campground near the city, and there are several B&Bs to choose from as well.

Winchester to Salisbury: 24 miles

You'll have another short but hill-studded riding day ahead as you leave Winchester on **Road A272** for **Stockbridge.** Climb a steep hill from town, and then ride through rolling farmland. Enter Stockbridge and follow the signs for **Salisbury** onto **Road A30,** then battle a grueling series of steep ups and downs.

The terrain levels off as you approach Salisbury. You'll soon spot the tallest spire in England, crowning one of the loveliest cathedrals you'll see on your entire ride. Enter Salisbury on the four-lane A30 and cycle through the city streets, using the cathedral spire as your guide. Salisbury Cathedral was built in the incredibly short span of 38 years, in an era when many cathedrals took centuries to complete. The church is well worth an afternoon of sightseeing, especially if you can tag along on a tour of the heights (tours

Bodiam Castle attests to England's war-torn past.

start at 11:00 a.m. and 2:30 p.m.). You'll never forget the stairs, the stones, or the stories you'll hear on the climb.

Visit the adjoining Chapter House, too, to view the Magna Carta, or walk across the grassy park surrounding the cathedral to take a look at Mompesson House, a nearby National Trust Property.

Salisbury's tourist office at 10 Endless Street can direct you to the local hostel or to one of the many B&Bs in the city. The campground near town isn't open to tents.

Salisbury to Bath: 42 miles

In Salisbury, we made the totally "untouristy" decision to pass up a visit to **Stonehenge** on our ride toward Bath, holding out for the National Trust's Avebury Circle instead. But if you feel that no tour of England is complete without a trip to its most famous stones, you can cycle **Road A360** north from Salisbury to reach the site. There are also frequent roundtrip buses between Salisbury and Stonehenge.

If you're skipping the stones, go **south from Salisbury Cathedral** and take **St. Nicholas Road** over the old bridge across the **Avon River.** Turn right on **Harnham Road** to gain **Road A3094** leading west out of town through **West Harnham** and on to **Netherhampton.** Then angle right for **Wilton.**

Cross the river as you enter Wilton, and turn left immediately onto **Road A30.** Stay on A30 through the city, recrossing the river, then follow signs for **Great Wishford** onto an unnamed secondary road along the south bank of the **River Wylye.** Pass through one lovely village after another, admiring homes built of the grey stone common to the area, their sturdy walls topped by thatched roofs and brightened by flower-filled yards. Light traffic and level terrain make the cycling pleasant.

Angle left onto **Road A36** just before **Warminster,** following the busy and disagreeable road for about 9 mi. Pass through **Beckington** and **Woolverton,** then escape to the left onto **Road B3110** toward **Norton St. Philip** and **Hinton Charterhouse.** Climb gradually through rolling terrain, descend a large hill to cross **a river,** then take the **first right** to pedal on to **A36** for **Bath.**

Follow A36 into the city and then follow **city center** signs. You can shorten the circuitous main-road route into Bath's center by turning right onto **Great Pulteney Street.** The tourist office is nestled in the busy city core.

You can wander Bath's streets for hours, looking at mansions and townhouses, museums and churches. Visits to Bath Abbey and the nearby Roman Baths are practically obligatory, and you can join the English tourists for a "cuppa" in the Pump Room above the Roman Baths.

The Bath Assembly Rooms are owned by the National Trust but administered by the city council, so you'll have to pay to visit the fine Museum of Costume inside.

You'll have to compete with scores of tourists for lodgings if you visit Bath in July or August. However, the city has a hostel, a campground (5 mi west on **Road A4**), and loads of B&Bs to choose from.

Bath to Lechlade: 57 miles

Leave Bath's center on **A4,** heading northeast for **Chippenham,** but veer right in **Box** onto **Road A365** toward **Melksham.** Climb a long, gentle hill through a wooded draw. At the top, turn left at a sign for **Road B3109.** Follow this road for about a block, then go right for **Neston.**

Continue on for **Gastard,** and then follow signs for **Lacock.** You'll enjoy the quiet country riding after the hubbub of Bath, and you'll gladly trade the big city's circus-like streets for narrow country lanes bordered by attractive, flat-stoned walls and rippling fields of wheat.

Both **Lacock Abbey,** established in 1232 and made into a country estate 300 years later, and the surrounding **Lacock Village** belong to the National Trust. The abbey and grounds are open to visitors in the afternoon, and there's a museum of photography inside.

Lacock's campground is outside of town on the southerly road to Gastard. Ask directions in town.

From Lacock, cycle east on the **secondary road toward Calne.** Climb a tough hill away from town. The incline is long and steep, but you'll have fine views out over the valley from the ridgetop. Turn right onto **Road A342** at **Sandy Lane,** a lovely town of thatch and slate, then angle left as you leave town, turning **off A342,** and crossing **Road A3102.** Follow signs for **Heddington, Stockley,** and **Blackland.**

After Blackland, keep **right to avoid Calne.** Cross the first road heading north for **Road A4,** but take a left on the next, to give up quiet riding for a short stint on A4. Cycle east on A4, turning left onto **Road A361** and climbing gradually for **Avebury** and another Trust visit.

Avebury Circle stands contentedly in the shadow of Stonehenge, its much-publicized neighbor to the south. Walk out into the 28-acre site, and stroll among the silent stones of one of the primary megalithic monuments in Europe. There's a small on-site museum with photos and exhibits that explain the history of the area.

Continue north from Avebury on **A361** toward **Swindon** and **Stow.** A brutal north wind sometimes makes this section of the ride trying, but without it, the relatively flat terrain will be a refreshing change. Suffer through Swindon with its traffic and turmoil, and keep to A361 toward Stow. (If you're looking for a room to shorten this long riding day, Swindon's tourist office can help you out.)

A brief detour off A361 leads to **Buscot Manor,** a National Trust country mansion set like a French château within wide lawns and radiating avenues. A bevy of grandmotherly guides watches visitors stroll through rooms filled with antique furniture and oil paintings by Rubens, Rembrandt, and Van Dyck.

To reach Buscot Manor, turn right off **A361** about 8 mi north of Swindon, following signs for **Buscot.** Continue about 1 mi past the town to reach the house and park. Ride back through Buscot on **Road A417,** and continue north for **Lechlade.**

To find Lechlade's pleasant, grassy campground, turn left in the small town onto A361 toward Swindon, cross the bridge, and watch for the campground on the left.

Lechlade to Stratford-upon-Avon: 49 miles

This portion of the tour has a handful of incredibly tough hills, half a day of very light traffic, and lots of looks at Cotswold stone villages and green fields cut by endless lines of piled rock fences.

Leave Lechlade on the main road (**A361**) north for **Burford,** but angle left on the edge of town toward **Hatherop** and **Bibury.** The riding is fairly level to **Hatherop.** Go left here to pedal for **Bibury** and hill country.

Stop to admire **Arlington Row,** a National Trust avenue of Cotswold cottages set in a little glen and bordered by a chortling stream. All the villages in the area are candidates for special attention, with fascinating slate roofs and stone-enclosed gardens.

Continue on a winding, rolling route through **Winson** and **Fossebridge** toward **Yanworth,** crossing noisy **Road A429** along the way. There's a large hill just before Yanworth, but you can avoid it by following a dirt road to the left along a creek. Regain the paved road after Yanworth and just before **Chedworth Roman Villa.** This Trust property has the excavated remains of a Roman mansion that dates back to the days when Britain was a Roman colony. Some of the best-preserved Roman mosaics in England are on display at this quiet, well-maintained site, and it will provide a welcome break from the hilly riding.

Leave Chedworth Roman Villa and go left at the main road, then turn right about 1 mi later toward **Compton Abdale** and **Road A40.** Struggle up two agonizingly steep hills, then **cross A40** and gain more level terrain. Continue north to an intersection with **Road A436** and turn right. Take a left about 200 ft later to gain the old **"Salt Way."** Follow a ridgetop, and revel in spectacular views of the valley below. The grazing sheep look like tiny cottonballs on the vast expanse of green.

Follow signs for **Winchcombe** until you reach a **crossroad** where the Winchcombe marker points left down a steep hill. **Continue straight** instead, and reach a **T.** Go left, then right 200 ft later, to descend a short and almost vertical hill to **Hailes Abbey,** another Trust site. One of the scores of ruined church buildings in England, Hailes Abbey is a picturesque spot with a small on-site museum. Stroll among the lonely stone arches, and give your legs a chance to recover for the final 20 mi to Stratford-upon-Avon.

The ride from Hailes Abbey to Stratford is fairly flat and traffic ranges from tolerable to heavy. From the abbey, ride 1 mi west to **Road A46** and turn right. Follow A46 through **Willersey** and **Mickleton,** and continue on to **Stratford-upon-Avon,** a town custom-designed for tourists. The route to the tourist office at 1 High Street is well marked.

Stratford has obvious attractions that any Shakespeare fan will want to explore, but there's also a Trust property in the area that's worth a visit. **Charlecote Park,** 5 mi east of Stratford, is a wonderfully landscaped reserve for sheep and deer (their ancestors were victims of Shakespeare's penchant for poaching, according to local tradition). A manor house dating from the 1500s commands the grounds, and there's fantastic carved furniture inside. To reach the park, follow **B4086** through Tiddington, then turn left at the sign for **Charlecote Park.**

Lodgings can be difficult to find in Stratford during the summer theater/ tourist season, so you may need advance reservations, a visit to the tourist office, or a diligent search in order to locate a B&B. There's a youth hostel in the city, too.

Stratford's closest campground is 1 mi northeast of town in Tiddington. It's clean and spacious and has wonderful hot showers. To reach the campground, turn right onto **Road B4086** for **Tiddington** just before crossing the River Avon into downtown Stratford. Pass a golf course on the right, and look for signs for the Elms Campground soon after.

Stratford-upon-Avon to Bridgnorth: 51 miles

Leave Stratford by cycling west on the busy **Road A422** toward **Alcester.** Angle left onto **Road B4090** after Alcester, and ride through **New End** and **Feckenham** on the route toward **Droitwich.** This section has moderate hills and light traffic.

Look for the change in architecture from the grey Cotswold cottages to red brick farmhouses topped by stout round chimneys. And check your member's guidebook for sightseeing options, since you'll be riding near a few more National Trust properties during the day.

In Droitwich, pass under the freeway, go **across Road A38,** and continue straight. Follow signs onto **Road A4133** toward **Tenbury.** After Droitwich, the terrain becomes more punishing, with several steep ups and downs. It seems there's always a sharp bend or a burst of road construction at the bottom of each dip, to ensure that all momentum is lost for the ensuing climb.

Make the long ascent of **Abberley Hill,** with the impressive form of a large bell tower above, then turn right onto **Road B4202** when you reach the top. Ride through **Clows Top** and continue on B4202 to merge with **Road A4117.** Then angle right onto **Road B4363** for **Bridgnorth.**

A series of roller coaster hills covers the 14 tough miles to Bridgnorth, a quaint town with busy streets, old gateways, and a hilltop castle. Reach a **junction** as you enter town, turn left up the hill, then go right to enter the old city at the top.

There's a tourist office in Bridgnorth, if you need help in your search for a room. We made our day a long one and pushed on another 8 mi to **Ironbridge** and a secluded municipal campground.

Bridgnorth to Nantwich: 49 miles

Leave Bridgnorth on **Road B4373** for **Ironbridge.** Descend and pass a golf course as you leave the city, then cycle the moderately hilly 8 mi to Ironbridge. This town has few tourists, an interesting history, a 200-year-old pub, a free city campground, and the "first iron bridge in the world" (if you can believe the locals).

If you're camping, Ironbridge is a great place to spend an evening talking about the region's industrial history with the dart-playing customers in the local pub, The Boat. To reach the campground and the pub, turn right along the **south bank** of the **Severn River** instead of crossing the main bridge into the city proper. Ride about 1 mi over rough road to reach the campground. It's on a small, grassy slope beyond the pub.

Backtrack toward the main road, and continue riding **west** along the south bank of the river to reach the **old iron bridge** spanning the Severn. There's an information office with excellent literature here, and you can walk your bike across on the old bridge to regain the main road. Once across the river, turn left on the **main road**, then right on **Road A4169** up a mile-long hill toward **Wellington**. Share the stiff climb with lots of traffic. The terrain is more agreeable after the hill. In Wellington, follow signs for **Road A518** and **Stafford.**

At **Newport,** turn left onto **Road A41** toward **Whitchurch.** Angle right in **Hinstock,** turning onto **Road A529** for **Market Drayton.** Newport, Market Drayton, and Audlem are attractive small cities with interesting brick houses. Stay on A529 through **Audlem,** and pedal the final 8 mi to **Nantwich.**

There's a tourist office in Nantwich where you can get a listing of B&Bs. There's a campground near the city as well. Explore the shop-lined streets around the Nantwich church, a somber-looking building of dark red stone. Or sit on a bench near the city library and wait for one of the friendly townfolk to invite you home for tea.

Nantwich to Leigh: 40 miles

Leave Nantwich by following signs for **Middlewich** onto the busy **Road A530.** At the **junction** in Middlewich, turn right onto **Road A54** toward **Holmes Chapel.** Take the next left onto **Road B5081.** Cycle 7 mi to a junction with **Road A50** and turn left for **Knutsford** and a visit to Tatton Hall, a superb spot for a midday picnic.

Watch for the Knutsford tourist office on the left (across from the train station) as you enter the city. Get a free map of the town and the adjoining park from the people there. Pick up a chunk of Cheshire cheese, a tin of corned beef, and a loaf of brown bread for a festive picnic lunch, and then follow **King Street** to the edge of town and the entrance to **Tatton Park.**

Though owned by the National Trust, Tatton Park is administered by Cheshire County, so you'll have to pay a whopping 25 pence to cycle through. This 1,000-acre deer park and garden is a treat to explore. Park your bike near the manor house and take a look at the collections of china, furniture, and paintings. Be sure to visit the museum assembled by the last lord of the line. An amazing collection of hunting trophies and weapons covers its walls.

If you'd like to visit Manchester, you might consider using Knutsford as a base and simply (and safely) riding the train into the growling metropolis. We were headed for the serenity of the Lake District and the wild north country, so our route from Knutsford is basically a tightrope journey between the industrial sprawls of Birmingham and Manchester.

Pedal through Tatton Park, and leave by the **Rostherne exit.** Go straight as you leave the gate, and cycle on to **Road A556,** a humming four-lane thoroughfare. Turn right and ride along A556 for about 1 mi, passing **over** the M56 freeway. Continue straight through a hair-raising roundabout and go left onto **Road B5160** at the next light.

Follow B5160 to a junction with **Road A6144** and turn left for **Warburton.** Angle right when the road branches, about ½ mi later. Ride through Warburton and turn right for the toll bridge across the **Manchester Ship Canal.**

There's a nice campground on the right just across the bridge. Turn right on **Road A57,** then go left onto **Road B5212** about ½ mi later. Cross **over the M62** freeway and come to a junction with **Road A574.** Turn right to cycle the final 4 mi to **Leigh,** a midsized town where you should be able to claim a B&B.

Leigh to Lancaster: 53 miles

This ride is a run through the industrial "gauntlet" of England. It keeps to secondary roads as much as possible, but there are brief skirmishes with Leyland and Preston, so keep your helmet cinched and your reflexes ready.

From **Leigh's center,** turn right onto **Road A572.** Soon after, go left onto **Road B5235** for **Westhoughton.** In Westhoughton, turn left onto **Road A58** for a short distance, then go right when A58 makes a sharp bend to the south. Reach **Road A6** at **Wingates** and turn left. Cycle about 1 mi on A6 before turning left onto **Road B5239** for **Aspull.** Continue on through gentle hills to **Standish,** then follow signs for **Road B5250** and **Eccleston.**

There's a Trust property (**Rufford Old Hall**) on a parallel road to the west, and you can easily alter the route to cycle past it if you wish. Continue north through Eccleston, go right onto **Road A581,** then veer left onto **Road B5253,** following the signs for **Leyland.** Look out for the fleets of whizzing Leyland trucks as you negotiate two roundabouts, continuing straight for **Bomber Bridge.** Reach **Farington** and **Road A582** (not well marked) after Leyland. Turn left on the busy A582, cycling to a junction with **Road A59.** Go right toward **Preston.**

To avoid the downtown jumble of Preston, follow signs for **Lancaster.** Go left off A59 just after crossing the **Ribble River,** then climb a hill away from the city's core. Hop onto **Road B5411** for **Woodplumpton** and follow the signs to that town. Watch for the old wooden stocks by the town church — and stay out of trouble!

Go left onto **Road B5269** just past Woodplumpton, then swing right about ¼ mi later for **Barton.** Small bicycle route signs lead to **Road A6** and **Bilsborrow.** Traffic on A6 isn't too bad, as the nearby M6 freeway takes a good share of the load. Cycle north on A6, dive off onto **Road B6430** through **Garstang,** then rejoin **A6** once more.

There's a **campground** turnoff before Lancaster, on the right 2 mi beyond **Garstang.** Follow a rough road through fields to an excellent campground, complete with game room, store, washer and dryer, hot showers, and a gang of hungry ducks.

To reach **Lancaster,** continue along the increasingly busy **A6** into the **city center.** The tourist office is at 7 Dalton Square. A city museum, several churches, and a dark stone castle on a hilltop will make your visit interesting.

Lancaster to Ambleside: 43 miles

From Lancaster, follow signs toward **Kendal** as you cycle **A6** out of town. Hills are scattered and small, and the lure of the Lake District will power your pedaling. Pass through **Milnthorpe,** and reach a junction with **Road A590,** a four-lane road with steady traffic. Go left on A590 and hug the shoulder. You can get on a parallel road for about 2 mi by taking the **first right** after the turnoff for **Road A5074.** Or you can stay off A590 for even longer and get in some scenic, quiet, but very steep riding by veering right at the end of the 2-mi-long **parallel road.** Pass through **Witherslack,** and follow signs for **Newton.** Just before Newton, you'll come to a 20-percent hill. From the bottom, it's a ¾-mi "push" to the Lake District above. Rejoin **A590** at Newton.

If you stay with A590 all the way, you'll have a more gradual climb to **Lake Windermere,** but climb you will. The Lake District quickly quiets groaning muscles with the beauty of its rugged, rock-studded hillsides, its grassy dales, and its lovely stone farmhouses surrounded by pink-blossomed fruit trees. Coast into **Fell Foot Park** on the southern tip of Lake Windermere to visit the National Trust information center and load up on Lake District literature.

From Fell Foot Park, cycle north on **Road A592** along the eastern, more touristed shore of Windermere. Traffic is heavy, but views of the bluebell-carpeted forests and scattered lakeside resorts provide a pleasant distraction. If you prefer solitude to tourist sights, take the quieter roads along the western shore. We opted for the counterclockwise loop, catching the tourist towns of **Bowness** and **Windermere** on the ride north and exploring the opposite shore the next day.

Cycle north on A592, passing several campgrounds along the way. There are B&Bs in Bowness and Windermere, and there are youth hostels in **Troutbeck** and **Ambleside** (take **Road A591** left at the junction). Continue to circle the eastern shore of the lake on A591, stopping to admire the rhododendrons and azaleas at the Trust's **Stagshaw** property on Windermere's northern tip.

If you want an especially beautiful spot to camp, continue around the lake past **Ambleside,** and turn left onto **Road B5285** toward **Wray Castle.** Follow signs onto a small road beside the lake to reach the castle and Low Wray Campground. The campground is beautifully situated on Windermere's northwest edge, about 2½ mi beyond Ambleside. It's open only to tents, a pleasant change from life among the caravans.

Ambleside to Keswick (via Sawrey): 29 miles

From Ambleside, follow the route to Wray Castle and continue on through **High Wray,** turning right for **Hawkshead** to leave the lake shore. Go left on **B5285** and ride beside the pretty **Esthwaite Water** on a narrow, undulating road. Beatrix Potter's **Hill Top,** in the tiny hamlet of **Sawrey,** is a delightful National Trust stop. The house where Potter wrote many of her best-loved children's stories is still furnished with her desk and stove, and the wood-scented rooms offer visitors a touching glimpse into the writer's life.

Backtrack from Sawrey to the Hawkshead junction, and continue into **Hawkshead.** Follow signs for **Ambleside** out of town and turn left about 1 mi later to cycle a **small, scenic road.** Ascend a gradual hill, then coast down, following signs for **Skelwith.** Turn right on **Road A593,** then go left to follow **Road B5343** as you climb beside a sparkling creek. After about 1 mi, veer right up a short hill. Keep to the right, **merging** with another unmarked road. Go left at the next **junction** and pedal up and over the hill to **Grasmere.**

The descent into town is dangerously steep, so be careful. Grasmere is a small Lake District town trampled by hordes of Wordsworth fans, come to pay homage to Dove Cottage, Rydal Mount, and the poet's grave. Unfortunately, Grasmere's beautiful setting isn't poetry enough to turn the tourist tumult into verse.

Continue north on **Road A591** for **Keswick,** and climb a long, challenging hill (about 1½ mi) to **Thirlmer Lake,** where the road narrows. Both shores of the lake offer good roads, but the western route has a bit less traffic. Continue following signs for Keswick, and ascend a final hill with breathtaking vistas of green fields cut by crazy rock walls. There's a fine view of Derwent Water and Keswick from the top.

Descend into Keswick and follow **city center** signs to the tourist information office. This is a great area to abandon your cycling for a few days to do some wandering in the countryside. Keswick's tourist office has information on area hiking trails. Make an afternoon trek to the top of Mount Skiddaw, and you'll get a beautiful look at what makes the Lake District one of England's best-loved parklands.

There's a crowded, overpriced, but convenient city campground in Keswick, as well as a youth hostel and loads of B&Bs.

Keswick to Carlisle: 40 miles

Leave Keswick to the **west,** following signs for **Cockermouth** on **Road A66** and skirting along the flat shoreline of **Bassenthwaite Lake.** Turn right off A66 when it leaves the shore near the lake's **northern tip,** and go left immediately after, to ride through **Dubwath,** a tiny village with a handful of houses.

Take the **first right** turn after Dubwath, then take the **second left** (unmarked) to pedal a quiet road along the **Derwent River** into **Cockermouth.** The **Wordsworth House** is on Main Street in this midsized city. This serene Trust property was the boyhood home of William Wordsworth, and is Cockermouth's major claim to fame.

From Cockermouth, climb a long hill to the ridge above town and pedal along **Road A595** toward **Carlisle** for the final 25 mi of the day. Pass through gently undulating farmland as you draw away from the mounded blue hills of the Lake District.

There's an excellent campground 4 mi before Carlisle, just past **Thursby** on A595. It's well marked from the road. This is the closest camping to Carlisle.

Continue on A595 into the city. When you draw abreast of **Carlisle's castle** (on the left), turn right off the main road to reach the tourist office.

Carlisle is worth a visit for its castle, cathedral, and museum. Take time to view the Roman artifacts and exhibits in the museum, to lay the groundwork for your ride along Hadrian's Wall. Then stroll the streets of Carlisle, letting the lyrical language of its inhabitants remind you that Scotland is only a day's ride to the north.

Carlisle to Hexham: 39 miles

From Carlisle Castle, continue on A595 and veer left toward **Road A7,** but go right after crossing the **River Eden** to cycle **Road B6264,** climbing gradually and following signs for **Road A69.** The day's route leads along the hilly line of defense known as Hadrian's Wall, built by the Romans between 122 and 128. The Wall spans the narrowest part of Britain from shore to shore, serving as a barrier against invasion. Throughout the day, you'll have views of this amazing ribbon of stone, a monument to Roman tenacity and to the rebelliousness of the warriors to the north.

In **Brampton,** join **A69** and gain heavier traffic and steeper hills. Leave A69 by turning left at **Low Row,** and then cycle along the river to **Gilsland** and on to **Greenhead.** Take **Road B6318** from Greenhead and battle a very steep hill away from town. Ride through quiet countryside, sharing the road with occasional tour buses. Watch for traces of the Roman stones on the ridgeline to the left, and pass through **Once Brewed** before turning off for **Housesteads Fort.** This National Trust site contains 3½ mi of the Wall, several mile castles, and Housesteads Fort, one of the best-preserved Roman forts in Britain.

Visit the small museum on the site, and walk a portion of the wall if you have time. Stand on top of the square stones, looking north toward Scotland, and imagine the thoughts of the lonely Roman sentries who stood guard here nearly 2,000 years ago.

From Housesteads, you can stay on B6318 toward Newcastle if you want to cycle more of the Wall. A cold Scottish wind persuaded us to turn south instead, and we swung right off **B6318** just past Housesteads Fort, cycling toward **Haydon Bridge.** Go left for **Newbrough** off the **Haydon Bridge road** after about 1½ mi, and continue on through gentle terrain to Newbrough, following the river and signs for **Hexham.**

Cross the **Tyne River** and go left on **A69,** then veer right after 200 ft onto **Road A695.** Cycle the final 2½ mi into **Hexham.**

The hills begin in earnest after Hexham, and the next 12 mi to Allensford Park Campground are mercilessly tough, so you may want to stop in

Hexham for the night. There's a campground south of town, near the racetrack.

Hexham to Durham: 27 miles

Leave Hexham on A695, cycling toward **Road A68,** where you'll turn south toward **Darlington.** Climb a long, steep hill and pass through **Carterway Heads.** To reach the Allensford Park Campground, coast down the exhilarating descent to the river. The camping area is on the left, just across the bridge. It's a lovely spot, but a visit here means you'll have to climb again to leave the river, pedaling up a 1½-mi hill.

If you're not in the market for a tent spot yet, go left on **Road B6278** for **Shotley Bridge** after Carterway Heads. This will eliminate some of the uphill cycling, taking you into **Consett,** where a right turn will put you on **Road A691** for **Lancaster** and **Durham.** From Consett, enjoy 12 mi of easy, peaceful riding. Traffic increases as you draw near Durham.

Follow signs for the **city center,** crossing the **River Wear,** then take the first left after the bridge. Pedal up a ramp to an overpass above A691. The tourist office is left of the overpass; the castle and cathedral are to the right.

Durham is an attractive town, perched above a crazy loop in the River Wear. Walk down to the park along the river for a picnic, and enjoy a fine view of the cathedral. Then climb the hill to explore Durham's castle or the dark, squarish cathedral housing the bones of St. Cuthbert, one of England's many saints. The building's beautiful interior provides an interesting blend of Norman and Gothic architectural styles.

Durham offers several B&Bs and a youth hostel (limited opening times).

Durham to Ripon: 65 miles

Leave Durham by recrossing the bridge above the River Wear and continuing west on **Road A690** toward **Crook.** Climb a hill away from town. Cycle into **Willington** and turn left on the road for **Hunwick.** Pass through Hunwick to where the **road veers** sharply left. Go right here, then turn left for **Witton-le-Wear** about ¼ mi later. Descend steeply to **Road A689** and turn left. Pedal about ¼ mi and turn right for Witton-le-Wear. Pass through Witton-le-Wear, then turn left on **Road A68.**

Stay on A68 to **West Auckland,** then turn right onto **Road A688** toward **Staindrop** and **Barnard Castle.** Pass by the handsome Raby Castle on the way.

The tourist office in Barnard Castle is on the left as you enter town. The city and its surroundings have much to offer, from the ruined castle in the city's heart to the nearby Bowes Castle to the striking ruins of Egglestone Abbey a little farther on.

We chose a sunny picnic by the quiet stones of **Egglestone Abbey** for our sightseeing stop. To reach the abbey, continue on the main road through Barnard Castle (with a quick visit to the city castle along the way), then

The ruined walls of Egglestone Abbey stand open to the sky.

follow signs for **Bowes Castle and Museum** out of town. Cycle past the French-inspired English château and turn right for **Egglestone Abbey** and **Road A66.** Go right again just after crossing the bridge over the **River Tees** and ride the final ¼ mi to the ruined abbey.

After your lunch break, return **past the bridge** (don't cross) to reach A66, a busy road with lots of trucks. Turn left on **A66,** but escape it after about 2 mi, veering right for **Newsham.** Then follow signs for **Dalton, Kirby Hill,** and **Richmond.** Climb to a ridge above the river, cycling on rolling country roads through peaceful farming villages. Go up and over a final steep hill before descending quickly into Richmond, with its large church, ruined castle, and lovely park.

Cross a small bridge on the **Swale River** below Richmond's castle and go straight, following signs for **Road A6136** and **Catterick Garrison.** Climb away from Richmond for about ½ mi of tough pedaling, then merge right onto **A6136** for Catterick Garrison. The terrain softens to roller-coaster hills as you ride past large, unattractive military encampments. Follow signs for **Scotton** from Catterick Garrison. From Scotton, continue on for **Masham,** then pedal toward **Kirkby Malzeard.** From Kirkby Malzeard, ride for **Galphay** and continue on the route signed for **Ripon.**

If you want to camp before Ripon, you can find a convenient base for visiting Fountains Abbey by going right for **Grantley** after **Kirkby Malzeard.** You'll reach a pleasant campground about 1 mi later. If you stay at the campground, you can get fresh milk and directions to the abbey from the friendly owner.

To reach the Trust's **Fountains Abbey,** go **west** from Ripon on **Road B6265** and turn left at the sign for **Studley Royal Park.** Ride most of the way to the ruins through the surrounding deer park, then walk the final ¼ mi through the landscaped grounds. Fountains Abbey is the largest monastic ruin in England, and it's surrounded by the lawns and gardens of Studley Royal Park. This is one of the most enchanting Trust properties you'll visit. Plan to spend at least two or three hours exploring the grounds.

Ripon to York: 25 miles

Leave Ripon heading **east** on **B6265** for **Boroughbridge.** Stay on B6265 through Boroughbridge, following signs for York. About 4 mi past town, turn left at a sign for **Ouseburn.** Pedal through Ouseburn, angling left for the **toll bridge** and turning right just across it to follow signs for **Beningbrough Hall.** You can reach this Trust mansion and garden from **Newton-on-Ouse.** Watch for signs in town.

Continue on for **Shipton** and turn right onto the hectic **Road A19** to cycle the final miles to **York.** There's a campground 2 mi before the city at **Rawcliffe** (well marked from the main road), if you'd prefer to camp outside town. Otherwise, continue into **York** on A19. You'll see signs for the tourist office as you approach the walled old town. Go right at the **Y.** The tourist office is on the left, across from the York Art Gallery.

It's a short walk from there to York Minster, one of England's most magnificent cathedrals. For a fine view of the cathedral and the city, climb to the walk along the city wall and make the circuit of the town. Don't spend all your time outdoors, though, because the grand interior of York's cathedral boasts a spectacular collection of stained glass you won't want to miss.

If you're ending your cycling in York with a train ride back to London, reach the train station by continuing to the right past the tourist office and across the Ouse River. If you're staying awhile, there are two youth hostels in York, and there's a campground on the banks of the Ouse, not far from the Castle Museum.

A smiling angel welcomes worshipers to the cathedral in Reims.

TOUR NO. 2

WAFFLES, CHAMPAGNE, AND CHÂTEAUX

Brussels, Belgium, to Angers, France

Distance:	1,115 kilometers (692 miles)
Estimated time:	16 riding days
Best time to go:	May, June or September; avoid July/August tourist crunch
Terrain:	Gentle hills; lots of quiet secondary roads
Connecting tours:	Tour No. 16

"Are the French people really as unfriendly as everyone says?" We were asked that question a dozen times during our first month of European cycling. Our phone calls home were interrupted with the query, the letters we received from family and friends repeated it, and other travelers we met along the way wanted to know if we'd had problems with the supposedly stuck-up French. To all concerned we enthusiastically answered, "No, no, no!"

In fact, the three weeks we spent riding from Brussels south through French-influenced Belgium and on into France provided us with some of the most heartwarming experiences we were to have on our entire trip. First, there was the young man in Laon who, when we stopped to ask for directions at his flower shop, offered to lead us to the city campground, but changed his mind en route and took us home instead. That meeting yielded an afternoon of laughter and talk, an evening meal of steaming homemade *crêpes,* and a warm night's sleep on his living-room couch.

Then there was the French dairy farmer who offered his front lawn for our tent, pulled a thick mattress from his attic, and poured tiny cupfuls of strong black coffee to support our drooping eyelids while we talked late into the night. And then there was the schoolboy who found us camped beside a soccer field and took us home to his smiling parents, who graciously offered us hot baths and a warm bed for the night.

No, the French are not as unfriendly as everyone says. Savor the small towns, the farmhouses, the quiet parks just off the beaten track, and you'll find a treasure of friendly, smiling people just waiting for you to say the first *"Bonjour"*!

French roads are among the best in Europe. The secondary road system is excellent, with well-maintained surfaces, light traffic, courteous drivers, and surprisingly direct routes. Often, we found that our "sacrifice" in using the small French roads instead of the major ones actually resulted in fewer kilometers to pedal rather than more. Generally, both the Belgian and French drivers travel entirely too fast, and you'll be shocked by the "rockets" that catapult past you during your first days on the road. But you'll love the careful courtesy extended to cyclists.

CONNECTIONS. The busy Zaventem Airport in Brussels is a major European entry point for travelers from the United States and Canada. Airfares to Brussels are competitively priced, so it's an economical spot to begin your cycling trip. If you choose to begin your trip elsewhere, Brussels also has convenient rail service from other European cities.

INFORMATION. Write to the Belgian and French national tourist offices before you leave. They'll send bundles of literature, plus campground and tourist maps. The address for France is French National Tourist Office, 610 Fifth Avenue, New York, New York 10020. Be sure to make use of the local tourist offices in France as well, to collect English-language literature and regional campground and accommodation listings. These offices are called *Office de Tourisme* or *Syndicat d'Initiative.*

For information on Belgium, write the Belgian National Tourist Office at 745 Fifth Avenue, New York, New York 10151. Ask for a street map of Brussels to make your arrival go more smoothly.

Michelin's *Green Guide Belgium and Luxembourg,* Rand McNally's *Blue Guide Belgium and Luxembourg* and *Baedeker's Netherlands, Belgium, and Luxembourg* are three excellent guidebook options for your visit. Michelin divides France into 19 regions, each covered by a separate *Green Guide.* Guides for the Loire and Paris are applicable to this tour, and are published in English. Two *Blue Guides* and *Baedeker's France,* as well as *Let's Go: France,* are other possibilities.

MAPS. Michelin produces an excellent map series for route finding in Belgium and France, and the 1:200,000 detail will satisfy all your needs. Maps are readily available in bookstores, and they're considerably cheaper than the Michelins in the United States. If you're conserving *francs,* wait until you arrive to buy.

ACCOMMODATIONS. Campgrounds abound in both France and Belgium, but they're scarcer in the rural areas of France and the less-toured parts of Belgium. Prices are low and facilities are adequate, if somewhat spartan at times. (Bring your own toilet paper, and resign yourself to occasional cold showers and lots of pit toilets.)

The hotel systems of Belgium and France are markedly different. In France, rooms in one- or two-star hotels are usually less than $10. In Belgium, you'll be lucky to claim budget lodgings for less than $15. Room prices are usually posted at the front of the hotel, either on a window or in the lobby, and they often include a continental breakfast consisting of a beverage (coffee, tea, or chocolate) and bread, butter, and jam.

SUPPLIES. Shopping hours in Belgium and France can be troublesome, especially outside of the big cities. In Brussels and Paris you'll be able to find stores open at almost any hour, but in rural areas the shopkeepers adhere to

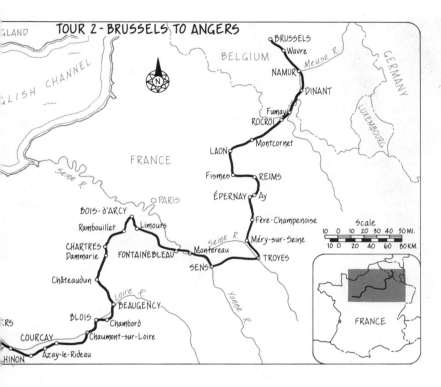

a strict set of opening and closing times that will have your stomach growling in dismay. Watch out particularly for Sunday afternoons and Mondays. These are sacred times to shopkeepers, and you can often search high and low for sustenance without luck. Also, the hours between 12:00 noon and 2:00 p.m. are dedicated to crazily hung *fermé* signs and lots of locked doors. But if you shop for lunch early, shop for dinner by 6:00 p.m., and buy for the weekend on Saturday, you'll be able to enjoy some of the most delicious food you'll find anywhere in Europe.

If you're a cheese and bread lover, France is just short of heaven. If pastries are your weakness, it may be even closer! Hunt down breakfast feasts of buttery *croissants* or *pain au chocolat;* enjoy wonderful picnic lunches with crusty brown *baguettes* and creamy cheese; and make your dinners special with a glass of one of the outstanding regional wines.

Cycling is extremely popular in both Belgium and France, and you won't have difficulty finding bike parts in large cities. Of course, racing has priority and 27-in tires aren't common, so you may have to do some scouting around to meet special needs.

Brussels to Namur: 78 kilometers

Belgian tourist literature laments the fact that many travelers consider Belgium to be simply a place to set off from on their way to other European destinations. Indeed, it's a shame to skip the things that Brussels has to offer in your haste to hit the cycling trail. So, if you won't be returning to Brussels for your flight home, plan to delay your cycling a few days and take a look around while you recover from jet lag.

If you arrive at the airport, located in the area of the city known as Zaventem, you'll have several options for accommodations. (Pick up a map and information on the city at the airport information office.) If you're in the market for a hotel room on your first night out, there's an excellent spot about 15 minutes' ride from the airport — the Hotel Residencie Z, on the left as you cycle through Zaventem. Rooms are spotless, and the proprietress is friendly and speaks excellent English.

The closest campground is at Wezembeek-Oppem, about 6 km from the airport. It opens on April 1, has nice facilities with hot showers and a cozy clubhouse, and provides a good base for trips into Brussels via public transport. To reach the campground from the airport, follow the signs to Zaventem. Turn left at the **first light** and stay on the main street, passing a park on the left, then turn left at the **next light**. Go left on **Road N2**, then swing right onto **Road M3**, to pass under the freeway, and angle left at the **Y**. Keep to the right, passing a large American School and descending a **short hill**. Turn left at the bottom and reach a **camping sign** pointing to the right. Go right up a slight hill, following the road past another camping sign and on to Paul Rosmant Campground.

If neither camping outside the city nor a room in the suburbs appeals to you, you can find plenty of accommodation options in Brussels, including a youth hostel. You'll find lots of cars and congestion in this very international city, home of the European Economic Community and NATO staffs, so enter with caution.

After you've gotten dizzy spinning and staring in the Grand'Place, overwhelmed your senses in a few of Brussels' superior museums, and had your first taste of sugar-crusted Belgian waffles, Belgian *frites* topped with mayonnaise, or a bar of the country's famous chocolate, you'll be ready to pedal.

From Zaventem, continue south to **Road N2** and turn left. Pedal N2 to **Nossegem** and veer right onto **Road N227**. Cross over the freeway, descend a hill, and turn left for **Moorsel**. Ride 4½ km to **Road N3**, turn left toward **Leuven**, then go right soon after for **Vossem**. Cycle into Vossem and cross the creek. Go right at the T, then immediately left to climb steeply for **Duisburg**.

Continue to Duisburg and turn left toward **Veeweide** and **Huldenberg**. From Huldenberg, continue on up a steep hill toward St.-Agatha-Rode. Turn right at a sign for **Terlanen**, then descend and go right again to arrive in the small town.

Follow the road toward **Ottenburg**, and turn right in Ottenburg for **Wavre**. Swing left on the main road (**Road N4**) after crossing the tracks and entering Wavre. Shortly after, turn left onto **Road N43,** making your way toward **Perwez,** 19 km farther on. The route to Perwez climbs and descends through mild hills and farmland. There's a bike path on the left side of the road, and heavy traffic will encourage you to use it. Watch out for the speeding mopeds you'll have to share it with, though.

In Perwez, turn right on **Road N42** for **Aische-en-Refail,** and continue through **Liernu** for **St. Germain.** Cycle through St. Germain and turn right on **Road N411.** Cross over the freeway, then abandon N411 by veering left onto **Road N534** for **Villers-lez-Heest.**

Cycle on through Villers-lez-Heest and descend on N534 into **Namur.** You'll want to explore the Citadel that rules the city, and you can stop at the tourist office at the confluence of the Meuse and Sambre rivers to gather information on the city and accommodations.

There's a youth hostel in Namur, as well as several hotels. The closest camping is at Suarlée, about 9 km from the city.

Namur to Dinant: 28 kilometers

From the Citadel and the tourist office, cross the Sambre River and turn right onto the **Ardennes Bridge** to cross the Meuse. Continue to the roundabout and go right on **Avenue Bouvesse,** following signs for **Dinant** along the pleasant, somewhat narrow **Road N47** and climbing into the hills above the river. You'll have pretty views of the opposite shore and the meandering river below as you ride. This part of the Meuse Valley has lots of tourists, so if you're cycling on a weekend or in midsummer, you may have plenty of company.

Follow N47 to Dinant, a charming small city nestled beneath a fortress on the lazy river. A bizarre church with an onion-shaped bulb adds to the overall interest. Although it's small and touristy, Dinant is worth exploring. Climb the steps to the clifftop fortress for a stunning view of the church and city below. Take the 20-minute tour of the Citadel and listen to your guide tell jokes in two or three languages. Then descend to admire the striking stained glass in Dinant's church or join the crowds of tourists strolling the narrow streets.

There are campgrounds at both ends of the city, and there are several hotels tucked into the downtown core.

Dinant to Rocroi: 64 kilometers

Cross the **Meuse River** from Dinant's church and turn left for **Givet.** Follow the flat riverside route, admiring the churches and luxurious homes along the way. The road has very little traffic on weekdays, so you can watch the swans sailing on the Meuse and enjoy peaceful cycling as you anticipate your entry into France.

The **border station** at **Givet** is small and unimposing. It's also the only spot on our yearlong trip where our bicycle bags were searched. We were asked to remove our bags and carry them inside so the guards could examine them. Ten minutes later, after a somewhat shaky welcome, we were pedaling in France.

Follow the Meuse and **Road N51** toward **Fumay.** Climb steeply a few kilometers past Givet, then descend gradually to follow the river once more. At Fumay, another climb awaits as you turn up the hill (still on N51) for **Rocroi.** Admire the view of Fumay and its church as you labor up a steep grade from the city, then ascend more gradually through quiet forestland for the next 10 km. The road levels out before you reach Rocroi, a small settlement on a wide agricultural plateau.

There's a campground (open mid-April through September) in Rocroi, as well as a handful of small hotels.

Rocroi to Laon: 90 kilometers

In Rocroi, angle left on **N51** toward **Tremblois** and **Signy l'Abbaye.** Enjoy easy, level riding for awhile, then descend quickly after **Tremblois** on **Road D985** for **Rouvroy.** After Laval-Morency, the terrain flattens again. Continue **through Rouvroy** and turn right onto **Road D978** for **Rozoy.** The next 29 km provides excellent riding through rolling farmland with sparse traffic.

At Rozoy, follow signs onto **Road D946** for **Montcornet** and enter Montcornet 8 km later. Climb a steep hill as you leave town on **Road D977** for **Laon.** Traffic increases for the final 32 km into the city. Take a break to admire the pretty church in **Liesse** if the pedaling gets too hectic along the way.

Reach a junction with **Road N2** just outside of Laon and turn left for a brief but harrowing ride toward the city. Go right at the next intersection, following signs for Laon's **center** (*centre*).

There's a municipal campground sign pointing to the left at the next traffic light. Continue into the city if you want to hunt for other accommodations.

Laon's tourist office is next to the hilltop Cathedral of Notre Dame. This early Gothic church has one of the most incredible exteriors you'll see in France, and the bovines that moo from its heights represent the epitome of Gothic stonework.

Laon to Reims: 70 kilometers

Leave Laon via the small suburb of **Ardon** and continue on **Road D967** toward **Fismes.** Keep to the hilly but lightly traveled road through Bruyères-et-Montbérault (steep climb from town), Chamouille (another climb), and Longueval-Barbonval (one more time). There's a nice park in Fismes, if you're looking for a picnic spot.

Go straight through Fismes onto **Road RD386** for **Faverolles.** From Faverolles, continue **through Tramery,** go under the A4 freeway, and ride to Sarcy. Angle left in **Sarcy,** then go right, staying on **RD386** for **Chaumuzy.** Reach a junction with **RD380** and turn left to pedal the final 16 km into Reims. Cross the **Andre River,** then climb past one of the many military cemeteries in the region. Descend, then pedal up a final hill to **Pargny.** The last 8 km into **Reims** are level.

Begin following signs for the **city center** and the cathedral as you negotiate the busy city streets. The rue Libergier will deposit you in the Place du Cardinal-Lucon, with a magnificent view of the cathedral's west front to recompense you for all the exhaust you've just inhaled. The tourist office, two blocks from the cathedral, offers lots of literature on the city and the surrounding Champagne region. You can buy a street map for Reims there as well.

We carried the memory of the city's Cathedral of Notre Dame with us for an entire year of cycling. Its golden stone exterior and breathtaking interior will make an indelible mark on your heart. Take time to appreciate this masterpiece of the 13th century, with its matchless stained glass and the stone-faced company of angels, animals, and saints that guard its doors.

There are lots of inexpensive hotels in Reims, or you can stay at the campground about 2 km southeast of the city center. It's open from Easter until the end of September.

Reims to Épernay: 33 kilometers

Leave Reims to the south on **Road D9** for **Ay.** The quiet, scenic route will take you through acres of champagne vineyards and forested hills. There's a long, steady climb through trees to **Craon-de-Ludes,** then easier riding and more vines leading on to Ay. Look for signs for **Épernay** in Ay. Follow a **bike path** from Ay to **Épernay** as you pedal **Road D201** to a junction with **Road N51.** Go left and cross the **Marne River** into the city.

Check with the tourist office across from the train station for information on tours of the champagne cellars that give Épernay its major claim to fame. We tried out Moet et Chandon, wandering the extensive caves with a group of British tourists. Then we continued on to Mercier, where visitors ride an underground trolley and marvel at old statuary and a huge wooden cask built in the 1800s for a world exposition in Paris.

You can also ask at the tourist office for information on hotel rooms. If you prefer to use Épernay's campground, take the first right after you cross the **Marne River** coming into the city. You'll pass a gigantic **supermarket** on the left. Swing left on the **second street** past the store, then left again at the Y and follow campground signs to the site. Although it's in an industrial area, the campground is clean and pleasant, and it's just a 10-minute ride to the champagne cellars.

Épernay to Troyes: 100 kilometers

Cycle south through Épernay on **Road RD51** toward **Sézanne,** but angle left onto **Road D40** before you actually leave Épernay, following signs for **Cuis** and **Avize.** Climb a gentle hill covered with vines, then pass through the picturesque towns of Cramant and Avize.

From Avize, continue **through Oger** and keep right for **Vertus** when the road merges with **D9.** Vineyards give way to rolling wheatland, and you can watch dozens of tractors crisscrossing the fields as you exchange waves with the dust-covered drivers. Cross **Road RD33** at **Bergères** and stay on D9 toward **Fère-Champenoise.** Traffic is light, the road surfaces are good, and the hills are gentle swells on the horizon as you pedal through acres of farmland.

Follow signs for **Euvy** and **Road D43** in Fère-Champenoise, but take time to explore the cool stillness of the town church if you get a chance. Then cycle D43 through Euvy and Gourgançon to **Salon**. Go left, then veer right onto **Road D7** for **Champfleury** and **Plancy-l'Abbaye**. There's a nice riverside park in Plancy, if you need a picnic spot.

From Plancy, you'll see signs for Troyes. Cross the **Aube River** as you ride toward Charny-le-Bachot. Go right on **Road D8** in **Charny,** then left back onto **D7** for **Méry-sur-Seine**. Just before the road crosses the Seine, swing left again onto **Road D78** for **Droupt**.

Pass through many small farming towns on the 31-km, up-and-down ride along the Seine. Each settlement has its own church, graveyard, and war memorial. At Pont St. Marie, turn right on the main road (Road N77) for Troyes.

There's a large campground on the right before you cross the river into Troyes, or you can check at the tourist office near Troyes's cathedral or near the train station for accommodation listings and information on the city.

Continue into Troyes, following signs for the **center,** and arrive at the Cathedral St. Pierre et St. Paul. Enter the cool interior and watch the lines of stone pillars unfold before you, dappled with colored sunlight and stained by windows of brilliant glass.

Troyes is a wonderful city for strolling. Visit the old town to walk along the rue des Chats, lined by half-timbered houses, or explore the churches of St. Urbain, St. Jean, and St. Madeleine.

Troyes to Sens: 70 kilometers

This ride leads through the breadbasket of France, with endless acres of rolling wheatland, lots of quiet roads, and an often troublesome west wind. Leave Troyes's center on **Road N60** toward Estissac. Cross over the **train tracks** and take the **first right,** to gain **Road D60** out of town. Go across the busy main road on the edge of Troyes, following signs for **Grange l'Evêque.**

Stay on D60 through Dierrey St. Pierre and continue on to **Faux-Villecerf,** then angle right onto **Road D23** before going left onto **Road D29** for **Villadin.** Turn left in Villadin, then right to climb for Pouy-sur-Vannes on D29 once more. Swing down through town at **Pouy-sur-Vannes** to pedal past a lovely château, then regain the main road (now **Road D84**) for **Courgenay.** There's a campground in Courgenay, if you want to end your day early. Otherwise, continue on D84 past Courgenay and take a right soon after onto **Road D328** for **la Charmee.** Cycle through la Charmee and stay on D328, then go right onto **Road D28** for **la Postolle** and **Thorigny-sur-Oreuse.**

In **Thorigny,** angle left to ride the final 15 km to **Sens** on the up-and-down **Road D939.** Descend a moderate hill before Soucy, then continue on for Sens through St. Clément, arriving in Sens right by the tourist office. The mass of the cathedral will rise out of the city before you.

There's a campground in Sens, as well as several hotels sprinkled throughout the shop-lined streets.

If you would prefer to pedal south now, along the Rhône River toward the French Riviera, Provence, and Spain, you can hook up with Tour No. 16 in Sens, and ride that route in reverse.

Sens to Fontainebleau: 64 kilometers

Leave Sens by **retracing** the route north to **St. Clément,** then angle left onto **Road D23** toward **Cuy** and **Gisy** just after crossing the **N6** autoroute. Go left again after about 2 km to follow the small road through Cuy, Evry, Gisy, and Michery, paralleling the winding **Yonne River** along the way.

Go through **Saichery** and continue on D23 through **Serbonnes** and **Courlon,** riding northwest toward Montereau. At **Misy-sur-Yonne,** there is a pretty riverside resort with a campground and an attractive park. In **Marolles,** 6 km farther on, turn left onto **Road D411** and ride toward **Montereau.** Cross the confluence of the Yonne and Seine in Montereau, a city with a large church. Turn west onto **Road D39** immediately after crossing the river, following signs for **Champagne.**

This part of the ride is dull, with lots of industrial development, but the scenery improves soon after. From Champagne, **recross the Seine** to **Thomery** (there's a campground here), and climb out of town on **Road D137** through the lovely **Forêt de Fontainebleau.** Reach Fontainebleau 8 km later, and follow signs for the **center** to reach the heart of the city and the château that housed French rulers from Louis VII through Napoleon III.

There are several hotels in Fontainebleau. Find a room and then plan to spend several hours wandering the immense grounds of the château. Enjoy a picnic dinner of a *baguette* and a chunk of pungent goat cheese (*Chèvre*), and watch the strollers in the neatly trimmed gardens. Or take a tour of the château's lush interior to end your royal afternoon.

Fontainebleau to Bois d'Arcy: 95 kilometers

The route from Fontainebleau will take you along the southern edge of the Paris sprawl, zigzagging on quiet roads and getting close enough to France's overwhelming capital for a visit to Versailles.

You can take the rapid-transit train into Paris to sightsee from your campground base in Bois d'Arcy. If you're not camping, you can stow your bike and gear at Fontainebleau or Versailles before heading into Paris. Many French train stations offer a baggage storage service. Friendly hostel or hotel keepers are another option. Thinking of cycling into the city? Well, you're braver than we were.

Leave Fontainebleau on **Road D409** for Étampes, passing through fragrant forests on the way. Turn right on **Road D11** for **St. Martin** and forsake the busy road for quieter riding. In St. Martin, go left for **Courances,** crossing **under the A6** autoroute. You can make a short detour from St. Martin to peek at the château in nearby Forges. Follow the quiet country road to Courances. The city offers a beautiful château with extensive gardens and lawns that practically demand a picnic.

Go left onto **Road D372,** then swing right onto **Road C3** to continue on to Moigny-sur-École. Take the hilly Road C3 west toward **Courdimanche.**

Merge with **Road D105,** going right, then turn right again onto **Road D449** for **d'Huison.** There are many lovely châteaux to entertain you as you follow the Essonne River. Turn left for **Longueville** in d'Huison. Ride through Longueville, continue on to **Boissy,** and take **Road D148** to **Villeneuve, Etréchy,** and **Chauffour.** Angle right in Chauffour onto **Road D132** for Souzy. Cycle through Souzy and continue for St. Chéron and **Marais.**

Turn right onto Road D27 just before Marais, catch a glimpse of another château, then swing left to regain D132 to Angervilliers. Go right on Road D838 for Limours in Angervilliers. From Limours, climb steeply on **Road D998,** then turn left onto **D838** again, following signs for **Versailles** toward **St. Remy.** Follow the signs for Milon-la-Chapelle through St. Remy, turning left onto **Road N306** in town, then swinging right for **Milon-la-Chapelle.**

Reach the picturesque city of Milon and climb a tough hill toward **St. Lambert** on **Road D46.** There are several luxurious homes scattered along the way. You'll have lots of time to look at them as you labor up the hill. Go right onto **Road D91** after St. Lambert and climb some more. At the top of the ridge, turn left for **Montigny-le-Bretonneux,** then turn right about 3 km later onto a **smaller road** that runs parallel to the **train tracks** (tracks will be on your left). Go under a **bridge** crossing the tracks, and turn right. Then go left at the **main road.**

Follow signs for **Bois d'Arcy** and turn left to get onto a **bridge** over the tracks and freeway. Descend a short hill and look for signs for the campground at the **next intersection.** Go left and follow the road to the large, modern, and sparkling clean Parc Étang Campground. It's a 15-minute walk from the campground to a huge Euromarche shopping complex and the train station. You can ride the train into Paris in less than an hour. It's also a short train trip to Versailles from here, and there are a campground and hotels in Versailles, if you'd prefer to stay there.

Ask the helpful campground staff of Parc Étang to explain the complexities of train fees and schedules before you set off for Paris. Then lock up your bike, grab your camera, and make your pilgrimage to Paris. A few exhausting days of sightseeing in the "heart of France," and you'll be ready to head for back roads and farmland once again.

Bois d'Arcy to Chartres: 69 kilometers

Retrace your route through **Montigny,** and turn right on **D91** for **Dampierre** and **Rambouillet.** You'll face scattered hills along the way, with a real steepie just before Dampierre. Handsome châteaux in pretty settings will greet you in Dampierre and Senlisse. Road D91 leads into **Road N306.** Turn **right** to pedal the final busy kilometers to **Rambouillet.**

Cycle into Rambouillet's **center** to arrive at the luxurious grounds of the château. This part of France has an abundance of scenic picnic spots. All you need is a loaf of bread, a cool beverage, and a château. Rambouillet provides all three. If you're drinking wine, be sure to dilute it with water the way the French people do, or your legs won't carry you through the afternoon.

Depart Rambouillet along the **main road south** (Road N10), and turn right onto **Road D150** for **Orphin**. Cycle **through Orphin** and go right, then veer left on **Road D150** (becomes **Road D32**) for **Ecrosnes and Gallardon**. Stop to explore the large church in Gallardon before pushing on along D32 for **Chartres**. You'll see the lovely silhouette of the twin-towered cathedral of Chartres as you approach the city. Road D32 dumps you onto the growling **Road N10** just before town. Follow this road to the center and the cathedral.

The famed stained-glass windows of Chartres Cathedral glow like a thousand jewels in the velvet-vaulted heights, and the carvings around the front altar are masterpieces of detail, reciting the life of Christ in stone. With its parks and churches, its hilly old quarter, its narrow streets and its tantalizing alleys, Chartres is a gem of a city to visit on your journey to the Loire.

If you want to camp, Chartres has a great municipal campground within walking distance of the cathedral. To find it, follow the path along the Eure River from the cathedral, heading south to reach a large sports complex/park/camping area. There's a youth hostel in Chartres, as well. Check at the tourist office next to the cathedral for information.

Chartres to Beaugency: 94 kilometers

From the campground at Chartres, turn right onto the **main road**, then go left on **Road D935** and ride the 10 km to **Dammarie**. On the far side of Dammarie, take **Road D127** right toward **Fresnay-le-Comte**. Swing right into Fresnay soon after, and follow signs to **Meslay-le-Vidame**, a small town with a big château. From Meslay, continue on for **Bronville**, and go right on **Road D154** for **Bois-de-Feugères**.

Cross **N10** and angle left on D359 for **Alluyes**, riding through flat farmland. Leave Alluyes on **Road D153** and pedal to **Dangeau**, then go left on **Road D941** toward Logron. Veer left in **Logron** onto **Road D955** for **Châteaudun**. Riding is flat and effortless for most of the day, and you'll spot the fortress-like château of Châteaudun peering out over the plain long before you cross the Loir River and climb the hilly, narrow streets to the château.

There's a well-signed campground 1 km off the road as you approach the city, if you're looking for a spot to spend the night.

Stop to explore the city's tangled streets and get a closer look at the stout walls of the château before continuing on **Road N10** for **Cloyes**. Turn left onto **Road D924** for **Blois** just outside of Châteaudun, and angle left again a few kilometers later onto **Road D925** for **Beaugency**. Follow this road through Verdes, Binas, and Cravant.

Ride the final 7½ km along D925, and enter Beaugency. You can wander the streets of this interesting little town on the banks of the Loire River and visit the ruined 15th-century château.

There's a campground just across the river from the city. The tourist office at 88, Place du Martroi can direct you to the youth hostel or recommend hotels in town.

Chambord Château scrambles toward the sky in a rush of towers, pinnacles and roofs.

Beaugency to Blois (via Chambord): 44 kilometers

If you prefer smooth (but busy) roads, take **D925 south** from Beaugency and ride to **la Ferté St. Cyr,** then turn right onto **Road D103** and follow signs for the 15 km to **Chambord.** But if you'd rather gain a bit of dirt road and lots of solitude, leave Beaugency on the small road along the **north shore of the Loire.** Cycle through **Tavers** and on to Lestiou and Avaray, where you can peek through someone's front gate at a luxurious private château. Continue south to **Herbilly,** and turn left to ride through farmland toward the bending river.

Come to a **bridge** across the Loire a little farther on, and go left on **Road D112** to cross to **Muides.** Follow signs for **Chambord** and pedal the last 7 km to the château through the delightful Parc Chambord. Sunny April weather, a fragrant forest, and the waves from picnicking French families made the ride a joy for us. Be sure to stock up on lunch supplies before you enter the park, as you'll surely want to have a picnic of your own on the lovely grounds.

The Château de Chambord, set on vast green lawns and framed by carefully trimmed plane trees, is a fanciful building, reputedly designed by Leonardo da Vinci. You may have to deal with unusually large hordes of tourists here, but the beauty of the grounds will enthrall you for hours. Take the tour of the interior, too, if you can bear to leave the view outside.

Leave the château by backtracking to the **junction** of **Roads D84** and **D112** and angle left for **Maslives** and **Blois.** Go left at **Montlivault,** 8 km later, onto the busy **Road D951** along the Loire. Follow this main road toward **Blois** and sneak some glances at the pretty river vistas while the cars whiz past.

There are two campgrounds before Blois. The first is on the right about 4 km from town. It is big and noisy, with chilly showers and primitive toilet facilities, so you might want to try your luck down the road at the second campground, on the left 2 km closer in.

You'll have a fine view of Blois as you pedal into the city on **D951** along the south side of the river, and the streets you'll explore after crossing the Loire are a delight as well. The Château de Blois has one of the best-preserved interiors of all the Loire châteaux, and the tour is well worth your time. Visit the tourist office on Avenue Jean-Laigret to get a list of the city's churches and find out about accommodation options. There are several hotels in town, and there's a rural youth hostel about 5 km from the city center.

Blois to Courcay (via Chaumont and Chenonceaux): 67 kilometers

From Blois, continue on **Road D751** on the south side of the Loire toward **Chaumont-sur-Loire.** The 21-km ride to Chaumont is quick and effortless.

Lock your bike at the entrance to the park that surrounds the château and climb to the hilltop fortress/mansion to enjoy a spectacular view. The inexpensive tour of the drawbridge-equipped château includes a visit to the stables and a self-guided stroll through the mansion. But don't linger past the lunch-hour break or you may find yourself locked inside with the drawbridge drawn!

Retrieve your bike and climb away from Chaumont and the Loire on **Road D114** toward **Montrichard.** Branch right soon afterward onto **Road D27** for **Vallières** and **Chissay-en-Touraine.** Climb again after Vallières, staying on D27 for the 10 km to Chissay-en-Touraine and the Cher River and watching for the homes burrowed into the hillsides along the way. In Chissay-en-Touraine turn right onto **Road D176** for **Chenonceaux.**

Chenonceaux is an impressively situated château that spans the Cher River with elegant arches. Hand over the entry fee for grounds, gardens, and interior, and savor the matchless setting in the company of floods of tourists doing the same.

There are hotels in the nearby town if you need a room, but the prices will reflect their proximity to one of France's most popular châteaux. Chenonceaux also has three campgrounds.

You may want to consider continuing along the Cher toward Tours and its St. Gatien Cathedral from Chenonceaux, but Tours is a big city with big-city traffic. We were ready for a break from cities and sights at this point in our ride, so our route from Chenonceaux was an end run south of Tours and its sprawl. Leave Chenonceaux by continuing west on **Road D176.** At **Civray,** turn left for **Blére** and cross the Cher. Go left at the **Y** for **Thoré,** cross under the **main road,** and climb past Thoré and les Fougères before turning right for **Sublaines.**

Leave Sublaines on **Road D25** toward **Chédigny,** then turn right onto **Road D10** to follow the pretty river route through **Reignac** and on to Courcay.

There's a great spot for picnics along the river in Courcay, and there's a city campground, as well.

Courcay to Chinon: 64 kilometers

Leave Courcay on **Road D17** along the **south shore** of the Indre River, and pedal the 4 km to **Cormery.** From here, you can choose between the main road for **Veigne** on the north side of the river or the hilly, smaller roads to the south. It's 8 km to Veigne by the northern D17 route. Veigne has a pleasant municipal campground.

The remaining 54 km to Chinon are mostly level, with some short climbs out of the scattered towns along the way. From **Veigne,** stay on **D17** to pass through **Montbazon,** a busy town with an open market in its central square and a striking hilltop ruin. Continue on D17 along the **Indre,** and watch for the caves and dwellings tunneled into the limestone cliffs along the water's edge. After **Artannes,** veer right onto **Road D84** and proceed straight through the following junction to stay along the north side of the Indre for the final 9 km to **Azay-le-Rideau.** The moated Renaissance château of Azay-le-Rideau is open for tours.

From Azay, cross the Indre for **la Chapelle St. Blaise,** and turn right on **Road D17** for **Usse.** Pick up more traffic as you merge with **Road D7** to pedal the remaining 6½ km to the castle/château at Usse. Go to the bridge spanning the Indre River to get an excellent view of the fairy-tale structure said to be the inspiration for Sleeping Beauty's castle.

Continue pedaling on D7 to **Huismes,** and veer left to follow **Road D16** the 10 km to **Chinon,** a small city with a rich history. Chinon offers a superbly situated campground on the south bank of the Vienne River, with a great view of the medieval town beneath its impressive hilltop fortress. Climb the hill to explore the ruined château and savor the view of the city, the river, and the surrounding vineyards. Then wander the steep hillside below to stare at the homes burrowed into the rock, before returning to your tent for a dinner of bread and Port Salut cheese.

Chinon has a youth hostel and several hotels. The tourist office is on rue Voltaire in the heart of the old town.

Chinon to Angers: 85 kilometers

Leave Chinon on **Road D749 south,** crossing the Vienne and turning right onto **Road D751** when the road branches. Go left after 3 km onto **Road**

D759, then turn right for **le Coudray-Montpensier.** Angle right again for **la Devinière.** As you pedal along **Road D117,** you'll spot the châteaux of la Devinière and Chavigny on the right and the bulk of Coudray-Montpensier commanding a hill to the left.

Just after **Chavigny,** turn right for **Couziers** and **Fontevraud,** cycling through a military area of forest, rolling hills, and rough pavement. Cruise through Fontevraud and continue on **Road D145** through the Forêt de Fontevraud. Go straight in Champigny and pedal into **Saumur** along a ridge above the Loire River.

Arrive at the lofty château of Saumur, a beautiful towered fortress with a spectacular site above the river. Plan to enjoy a picnic on the grassy grounds while you savor the château and the view. Then proceed through Saumur, following signs for **Gennes** onto **Road D751** along the south bank of the Loire. Riding is pleasant for the 15 km to Gennes, once you escape the industrial suburbs of Saumur. You can stop at one of the wineries or visit the famed mushroom caves of the Musée du Champignon along the way.

Saumur has a hostel, a campground, and several hotels, if you decide to linger. The tourist office is at 25, rue Beaurepaire.

In **Gennes,** angle right to stay along the Loire's flat **southern shore.** Ride on **Road D132** and pass through the quiet towns of le Thoureil, St. Remy, and St. Jean. Go right onto **Road D751** in **St. Jean,** then ride to **Juigne** and continue straight to regain **D132.** Pedal the last few km to a junction with **Road N160** and turn right on N160 to gain the bridge across the Loire toward **Angers.**

If you want to camp at Angers, you can stop at les Ponts-de-Cé, about 6 km before the city center. Or continue into Angers by pedaling along the busy **Road N160** and following signs for the **center.** The somber black towers of the château, its flower-filled moat, and its museum displaying the Tapestries of the Apocalypse will combine to make your visit to the city a memorable one.

There are tourist offices near the château and the train station where you can get information on the city's hotels, hostel, and campgrounds.

Angers offers good rail connections to other parts of France, if you're ending your cycling here. The train-station workers are used to handling lots of bikes in this heavily cycled region of France, so your hassles should be limited.

In our case, our ride continued northwest from Angers, so we cycled away from the magical Loire Valley and on to green and windy Normandy and Mont St. Michel on the Normandy coast. Then we pedaled east for Rouen and north to Dieppe to catch the ferry to England, bidding a fond *"au revoir"* to France.

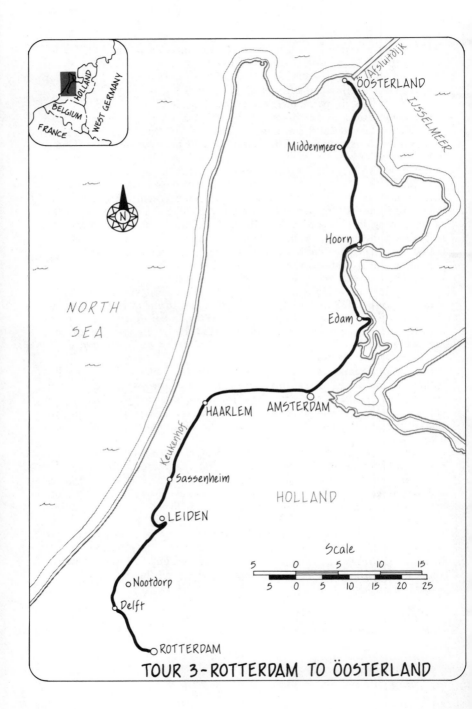

TOUR 3-ROTTERDAM TO ÖOSTERLAND

TOUR NO. 3

SAY CHEESE
Rotterdam, Holland, to the Ijsselmeer

Distance:	162 kilometers (100 miles)
Estimated time:	4 riding days
Best time to go:	May for tulips, June for sun, September for solitude
Terrain:	Flatly undemanding
Connecting tours:	Tour No. 1

If you're unsure of your conditioning or courage for bicycle touring in Europe, there are few countries more ideal to "get your feet wet" than Holland, a land so flat it's practically underwater and so overrun with bicycles that cyclists rule the road. If you're seeking adventure, wide-open spaces, or great physical challenge, however, perhaps you can combine this ride with a more demanding tour in England or West Germany.

Holland will reward you generously for the time you invest in it — whether it's a month-long exploration of the country's 30,000 km of cycle routes or a quick zip through on your way to West Germany or Belgium. The Dutch are hospitable, helpful and amazingly skilled in languages. Dutch food is hearty and simple, from the famous cheeses such as Edam and Gouda to pickled cabbage and salty herring. And Dutch beer is famous throughout the world.

Bicycling is a national pastime in Holland. You'll see women toting tots and groceries and men hauling briefcases and hoes. The country's bicycle path system is incredible, and most cities are crisscrossed with scores of bike lanes and illuminated with dozens of bicycle traffic lights. Watch for signs showing a white bicycle on a blue background — they mean that use of the bike paths they mark is compulsory. Dutch cyclists are conscientious about complying with traffic laws — you should be, too.

Be forewarned that this "cyclist's paradise" is sometimes less than heavenly. The bike paths are convenient and safe, but their rough surfaces will drive you batty, and their proximity to main roads will punish your senses with traffic noise. Dealing with Holland's bicycle rush hours can be unnerving, too, especially when you're being passed on all sides by older cyclists in wooden shoes.

CONNECTIONS. If you arrive in Holland at Amsterdam's busy international airport, you may want to begin your trip with a brief train ride to pick up the start of this tour in Rotterdam. Train travel with bicycles is delightfully hassle free in Holland, and many trains have baggage cars where you can simply wheel your bike aboard, secure it snugly for the ride, then unload it yourself at your destination.

If you land at Hoek van Holland via ferry from Harwich, England, as we did, there's a well-marked bicycle route for the 35-km ride to Rotterdam. Or, if you'd rather not make the detour south to Holland's second-largest city, you can simply hop onto the tour route at Delft, about 25 km from Hoek van Holland. There's an excellent city campground 1 km from the ferry terminal at Hoek van Holland.

INFORMATION. Write in advance to the Netherlands National Tourist Office, 576 Fifth Avenue, New York, New York 10036, and ask for information on sightseeing, camping and bicycling, as well as free maps for Rotterdam and Amsterdam. Check on getting a Holland Culture Card through the National Trust Office, too. For about $10, the Culture Card provides free admission to more than 200 museums and gives discounts on many other services.

For additional reading material on Holland, turn to *Baedeker's Netherlands, Belgium, and Luxembourg* or the *Blue Guide Holland*.

MAPS. For route finding in Holland, the 1:300,000 tourist map *Nederland CIB,* published by N.V. Falk, is a good choice. It's easy to use and shows hostels and campgrounds. Michelin also offers its usual high-quality 1:200,000 maps for the country.

ACCOMMODATIONS. Dutch campgrounds are pleasant, abundant, and affordable, and you can get listings of sites from the Dutch tourist offices (look for their *VVV* signs). The VVV staffs are helpful and usually speak excellent English. Many of the offices charge a slight fee for literature, and almost all charge for room-finding services.

Lodgings in hotels range from affordable to expensive. Look for youth hostels, student hostels, sleep-ins, or unpretentious hotels if you're on a budget.

SUPPLIES. Shopping is effortless in this modernized country. Stores generally stay open Monday through Saturday from 9:00 a.m. to 5:00 p.m., with an occasional afternoon or morning off, and banks keep similar hours.

Finding bike parts isn't difficult in Holland. Locating high-quality touring gear will be a challenge, however. You'll see Dutch tourers on balloon-tired bikes with suitcases strapped behind their seats, and most of the bicycles here use 26- or 28-in wheels, so you'll have to hunt for tires and tubes. There are several large bike shops in Amsterdam where you can find most replacement parts you'll need.

Rotterdam to Leiden: 50 kilometers

Rotterdam is a huge port city that plays host to more than 30,000 oceangoing ships a year. Despite its size, its industry, and its half-million-plus population, the city isn't too awful for cycling. But then how could it be? It's in Holland!

If you arrive at Rotterdam's main train station, there's a VVV office there where you can stock up on maps and literature. The Rotterdam

A quiet bike path near the coast of Holland.

campground is at the Roel Langerakpark, about 3 km from the train station. It's not marked with a camping symbol on the city map, so ask at the VVV for help locating it. There's a youth hostel in Rotterdam, too.

While you're in the city, check out a few of the dozen museums in town — Holland has more museums per capita than any other country in Europe. You might want to explore the Rotterdam zoo (Blijdorp), take a boat tour of the vast harbor, or go for a walk through Delfshaven, Rotterdam's old port district.

From Rotterdam's train station, go west on **Weena** and turn right at the

Staten Tunnel to pass under the train tracks. Cycle along Statenweg, and go left on **Stadhoudersweg** to pass the zoo and the campground. Gain a **bike path** leading out of the city as you follow bike path **signs for Den Haag and Delft.** Many of Holland's bike paths are simply small roads paralleling big roads, and the path from Rotterdam to Delft is a perfect example.

Cycle beside the northbound A13 freeway as you make your noise-flooded way out of Rotterdam. Turn left off the main bike network to ride for **Delft,** following signs for the **city center** as you approach Delft. The impressive town square, ringed by countless shops stuffed with the famed Delft Blue China, has a charm that even the oppressive tourist trade can't shatter.

Walk along Delft's cobblestone streets and admire placid canals running past handsome housefronts. Visit Nieuwe Kerk and Oude Kerk, Delft's most prominent churches. Their exteriors of somber red brick seem unnaturally glum in the midst of all the glittering china. Seek out Delft's tourist office in the **main square** to pick up literature on the town.

The city offers an abundance of inexpensive rooms in July and August, when the large student population disappears. There's also a campground on the north edge of town, if you decide to stay.

Leave Delft, following signs for **Nootdorp.** Pass Delft's campground and sports center, then cycle through Nootdorp and follow signs for **Leidschendam.** If you have trouble with your route finding along the way, stop at an intersection and pull out your map. Friendly locals will descend on you in hordes, eager to offer directions.

As you approach Leidschendam, cross under the **freeway** and turn right to parallel the **canal** toward **Leiden.** Keep the canal on your left for about 9 km, and continue on the small, car-free road past attractive homes with lace-filled windows and trim, flower-bedecked yards.

Cross the canal on a **bridge** at the edge of Leiden. Follow signs for the **city center** into town. Leiden's VVV is across from the train station. You can get a free city map and a brochure to help you negotiate the town's people-packed streets (be prepared for the huge street market on Wednesdays and Saturdays). Leiden has 11 museums to tempt the curious, and its rich intellectual heritage dates back to the founding of Holland's first university here in 1575. Leiden is also the city of the Mayflower pilgrims, and there's a special pilgrim museum in town.

Get help at the VVV to find a room. There are several inexpensive pensions and rooms in private homes to choose from, as well as a youth hostel and a campground. The campground is a short distance north of town.

Leiden to Haarlem: 28 kilometers

Leave Leiden from the VVV, cycling past the **train station,** then turn left under the **train tracks** to follow signs for **Haarlem** and **Amsterdam.** You'll come to a confusing sign directing bicycles and cars straight for Amsterdam. As the road branches into a **Y,** angle right toward **Sassenheim,** then follow the **bike signs for Haarlem.**

As you cycle north toward Haarlem, you'll be passing through the **Keukenhof,** the heart of Holland's bulb-growing industry. If you're lucky enough to ride through when the flowers are in bloom (late April and early May), you'll be rewarded with a dazzling display of daffodils, hyacinths, and tulips.

Enter Haarlem and follow signs for the **center and VVV** along the canal. Cross the **train tracks** and the **canal,** and turn right on **Staten Bolwerk.** Then follow signs to the **train station** and the VVV.

You can pick up a free map of the city, English-language literature, and a list of accommodations at the VVV. There are several campgrounds and two youth hostels near Haarlem. At the VVV office ask for directions to the campground at Liewegje 17, a few kilometers east of town. Even if you're not camping, it's the best way to get on the right road for Amsterdam.

While you're in Haarlem, be sure to visit St. Bavo's Church (Grote Kerk) and the adjacent Grote Markt for a look at some of the architecture that gives the city its charm. Or walk to St. Bavo's Cathedral, a strange jumble of architectural styles that's quite stimulating compared with some of the rather stuffy Dutch churches you'll see.

Haarlem to Amsterdam: 20 kilometers

Before you leave Haarlem, shop for the N.V. Falkplan/CIB street map of Amsterdam. It's a good reference to have for your ride into Holland's largest city. If you follow the abundant bicycle path signs, you'll probably do fine without it, but you'll want a map for your sightseeing in Amsterdam anyway, so why not get it in advance?

From **Haarlem's station,** cycle east along the canal and follow **signs for Amsterdam,** pedaling on the **bike path** away from the city. You'll parallel the N5 freeway for much of the ride to Amsterdam. The campground at Liewegje 17 is just off the bike path a few kilometers outside of Haarlem. The busy proprietor at the canalside site will squeeze your tent in with the scores of trailers that rule the place, if you decide to stop.

Continue on the well-marked bike route, following signs for **Amsterdam Noord** (north). You'll end up pedaling along **Road S103 (Haarlemmerweg)** with the canal on your left as you enter Amsterdam's urban sprawl. Cycle into the city core and head for the huge **Amsterdam train station** (a few blocks to the **left**). An immense VVV office with piles of literature and long lines of confused tourists awaits you there.

Be particularly careful with your bicycle and gear in Amsterdam. It's a city of youth, travelers, and bicycle thieves. In fact, a recent canal cleanup yielded hundreds of stolen (and scuttled) cycles. You may want to get a room where you can lock things up while you're sightseeing, just for peace of mind. There are several hostels and student sleep-ins in Amsterdam. Don't be shy about asking the management for a safe place to stow your bike.

We camped at Kampeerterrein, one of Amsterdam's "youth campgrounds," and wished we hadn't. Although it's just across the harbor from the train station and very convenient (free ferries run every 6 minutes), it was incredibly crowded and noisy when we were there.

Amsterdam has far too many top-notch attractions to list here. Our highest recommendations go to the Van Gogh Museum, the Rijksmuseum, and the Anne Frank House. Of course, the city itself is a living museum you can explore for days. Plan to do lots of walking, or hop one of the canal boat tours to get an overall look at this maritime city.

Amsterdam to the Ijsselmeer: 64 kilometers

From Amsterdam's main train station, take the free ferry across the harbor. Cycle away from the **ferry dock** and angle left, then go right to follow a path along the **Noord Hollandsch Kanaal.** Cross the canal on a small bridge and continue straight to a **T** on Meeuwen Laan. Turn left and follow **Meeuwen Laan** past the campground turnoff and onto **Wadden Weg.**

Go right onto **Wadden Dijk** just before another small canal, and follow this road as you first parallel and then go up and over the waterway. Take the bike path and then turn right on **Werengouw,** then veer left on **Beemsterstraat.** Continue on Beemsterstraat through **Zunderdorp** and follow signs for the **Waterland Bicycle Route.** This is a heavily used bike route through flat polder fields. The scenery is enjoyable, despite the crowds of weaving cyclists.

Pass through Waterland and cross under the main road in a **bike tunnel,** following signs for **Hoorn.** Make the short side trip to Volendam and Edam by turning right for **Volendam,** a small fishing village with a lively waterfront. Cruise along the waterside route next to Volendam's yacht-filled harbor, and admire the traditional costumes of the tourist-pleasing locals. Take the road along the dike (*dijk*) toward **Edam,** another pretty town cut by serene canals.

Cycle through Edam and cross under the main road in another **bike tunnel,** then follow the bike path on to **Berkhout.** There are two campgrounds beside the bike route near Berkhout. Continue on for **Hoorn** and turn off the main bike way to swing through the city. The 17th-century streets and a Wednesday folk market make Hoorn an interesting spot to visit. From Hoorn, follow signs for **Leeuwarden and Middenmeer.**

Ride past Lambertschaag, Middenmeer, and **Wieringerwerf,** then swing right, following signs for the **dike.** As you ride the final kilometers to the Afsluitdijk, you'll pedal through a pleasant forested area where birds, picnickers, campers, and beach lovers abound. This 29-km dike is the reason the Zuider Zee (a sea) is now the Ijsselmeer (a lake). It's an impressive witness to the Hollanders' tenacious quest for farmland.

If you're pedaling back to Amsterdam from the Ijsselmeer, consider a route through Alkmaar and Purmerend for visits to two of Holland's major "cheese towns." If you're continuing this tour by cycling on toward West Germany, be sure to allow yourself plenty of time for the ride across the dike. There aren't any campgrounds along the way! However, there are both a campground and a hostel on the southwest end of the dike at Oosterland.

TOUR NO. 4

BIKING WITH THE VIKINGS
Stockholm, Sweden, to Copenhagen, Denmark

Distance: 632 kilometers (392 miles)
Estimated time: 8 riding days
Best time to go: June, July, or August
Terrain: Gentle hills; lots of easy pedaling
Connecting tours: Tour No. 5

For a leisurely look at two very different Scandinavian countries, a pleasant mix of solitude and big-city sightseeing, and lots of beautiful scenery, this tour from Stockholm to Copenhagen is hard to beat. To prepare for your ride, read the introductory material for Sweden provided here and the information for Denmark at the start of Tour No. 5. If you have time, combine the two tours for a more extensive Scandinavian experience.

Beginning a ride in a new country is always a bit unnerving, and one of the first tasks you'll have in Sweden is discovering a greeting to use for your friendly exchanges on the road. *"Hej-hej,"* Swedish hellos are fun! Practice your *hej-hej* (hay-hay) while you cycle, and enjoy the easy warmth and responsiveness of the Swedes you meet along the way. You'll have few difficulties with language here, since most young Swedes speak excellent English, and you'll find people to be hospitable, fun loving and friendly to cyclists.

Like most Europeans, Swedish drivers fly down the road at terrifying speeds. You may want to run for cover the first time you see the famed "car-passing-a-car-passing-a-car" maneuver, but you'll get lots of "hello" honks and waves to brighten your cycling days.

CONNECTIONS. Stockholm's Arlanda Airport draws in international flights by the dozens on a daily basis, so reaching the start of this tour should be effortless if you're coming by air. If you intend to stop cycling in Copenhagen (where this tour ends), rather than hooking up with Tour No. 5 and pedaling on, you may want to buy roundtrip airfare to Copenhagen. You can travel to Stockholm by ferry and train to begin your ride.

If you arrive in Stockholm at the airport, you'll have about a 40-km journey into the city. Your best bet may be to find an airport-city center bus that will carry your bicycle and gear into Stockholm for you, or to stow your things at the airport and make the bus trip in to pick up maps and information before you ride. If you plan to cycle into Stockholm, be sure to have a good map on hand before you challenge the urban sprawl.

INFORMATION. Write to the Swedish Tourist Board, 75 Rockefeller

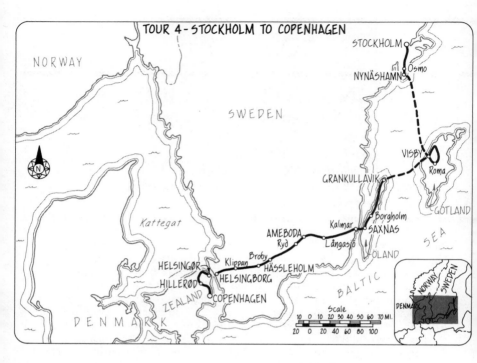

Plaza, New York, New York 10019, for information on Sweden, and request pamphlets on Stockholm, Gotland, the Stockholm Card, camping, and bicycling. Tourist offices within Sweden are well stocked with English-language literature, and be sure to also visit the superb library at the Swedish Institute when you call on Stockholm's main tourist office. Additional reading material can be found in *Baedeker's Scandinavia* for your trip.

MAPS. For route finding in Sweden, use either the inexpensive 1:1,000,000 FINA road map (available in FINA gas stations) or the costly 1:300,000 maps published by Esselte Kartor AB (available in bookstores at about $8.00 each). Although it's nice to have the detailed maps, you may discover, as we did, that many of Sweden's country roads are not paved and, consequently, not much use.

ACCOMMODATIONS. Although Swedish campgrounds cost more than those in most other European countries, they're still good accommodation bargains. And in Sweden you can also take advantage of "Everyman's right" (*Allmänsträtten*), a law that allows camping on unfenced land, and plop your tent down in a secluded spot for a free night's sleep. However, it's still wise and courteous to ask permission when you can.

Lodgings in hotels are expensive in Sweden. Youth hostels provide a more affordable option.

SUPPLIES. Sweden's reputation as one of the most expensive countries in Europe is well deserved, so you'll have to be sharp if you're on a tight budget. Grocery prices are slightly higher than in the United States, and prepared foods and restaurant meals are even more expensive. Stick to picnics and camp-cooked dinners (with an occasional splurge for local specialties), and your budget will survive.

Fortify yourself for long riding days with a hearty Swedish breakfast of whole-grain cereal doused with thick sour milk (*filmjölk*) and topped with lingonberries or wild blueberries. For delicious crunchy lunches, try the tasty and mild Swedish cheese (*ost*) on top of ripply brown crackers (*knäckebröd*). Dinner treats include reindeer stew (*renskav*) and a hearty potato, onion, and egg hash (*pytt i panna*).

Swedes are hard workers, and the Swedish economy is one of the healthiest in Europe. Stores keep long hours in this country where the almighty *kroner* stands tall beside the dollar, but you'll still have to look hard to find a grocery store open on Saturday afternoon, Sunday, or late at night, and banks are closed on weekends.

There are large bicycle shops in both Stockholm and Copenhagen where you'll be able to find a good selection of replacement parts.

Stockholm to Nynäshamn: 68 kilometers

Your first priority on arrival in Sweden's capital should be to head for the Sweden House (Sverigehuset) northeast of the train station. You can buy a detailed map of Stockholm's streets there, and you can get a free Stockholm map that shows major bike routes within the city. For a few dollars extra, the Sverigehuset offers a special Stockholm cycling map that provides more detail than the free map.

You'll see lots of bicycles on Stockholm's streets, and the extensive network of bike paths makes riding in the city pleasant.

The two campgrounds closest to Stockholm's center are both 10 km outside the city — one to the north and one to the west. We followed the "blue" bike path west to reach Ängby Camping. There are several youth hostels in Stockholm, as well. Ask at the Sverigehuset for directions.

After you've done your sightseeing in Sweden's sparkling capital, with walks in the old town (Gamla Stan) and visits to the islands of Skeppsholmen and Djurgården, you'll be ready to ride for Nynäshamn and the Gotland-bound ferry. Check on the Gotlandsbolaget ferry schedule while you're still in Stockholm. There's an office of the Gotland Tourist Association in the city, and you can get ferry times and prices there.

Hook up with the "purple" bike path (you can get onto it at **Slussen,** on the southern end of **Staden Mellan Broarna**) and follow the small **purple bike markers** through the city and onto a route paralleling **Road 226** south. Pass through Johanneshov, Älvsjö, Stuvsta, and Huddinge, and ride on to **Tumba,** where you'll cycle along the edge of the busy Road 226 toward **Nynäshamn.**

At **Vårsta,** turn left onto **Road 225,** again following signs for **Nynäshamn.** There isn't a marked bike lane along this 30-km section, and a weekend or holiday ferry rush might make things hectic. Pass through forested countryside and pedal gentle hills past clear lakes and countless red farm buildings. At **Ösmo,** swing right onto **Road 73** to pedal the final 11 km to the ferry. Traffic increases on this road, so ride carefully. Watch for signs for the **Gotland/Visby ferry** as you enter Nynäshamn.

The overnight Nynäshamn-Visby ferry may disrupt your sleeping schedule a bit, but you'll be able to catch a short snooze on the five-hour ride. The cost is about 100 kr per person, with no charge for bicycles. You'll have to wait to board until just before the midnight departure time, joining the crowd of restless cyclists making the trip. Entertain yourself by watching the vacation-bound Swedes around you, and marvel at the suitcases, guitars, and trailers lashed to their bikes.

Around Gotland: 70 kilometers

The ferry lands at Visby, the largest and loveliest city on Gotland. You'll see hundreds of cyclists in town and throughout the island. They have good reason to be there — Gotland is an enchanting spot for cycling. Its flat fields are carpeted with wildflowers, its Baltic beaches are ideal for lazy days in the sun, its weather is some of Sweden's finest, and its size allows cyclists to do as much or as little riding as they choose.

The Visby tourist office is a short distance from the ferry terminal at Färjeleden 5. Buy the tourist map (*Gotlands Karta*) at 1:200,000 scale. It shows campgrounds, churches, hostels, and sights of interest. Ask at the tourist office for information on hostels and camping on the island — there are nine youth hostels on Gotland (one in Visby), and there are several campgrounds.

If you want to camp near Visby, leave the ferry dock and follow the **bike path north** along the sea. The first campground you'll come to is open only to trailers. Continue on to the large and busy Snacks Campground, about 7 km from town. You can take the bike route up the hill just before the campground to enter at the main gate, or push your bike across a short stretch of sand and come in from below.

Plan to spend at least a day exploring Visby. The narrow streets lined with wooden houses and cascading rose trellises, the red slate roofs, and the ruined arches of naked churches against an invigorating backdrop of blue sky and sea will make your visit special. Don't linger in the tourist areas too long. Instead, visit Visby's churches, walk the walls, or explore the botanical gardens for a taste of the town.

You can easily choose your own day trip for cycling on the island. Or take your gear along and ride to a secluded beach to camp. We've included this sample day ride from Visby back to Visby to give you an idea of what Gotland has to offer.

Ride south through Visby on the main street and turn left just before the **old water tower,** gaining the road marked for **Roma.** Reach an **intersection** with a sign marked **Roma 2 km** straight and Dalhem to the left. Stop for a look inside the church beside the road. (*K:A* is Swedish road-sign terminology for church — *kyrka*.) Then turn left for **Dalhem** and go right just past the **church** onto a small paved road.

Follow the road to **Kungsgarden,** the ruin of a Cistercian abbey built in 1120. Retrace your route out from the grass-encircled ruin, and turn right for **Dalhem.** A wonderful series of biblical wall paintings graces the interior of Dalhem's church, and the quiet churchyard makes a great spot for a picnic lunch.

From Dalhem, ride toward **Ekeby,** then continue on for **Fole.** Turn left for **Bro** at Fole. Stop to inspect the painted interior of the ancient church at Bro, where a Norman tower rules a Gothic nave. Just past Bro's **church,** turn right for **Väskinde,** and pedal on past Väskinde through fields of shimmering wildflowers. Reach a **T** with a larger road and go right, then turn left for **Krysmyntagärden** to pedal south along the coast through **Brissund** and on back to Visby.

Grankullavik to Saxnas: 100 kilometers

The ferry from Visby to Grankullavik on the northern tip of Öland will further disrupt your ferry-flustered sleeping schedule with a 6:30 a.m. departure. The three-hour ride goes quickly, though, and you can stimulate your drooping eyelids with a cup of potent Swedish coffee on the way.

Öland is a long, skinny island connected to mainland Sweden by a 12-km bridge. It's as popular with the Swedes as Gotland is, and its accessibility results in heavier tourist traffic. Nevertheless, the unbroken vistas of sea and fields, wildflowers and windmills, make pedaling on Öland a delight.

Leave the ferry dock at Grankullavik and ride to **Byxelkrok.** You may want to stock up on groceries at the market in town, as it's the largest store for about 60 km. Continue on **Road 136** to **Boda** (there's an Öland tourist office here), then escape the main road for a time by turning right for **Byerum.**

The rough pavement on this quiet loop is its only drawback. At **Byerum,** angle back toward **Road 136** and **Löttorp.** Follow Road 136 to **Köpingsvik.** Truck traffic is light on Öland, but a seemingly endless line of cars and campers makes riding less than ideal on Road 136.

Öland's climate encourages the growth of more than 30 species of orchids (don't pick — they're protected), and it's also the temporary home of thousands of migratory birds. You'll be cheered by fields of glowing poppies and entranced by the silhouettes of dozens of wooden windmills as you ride.

Köpingsvik and Borgholm are two hectic tourist towns with what must be the highest per capita concentration of putt-putt courses in the world. Roll onto a bike path along the right side of the road after **Köpingsvik,** and follow it to **Borgholm.** Take the slight dogleg into town and stop at the busy tourist office for literature.

If you're looking for a room, you may want to end your day in Borgholm, as there are hotels and hostels there. Otherwise, you'll ride past several of the island's 27 campgrounds during your final 25 km to Saxnas and the bridge.

A stout windmill searches for a breeze on Öland.

Just outside of **Borgholm,** turn right off Road 136 to take a look at **Borgholm Castle** (*slot*). It has 12th-century origins and 300-year-old walls. The summer castle of Swedish royalty, Solliden, is a little farther down the secondary road past Borgholm Castle. Return to **Road 136** and continue south toward **Glömminge** for about 20 km. Turn right at the sign for **Saxnas** and its well-marked campground (a few kilometers north of the bridge) to end a long cycling day. The vast campground is quiet, clean, and inexpensive.

Saxnas to Ameboda: 109 kilometers

Leave the campground and continue on the secondary road to regain the **main route** toward **Kalmar.** Coast down a ramp onto the **12-km bridge** to the mainland, and claim a piece of the slow-vehicle lane as speeding cars fly by on the left. Bypass the first off ramp, then swing down from the second onto a **bike path** marked for Kalmar's **center** (*centrum*).

You'll be tormented by unmarked side paths shooting off the main bike route as you pedal toward Kalmar. Just continue following signs for the **center.** Kalmar's town hall and cathedral and the moat- and garden-encircled Kalmar Castle will greet you in the city.

From Kalmar, you can take a more northerly route toward Helsingborg and the Denmark ferry if you'd like to cycle through the heart of Sweden's glass district. It will mean busier roads, but will allow you to visit Orrefors (on Road 31) and Kosta (on Road 123), two of the best-known of Sweden's world-renowned glassworks.

We chose to continue our ride toward Helsingborg on the southern, secondary roads, cycling through quiet Swedish forests and shunning the traffic-heavy routes to the north and south. The result was three days of peaceful riding through forest and farmland, star-filled nights of camping in the woods and a welcome break from crowds and sightseeing.

From Kalmar Castle, follow signs for **Road E66** south. **Bicycle route** signs for **Smedby** will take you parallel to the main road for about 1 km. Then turn left for **E66** and **Karlskrona** and join E66 soon after. After about 8 km, veer right onto **Road 120** for **Långasjö.** Cycle kilometer after kilometer of gentle terrain, with only fern-covered forests and an occasional passing car for company.

Make the slight detour off Road 120 to pass through Långasjö. Be sure to stop at the small tourist office in town. If you need a room for the night, ask there. Continue on through town and turn left on **Road 124** to regain **Road 120** toward **Tingsryd.** We pulled off the road just past Ameboda to stake out a spot in the trees, sharing the cloudless night with mosquitoes, no-see-ums, and a host of stars.

Ameboda to Hässleholm: 112 kilometers

Continue on Road 120 until just before **Tingsryd,** then merge with **Road 30** into town. You can stop at the tourist office before hopping back onto **Road 120** for **Ryd.** In Urshult, stop to peek inside the city church. It has a wonderful painted interior that's a pleasant surprise. Pedal on to Ryd, a small town with a glass factory and a music museum, then turn left onto **Road 119** to pass through gently rolling forestland for the remainder of the day.

Lönsboda has another fine church with beautiful light fixtures. Ride through Glimåkra and **Broby,** cross Road 20, and continue on Road 119 for **Hässleholm,** a mid-sized city with a handful of pleasant churches and parks. To find the **campground** before Hässleholm, turn left onto **Road 23.** Go across the overpass and turn right to circle onto **Road 21** east. You'll soon reach the signposted campground at **Ignaberga,** and you can visit the on-site limestone grottoes if you have the energy. We opted for dinner and hot showers instead.

If you need a room in the city, stay on **Road 119** into **Hässleholm** and look for signs for the tourist office, located in a modern building complex to the left of the road.

Hässleholm to Helsingborg: 82 kilometers

Begin your last day of cycling in Sweden by leaving town on the busy **Road 21** through **Tyringe,** Perstorp, and Klippan. There's a wide shoulder most of the way, and there are several long, gradual hills. If you're fighting a persistent west wind, as we were, the going can be tough.

Abandon Road 21 about 3 km beyond **Kvidinge,** turning left for **Nord Vram.** Pedal up a gradual hill, then descend through forest to a T. Turn right toward **Astorp.** Continue on this road for **Gunnarstorp** (don't turn off for Astorp) and pass through Gunnarstorp. Then go left at the T. Turn right for **Hyllinge** soon after, pedal through the town, and follow signs for **Helsingborg.**

You'll come to an **overpass** and a ramp onto the **E4 freeway** for Helsingborg. Go straight for **Odåkra** instead, and climb a hill to reach a **roundabout** and signs for a **bike route** into Helsingborg. Follow this marked route into town, staying with signs for the **center.**

Helsingborg has an attractive core, centered around its castle, its park, and its Santa Maria Kyrka. Climb to the castle keep for a fine view of the harbor, then descend to the church. Unimpressive on the outside, this lovely building has a Gothic-arched nave of dark red brick supported on massive pillars. Look for the carved pulpit, the crystal chandelier, and the fleet of fascinating hanging ships inside.

From the church, it's only a few blocks to the ferry terminal, and there are frequent 20-minute crossings to Helsingør, Denmark. You can spend the night in Helsingborg or ride across to seek lodgings in Helsingør, calling a last *hej-hej* to Sweden.

Helsingør to Hillerød: 41 kilometers

The Helsingborg-Helsingør ferry lands in the shadow of Kronborg Castle, famed as the traditional home of Prince Hamlet. You can wander the grounds without charge or pay for a tour of the interior. Make the circuit of the castle and admire the view across the water to Sweden, then head north on the coast **Road 237** for **Hornbaek.** There's a large, noisy, crowded campground just off Road 237 on the outskirts of Helsingør. It's rather expensive, and all it has going for it is its proximity to the ferry and the castle.

Cycle along the coast, staring at sandy beaches and luxurious homes. Traffic can be heavy along the route, so try to ride early in the day before the sun seekers are out and about. In **Hornbaek,** a bustling seaside town awash in shops and tourists, turn inland onto **Road 235** toward **Espergaerde.** Veer right just past **Horneby** for **Havreholm,** and ride through lovely rolling farmland on small, almost traffic-free roads.

Continue on through **Plejelt,** go right onto **Road 205,** then left toward **Tikøb.** Ride less than a kilometer and swing right for Jonstrup and **Fredensborg.** Cycle along the quiet shoreline of Esrum Lake, surrounded by undulating fields of grain, and catch an occasional glimpse of a thatch-roofed cottage or a flower-flooded garden.

Enter Fredensborg, turning right onto the main road (**A6**), then go right at the **traffic light** in town to coast down a shop-lined street to Fredensborg Castle. The magnificent park surrounding the spring and fall residence of Danish royalty is worth a visit in itself, and if you're looking for a picnic spot, look no farther. The palace is open to visitors only in July (from 1:00 to 5:00 p.m.), but you can admire it from without as you explore the park and gardens.

Return to **A6** and turn right on A6 to cycle a nice **bike path** beside the road for the final 10 km to **Hillerød.** Follow the signs into Hillerød and turn right for Frederiksborg Slot. If you want to camp, follow campground signs to the south side of town to reach a pleasant, grassy site with great hot showers. It's an easy walk to the city center and the lakeside castle from the campground.

Hillerød's tourist office is in the center of town, across from the market area at 1 Torvet. If you'd like some help through the tangle of bike paths on the way out of town, pick up the inexpensive area bike-route map the tourist office offers. You'll be able to rent rooms in private homes through the tourist office, too.

Leave yourself a few hours for a visit to Frederiksborg Castle. It's one of Denmark's most magnificent palaces. Not only is the building itself outstanding, but the National Historical Museum inside presents a fantastic blend of furniture, paintings, china, and crystal that will take you hours to examine.

Hillerød to Lyngby/Copenhagen: 50 kilometers

We endured some frustrating wandering around, trying to find the best route out of Hillerød for Copenhagen, and road construction in the area added to the confusion. Decide on your own escape route with the help of the tourist office map, or try this option. Leave Hillerød on **Road 233** south toward **Lynge,** then turn left onto **Road 53.** Go past the intersection with **Road 19,** and veer right on the secondary road for **Karlebo.**

Cycle past a large windmill at Karlebo and continue on through moderately hilly farmland to **Avderød.** Go straight toward **Kokkedal** and **Hor-**

Signs of spring in the Danish countryside.

shølm, then angle right about 1 km outside of Avderød onto a larger road. Swing right again to get on **Road 229** for **Horshølm** after crossing the **E4 freeway.** Pedal along Road 229 for a few kilometers, then turn left for **Rungsted** and a return to the coast. The seaside **Road 152** has heavy traffic, but the route is scenic.

You can hop onto a **bike path** along the Copenhagen-bound train tracks if you prefer quieter riding. Watch for signs just before you reach **Road 152.** Cycle south through forests as you follow signs for **Klampenborg.**

There are several camping options in and around Copenhagen. We set up a base camp outside the city, then rode the train in for sightseeing. From **Skodsborg,** you can cycle inland 3 km on the **Naerum** road, then swing left after crossing E4 to reach a well-marked campground. Tucked in between the freeway and the train tracks, it's noisy and unattractive, but it's only five minutes from the train station — very convenient for sightseeing in Copenhagen.

There's a second campground just off the Copenhagen-bound bike path about 2 km south of **Skodsborg** (also signed from Road 152). This popular and crowded spot has a pleasant setting next to Dyrehaven, an immense deer park. You'll need to backtrack the 2 km to Skodsborg to catch a train into the city, however.

From either campground, you'll have easy access to an extensive network of bike trails, and you can explore the nearby attractions without your packs. For an enjoyable afternoon trek, follow signs for **Lyngby** on the gravel-surfaced bike ways. Lyngby (or Kongens Lyngby) has an old village centered around its 12th-century church, but most of the city is glaringly modern. Just north of town is the Frilandsmuseet, an open-air museum of Danish farm buildings and folklife.

From Lyngby, continue on bike paths for **Klampenborg.** You can swing off to the left to explore the forest paths of Dyrehaven. Entry to the deer park is free, and the well-maintained paths are open to bicycles. Plan to enjoy a picnic near the royal hunting lodge, or stop for a visit to Bakken, Denmark's 400-year-old amusement park. If you're camping at one of the spots we've mentioned, make your ride a loop trip by riding north through Dyrehaven and regaining the bike route along the train tracks at the northeast corner of the park.

Of course, all this suburb sightseeing will only increase your anticipation for Copenhagen. If you're ending your tour in Copenhagen, you'll probably cycle into the city center. Try to buy a detailed city map before you pedal in. There's an excellent 1:200,000 Copenhagen cycling map available at tourist offices, and it's a valuable reference for the host of bike paths in the city, especially for the approach routes from Klampenborg and Lyngby.

If you need a room, head for the tourist office next to Tivoli Amusement Park on H.C. Andersen's Boulevard 22 (a few blocks from the central train station) and let the staff there do your legwork for you. You may also want to buy a Copenhagen Card for your visit to the city. It's a good bargain if you're using public transit or exploring many of Copenhagen's myriad attractions.

Read the first few pages of Tour No. 5 for additional information on Denmark and on Copenhagen, its lovely, lively capital.

TOUR NO. 5

FERRY TALES IN DENMARK
Copenhagen, Denmark, to Kiel, West Germany

Distance:	266 kilometers (165 miles)
Estimated time:	6 riding days
Best time to go:	Late May through early September
Terrain:	Moderate hills; lots of pleasant, scenic cycling
Connecting tours:	Tours No. 4 and 6

There are few European countries better suited for the vacationing cyclist than Denmark. The road system is excellent, with more than 46,000 km of secondary roads and a vast network of bike paths. The country is small and the land is green and gentle, with friendly hills that break the monotony but not the spirit.

You may find the Danish language to be frustratingly unpronounceable, but the Danes are excellent linguists and you'll encounter many English speakers throughout your stay. People here are friendly and easygoing, and the Danes are blessed with a dry humor that will make your chance meetings a delight. We'll never forget the harried airline clerk at Copenhagen's Kastrup Airport who fielded our frantic inquiries as we faced a nationwide strike, a crippled airport, and one vacant seat on the last flight out. "Don't worry," he told us with a malicious twinkle in his eyes, "if a standby seat doesn't open up before the plane takes off, one of you will speak excellent Danish by the time you meet again."

CONNECTIONS. If you're beginning your Danish tour in Copenhagen, you'll probably arrive at the immense Kastrup Airport south of the city. Kastrup is a small city in itself — with restaurants, shops, showers, and beds. It's served by frequent flights from the United States and Canada.

You might choose to lock your bicycle in a safe spot at the airport and hop a bus into the city center to do your map and accommodation hunting before you mount up to do battle with the city streets. Once you're equipped with a Copenhagen street map or the cycle map we've recommended, your chances at a frustration-free introduction to this charming city will be much better. If you're cycling this tour as a continuation of Tour No. 4, you can pedal into Copenhagen on well-marked bike paths. Copenhagen also offers ferry connections to Malmö, Sweden.

INFORMATION. Write ahead to the Danish Tourist Board, 75 Rockefeller Plaza, New York, New York 10019, for general information about Denmark. They'll send brochures on camping, on Copenhagen, and on tour-group "bike holidays" at your request. You'll probably want to sup-

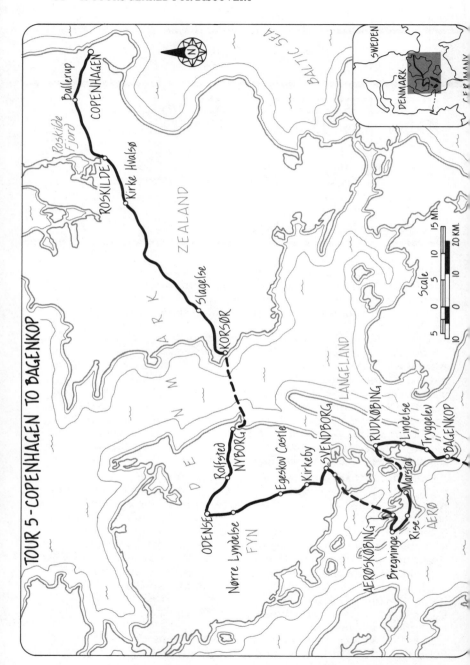

plement your knowledge of Denmark with a guidebook. *Blue Guide Denmark* and *Baedeker's Scandinavia* are two options.

The Danish Cyclist Federation publishes the information-packed *Bicycle Holiday in Denmark* and the *Bicycle Holiday Map*. While in Copenhagen, you can visit their office at Kjeld Langes Gade 14.

MAPS. A superlative four-map series for route finding in Denmark is published by the Geodesic Institute. The 1:200,000 maps are easy to use and well worth the 35-kr price. They show campgrounds, hostels and a plethora of tourist sights.

ACCOMMODATIONS. Campgrounds in Denmark are excellent. They're clean, convenient and well stocked with essentials like toilet paper and hot water. Coastal sites can be crowded and riotous with Tuborg-powered campers, however, and their prices are often surprisingly high. Check the fees and the noise level before you drive your stakes. You'll need an International Camping Carnet or a Danish camping permit to camp here. Review Part I for more details. Camping on your own in Denmark (with permission) is legal but less than ideal. The small country is overrun with tourists in the summer, and beaches and forests take a beating as it is. *Always* ask permission before you pitch your tent outside a campground.

Inexpensive beds are available in hostels, student sleep-ins, and private homes. Local tourist offices can help you make arrangements, and they'll supply lots of free literature for your bedtime reading, too. Because of the popularity of cycling in Denmark, you'll seldom get blank looks from tourist-office workers when you ask for cycle maps or route suggestions.

SUPPLIES. Prices in Denmark are roughly equivalent to those in Holland and England—less expensive than in Sweden but quite a bit more than in France, West Germany or Southern Europe. Shopping hours in the country are generally Monday through Saturday until 5:30 or 6:00 p.m., with Saturday-afternoon shutdowns and all-day lockups on Sunday.

Denmark is world famous for key elements of its cuisine, and you'll enjoy sampling sweet Danish pastries, flavorful and pungent Danish cheeses, and robust Danish beers. Open-faced sandwiches called *smørrebrød* make wonderful picnic fare, and you can pile on toppings of fish, meat, cheese, or vegetables to design your own feast. One warning about Danish cheeses— unless you're hauling a refrigerator on your bike, buy them in small quantities. The aroma of a warm chunk of day-old *h'avarti* can knock your socks off!

There's an excellent bicycle shop on Gothersgade, within a few blocks of the Danish Cyclist Federation office. (Ask at the office for directions.)

Copenhagen to Roskilde: 45 kilometers

There are several hostels and campgrounds in and around Copenhagen where you can stay while you go sightseeing in this wonderful city. The Copenhagen International Youth Hostel and an adjacent campground are on Sjaellandsbroen, a short ride west of the airport. (Read the final paragraph on Tour No. 4 for additional information.)

There is one drawback to beginning your cycling tour in Copenhagen—

Carved pews guard the shadowy corners of Roskilde Cathedral.

the city is so delightful, you may not want to leave! But after an obligatory visit to the Little Mermaid, a leisurely afternoon spent sitting with the silver-haired grandmothers on the benches in Tivoli Amusement Park, long hours of wandering the city streets, and a few cool evenings spent listening to jazz at a Copenhagen cafe, perhaps you'll be ready to ride.

From **Tivoli Amusement Park**, follow **H.C. Andersen's Boulevard** northwest, crossing the canal on **Gyldenløvesgade** and continuing on **Aboulevard** and **Agade** (same street — different names) until you run into **Borups Allé.** Turn left onto the bike lane along this street and continue past a campground (on the left) to **Frederikssundsvej.**

Go left here, riding through the districts of Brønshøj, Husum, and Herlev. Gain **Road 211** for **Ballerup** and go straight through an intersection with the road from Lyngby. Cycle into Ballerup, then turn left at the **first intersection.** Cross the railroad **tracks** and go right for **Smørumovre.** (If you're cycling from either of the campgrounds mentioned in Tour No. 4, you'll skirt to the north of Copenhagen proper and pedal through **Lyngby, Bagsvaerd,** and **Hareskovby** to join this route at Ballerup.)

From Smørumovre, follow signs for **Hove, Østrup, Gundsølille,** and **Store Valby,** cycling quiet secondary roads. We battled a tenacious headwind on this part of the ride, but hills are few and located mainly in the farmland beyond Smørumovre. After **Store Valby,** turn right for **Veddelev** to cross **Road A6** and reach a vast waterside campground. From this site, it's a short bike ride or a pleasant 3-km walk along Roskilde Fjord to reach the center of **Roskilde.**

If you're pedaling directly to the city to look for a room at the hostel or in a hotel, continue straight rather than turning off for Veddelev, and follow signs for the **city center.** Roskilde's tourist office is next to the twin-spired cathedral.

You'll be delighted by the skulls, crosses, swords, and angels that compete for space on the royal tombs that fill the church. Don't miss the woodwork in the choir, either. The intricately carved scenes give a beautiful summary of Biblical history. If you're still game for sightseeing after visiting the cathedral and taking a walk beside the whitecap-studded fjord, venture inside Roskilde's Viking Ship Museum before calling it a day.

Roskilde to Korsør: 84 kilometers

Follow the main road (**A6**) through Roskilde toward **Ringsted** and **Korsør.** Although there is an adequate-looking bike path beside the road, you'll do better to abandon the traffic noise for a secondary route through the green Danish countryside. On the edge of **Roskilde,** pass under the **A4 freeway,** and turn right onto the main road for **Holbaek** immediately after.

Go left about ½ km later onto a smaller road for **Lejre** and cycle through moderately hilly farmland past thatch-roofed houses and brilliant-hued rose gardens. The terrain becomes flatter as you pedal southwest throughout the day. From the **Lejre Road,** turn left at the sign for **Lejre ST** (station), cross the train **tracks,** and go right toward **Allerslev.** Come to a

T and take the **bike path** next to the **school** to gain the road toward **Kisserup.**

In Kisserup, follow signs for **Kirke Hvalsø,** then angle right onto **Road 255** to pedal through Kirke Hvalsø. Stay on the lightly trafficked Road 255 for about 20 km, then turn left just before **Stenlille** onto **Road 57** toward **Sorø.** Leave Road 57 a short distance later, swinging right onto **Road 203** toward **Slagelse.** As you approach Slagelse, follow signs for **C. Slagelse** and the **center** (*centrum*). The city has a pleasant downtown and a handsome church. There are a campground and a hostel there, if you need a place to stay.

Look for signs for **Korsør Road 150** to take you out of town. Cross the **A1 freeway** several kilometers later, then veer right at **Vemmelev** toward **Forlev.** Go straight through Vemmelev, keeping the freeway on your right. Cross a road signed for Korsør, continuing straight on the secondary route beside the freeway through **Halseby** and on into **Korsør.** Turn left when the road hits a **T,** and pedal under **two overpasses** before swinging right to reach the train station and **ferry office.**

Buy your ferry ticket for the one-hour crossing to Nyborg. You'll have to ride a short distance to reach the ferry landing, then squeeze aboard with the passenger train that runs into the middle of the ship's ample belly.

There are campgrounds at both Korsør and Nyborg. Make sure you have enough daylight left after the ferry crossing to make the 2-km ride to Nyborg's campground.

Nyborg to Odense: 33 kilometers

To reach Nyborg's campground, leave the **ferry harbor** and ride to a **T** with the main road. Turn right toward **Knudshoved,** then go left to cross **over the freeway** and follow campground signs to the jam-packed site. Hot showers, modern facilities, a small store, and lots of fellow campers await.

Retrace your route back into town from the campground (or turn left on the **main road** after leaving the ferry) and ride through Nyborg to where the **road branches.** Angle right toward **Road A8** and **Fåborg.** Come to a **junction** with A8 and go left, then turn right toward **Ferritslev** about 1 km later. Cycle through **Kullerup,** go past a turnoff for Pårup, then swing right at **Ellinge.** Stay right toward **Pårup** and go left for **Rolfsted** soon after. At Rolfsted turn right onto **Road 301** toward **Odense.**

Cycling is mellow throughout the day, with gentle hills and light traffic. Look for the wood-and-thatch country houses, the well-kept gardens, and the steeple-topped churches as you ride. The church at Fraugde is worth a visit if you can get inside. Beyond **Fraugde,** follow a **bike path** over the freeway (new construction — wasn't shown on our map), under a new road and onto the **old road** beside the busy auto route. Follow the old road through a **small town** and then back onto the **main thoroughfare.**

Turn left at the **junction** toward **Neder Holluf,** then swing right onto a **bike path** and parallel the main road into **Odense.** Cross a small **creek** and go left for the **university** (*Universitet*). You'll be cycling through a maze of bike paths around Odense's university. Many of the newer paths were still unsigned when we wandered through. Keep the school buildings on your left and the busy main road off to the right as you ride. Pass the **campus entrance** and angle right. Turn right when the bike path runs into a **small road.** Follow the road to an intersection with **Road A9** and go left a short distance to reach a large campground on the edge of Odense.

The forest-bordered site at Hunderup Skov is immense, but it has good facilities and a well-stocked store. It's an easy 4-km walk to the center of Odense from the campground. Take the footpath along the river and pass the city zoo and amusement park along the way. There are hotels and a youth hostel in Odense if you need a room.

Odense's tourist office is well prepared to handle the crowds that arrive to pay homage to Hans Christian Andersen's hometown and to visit the fine museum the city maintains in his honor. Stop at the tourist office in the town hall on Vestergade, then continue on to H.C. Andersen's House, where a collection of letters, photographs, illustrations, and manuscripts tells the tale of the author's life.

Odense is a pretty city with many handsome homes, a handful of interesting churches, and a host of tantalizing byways. So park your bicycle and let your feet roam freely.

Odense to Svendborg: 48 kilometers

Leave the campground (or the city center) by heading **south** on **Road A9.** Swing right for **Fåborg** just past the **campground,** and cross the train tracks. At the **roundabout,** follow a **bike sign** for **Volderslev** to cross under **Road 43** and up and onto its shoulder. Cycle through flat fields of wheat and barley, riding to **Nørre Lyndelse,** then going left for **Lumby.** Turn onto the **next road** to the right, go left at the **T,** and continue on for **Freltofte.**

Follow signs for **Gestelev** and **Herringe.** Ride through Gestelev, cross under **Road 323,** and go left after crossing the **creek.** You'll spot a large manor house on the right as you turn right, bumping over the train tracks and pedaling along the signed route for **Rudme.** Enter **Volstrup** and turn right for **Egeskov Castle.** Road signs will direct you to the castle entrance. This wonderfully preserved moated castle, still a private residence, offers an on-site museum with collections of airplanes, cars, motorcycles, and carriages, and it has an extensive garden area for strolling.

If you're more interested in finding a scenic picnic spot than in museum going, turn right off the road from Volstrup just before the castle turnoff and walk out to a tall stone column in the field. You'll have a great view of the castle while you munch your lunch.

Continue from Egeskov Castle onto **Road A8** toward **Fåborg,** but veer left on the **small road** just before the **Egeskov Windmill.** Then join a **larger road** to pedal south toward **Stenstrup.** Cycle through Stenstrup and go right at **Kirkeby** toward **Egebjerg** and **Ollerup.** At the next intersection, continue straight for **Hvidkilde.** Pedal a quiet, narrow road through forests, then turn left onto **Road 44** for the final 5 km to **Svendborg.**

A **bike path** will lead you into town (past the Svendborg campground). Continue straight for the **city center,** bypassing a turnoff for Rudkøbing. Follow signs for the ferry and **harbor** (*havn*) to reach the small ferry landing. Cost for the 75-minute ride to Aerø is about 48 kr. There are several crossings per day.

If you've got time to spare before departure, Svendborg is a spunky harbor town with narrow alleys and steep streets, half-timbered buildings, old churches, and a zoological museum. All of them are worth exploring.

Aerøskøbing to Marstal: 26 kilometers

Aerø is a small Baltic island, one of the more than 500 islands that make up Denmark. Although Aerø's main industry is agriculture, tourism is a primary source of revenue, and the island is a favorite with vacationing Danes and Germans. The ferry lands at Aerøskøbing, Aerø's oldest town. Its medieval streets are lined with wooden houses with geranium-filled window boxes, and its shops are hung with fascinating metal signs (look for the golden pretzels if you're hungry for bakery goods). Add Aerø's ever-present cobblestones to complete a delightful (albeit bumpy) journey back in time.

Follow **camping signs** to the west side of the city to reach the luxurious Aerøskøbing campground. With television room, cooking facilities, washers and dryers, spacious bathrooms, and a seaside setting, the site is a treat. You'll see lots of other cyclists here. Explore its gentle hills and discover its striking scenery, and you'll realize why Aerø is a very popular island for bicycling.

There are several hotels in Aerøskøbing. Aerø's only youth hostel is at Marstal, 13 km east. Ask at the tourist office near the church on Aerøskøbing's main square for more information on the city and the island. You may want to set up a base camp for a few days and explore Aerø without your baggage. We've written up our own meandering Aerøskøbing-to-Marstal ride, and you can follow it to Marstal and yet another ferry.

Leave **Aerøskøbing** on the secondary road **west** toward **Borgnaes.** (Turn right off the main road through town a few blocks past the **school** to gain the secondary road.) Stay to the right along the sea, with Aerø's windmill-studded backbone rising to your left and lovely vistas of the Baltic to your right. Pass through **Borgnaes** and turn at the **T.** Then climb a long, steady hill to the ridgeline of the island and the small town of **Bregninge.** Take a look at Bregninge's 13th-century church and the thatch-roofed houses on the streets around it.

From Bregninge, follow Aerø's **main road** southeast toward **Marstal.** You'll notice a slight increase in cars and bicycles on this route, and you can exchange greetings with whole families of bike riders, trailer-pulling couples, and lone tourers as you ride. Views of the sea, the rolling fields, and the quaint towns make the journey enjoyable.

At **Rise,** another old church invites exploration; then you'll negotiate a couple of moderate hills just before Marstal. Marstal lacks the charm of Aerøskøbing, but it has attractions of its own — a fine maritime museum, a handsome church, lots of shops, and a campground and hostel, if you decide to stay.

Follow signs through Marstal to the **ferry landing** and join throngs of cyclists awaiting the hour-long trip to **Rudkøbing.** There are several crossings per day, and the cost is the same as for the trip to Aerøskøbing.

Rudkøbing to Bagenkop (and Kiel): 30 kilometers

The final leg of Tour No. 5 and your ride in Denmark takes you south on the long, skinny island of Langeland from Rudkøbing to Bagenkop. From Bagenkop, you can take a ferry to Kiel, West Germany, and continue your cycling into the Sauerland with Tour No. 6. If time restraints and plane reservations are tugging you back to **Copenhagen,** you may want to pedal north from Rudkøbing instead. Follow **Road 305 north** for 29 km to reach Langeland's tip, and board a **ferry** in **Lohals** for **Korsør.** In Korsør, you can make direct **train** connections to Copenhagen, throwing bike and baggage aboard for the 107 km to Denmark's sparkling capital.

If you're riding on for **Bagenkop** and the ferry to Kiel, leave the **ferry dock** and turn right to walk through Rudkøbing's busy pedestrian core. Follow signs for the **campground** on the south edge of town and turn right on the **unmarked road** just past the site. Come to a **T** and turn right, then keep to the left for **Henninge** and pedal past a large manor house.

At Henninge, turn right onto **Road 305** and cycle on to **Lindelse,** where a large church dominates the town. On the **southern edge** of Lindelse, swing left for **Hennetved** and quiet countryside riding. Follow the road through Hennetved, go past a large **windmill** and **manor house,** and continue on through a sharp right turn. At the next **intersection,** go left and follow the signs to **Tryggelev.**

Turn left onto **Road 305,** then shoot right for **Kinderballe** and more lovely, lonely riding. Come to a **T** a few kilometers past Kinderballe. Go right and cycle along the coast to **Bagenkop.** There's a snazzy three-star campground just outside Bagenkop or a smaller, cheaper, more convenient site a stone's throw from the ferry landing. If you're planning an early-morning departure for West Germany, as we were, pass on the putt-putt and go for the somewhat dumpy ferry-side spot.

Buy your tickets at the **ferry terminal** near the dock. The Bagenkop-Kiel ferry makes the 2½-hour crossing two or three times per day. The cost is about 35 kr with a bicycle.

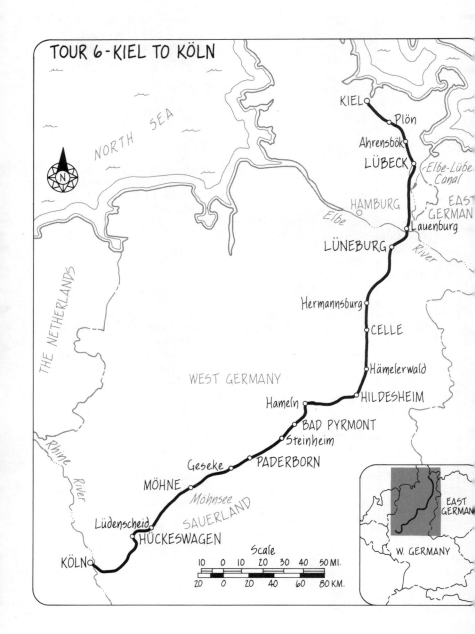

TOUR 6-KIEL TO KÖLN

NORTH SEA

N

KIEL
Plön
Ahrensbök
LÜBECK
Elbe-Lübe Canal

HAMBURG
Elbe
EAST GERMAN

Lauenburg
LÜNEBURG
River

THE NETHERLANDS

Hermannsburg
CELLE

WEST GERMANY
Hämelerwald
HILDESHEIM
Hameln
BAD PYRMONT
Steinheim
Geseke
PADERBORN

Rhine River
MÖHNE
Möhnsee
SAUERLAND
Lüdenscheid
HÜCKESWAGEN
KÖLN

Scale
10   0   10   20   30   40   50 MI.
20   0   20   40   60   80 KM.

EAST GERMAN
W. GERMANY

TOUR NO. 6

A HILL-STUDDED RIDE TO THE RHINE
Kiel to Köln, West Germany

Distance:	656 kilometers (408 miles)
Estimated time:	9 riding days
Best time to go:	June, July, or September
Terrain:	A balanced blend of moderate and difficult riding days
Connecting tours:	Tours No. 5 and 7

West Germany, despite its image as a European industrial superpower, its large population, and its diesel-powered fleets of flying Mercedes, is a delight for the cycle tourist. Secondary roads are well maintained and direct, and bicycle paths abound. Drivers are courteous, although the West Germans' fondness for raw speed can be downright terrifying at times. And the nation has swept away the rubble of World War II to reveal a treasure of matchless architecture, charming towns, and lovely countryside.

Search beyond the surface reserve of the West Germans you'll meet, and you'll discover a generous hospitality, a warm humor, and a stimulating interest in world affairs that will test your knowledge of current events and U.S. policy abroad. West Germans are some of Europe's greatest travelers, and you'll encounter them in every European country you visit. To meet the West Germans at home, though, it's best to do your cycling here in June, early July, or September. School holidays deplete the native population in August, and incoming flights replace the populace with scores of North American tourists.

CONNECTIONS. Kiel is served by ferries from Bagenkop, Denmark (end of Tour No. 5); Korsør, Denmark; Oslo, Norway; and Gothenburg, Sweden. You can also reach Kiel by train from other cities in West Germany and the Continent.

If you're cycling this tour as a continuation of Tour No. 5, you'll arrive in Kiel's center at the busy ferry dock. Enjoy one of the small benefits of being on a bicycle, as you cruise past the long line of waiting cars on your skinny mount and pass effortlessly through customs.

INFORMATION. West German tourist offices (*Verkehrsamt*) are good sources of free literature and city maps. They're usually located near the town church (*Kirche*), the city cathedral (*Dom*), or the main train station (*Hauptbahnhof*). Write in advance to the German National Tourist Office,

747 Third Avenue, New York, New York 10017, for preparatory reading, and take along a guidebook such as Michelin's *Green Guide Germany* or *Baedeker's Germany* to supplement the tourist-office offerings along the way.

MAPS. For route finding, *Deutsche Reisekarte,* a seven-map series published by Kümmerly and Frey, covers all of West Germany at 1:250,000 scale. These maps are available in offices of the German Auto Club (ADAC). Another map series, at 1:400,000 scale, is *Bundesrepublik Deutschland,* available at ARAL service stations. There are also excellent (but expensive) cyclists' maps for West Germany. Ask for them in large bookstores.

ACCOMMODATIONS. Camping in West Germany is convenient and comfortable. There are scores of sites, and most large cities have one or more municipal campgrounds. Avoid lakeside and seaside spots, however, as these are often expensive, crowded, and noisy. You'll sometimes have to pay camping "extras" in West Germany, such as city taxes, shower charges, or an occasional fee for your bicycle.

Youth hostels are a source of national pride in West Germany, and there are hundreds of them throughout the country. We were nearly always eagerly directed to the youth hostel when we stopped in a West German town, cheered on by robust gentlemen and sparkling-eyed women who waggled their walking sticks vaguely upward and muttered, *"Jugendherberge,"* with far-away looks in their eyes. However, though plentiful and inexpensive, West German hostels are often overrun with noisy teens, and they're invariably at the top of steep hills — never a welcome feature at the end of a long cycling day.

Rooms in pensions and hotels vary in price. You'll probably need help at the tourist offices to locate unfilled or inexpensive ones. Watch for *Zimmer Frei* signs in private homes as another option, but one-night boarders are sometimes turned away from these.

SUPPLIES. Shopping hours in West Germany are generally 8:00 a.m. to 6:30 p.m. on weekdays (with some Wednesday-afternoon shutdowns) and 8:00 a.m. to 1:00 or 2:00 p.m. on Saturdays. Some stores close for an hour or two at noon. Don't count on any stores being open on Sundays. With a good exchange rate, you'll find groceries in West Germany to be cheaper than in the United States. However, prepared foods are less economical than the basics such as meat, cheese, and bread.

German food is wonderful fare for a famished biker. Picnic lunches of dark rye bread, cheese, and salami will fuel your legs until the 4:00 p.m. ritual of coffee and cake (*Kaffee und Kuchen*) makes you consider applying for West German citizenship. And a dinner of *Kraut* and *Wurst* accompanied by strong German coffee or a bottle of local beer (*Bier*) or wine is a joy at the end of a tough riding day.

There are bicycle shops in almost every midsized West German city. Young people here do lots of cycling, but touring gear doesn't match the sophisticated equipment available in the United States. You'll probably have to do some hunting for special needs.

Kiel to Lübeck: 70 kilometers

Kiel is a big, industrialized city with little of the charm that makes other West German cities so delightful. Many of Kiel's buildings were leveled in the bombing raids of World War II, and the city is primarily a post-1945 rebuild.

You may want to explore the shopping area across from the ferry terminal before you cycle out of town, especially if you still need maps or a guidebook for your ride. Turn left (south) from the **ferry terminal** and follow the harborside road and signs for **Lübeck,** passing the main train station and a tourist information office on the way. Pedal on **bike paths** for most of the ride to **Plön.** Unfortunately, you'll be beside noisy, heavily-trafficked roads for much of the way.

When the road for Lübeck turns onto the **freeway,** abandon it and follow a road to the right signposted for **Wellsee** and **Rönne.** Then turn left onto a **bike path** that parallels the freeway. You'll spot **bicycle signs** for Raisdorf, Preetz and Plön as you pedal. Just beyond **Elmschenhagen,** the bike path goes to the right of the freeway. Turn left to cross **under the freeway** on a small road, then go right for **Raisdorf** and Plön. At Raisdorf, **cross the freeway** once more, and follow signs for **Preetz.**

Ride the **bike path** along the busy, two-lane **Road 76,** passing through Preetz, where a rose-filled city park and a tourist information office await. Continue on through rolling forestland to **Plön,** a tourist-packed lakeside town with a lofty castle and a large church. Bike lanes appear once more in Plön's congested core. Follow the **bike path** and cross **under Road 430,** then turn right up the dead-end street marked with a **bicycle symbol.** Look for signs for **Eutin.**

Rejoin **Road 76** for about 2 km, then turn right toward **Bosau** and **Pfingstberg.** Keep to the left rather than angling right for Bosau, and cycle through **Pfingstberg, Börnsdorf,** and **Brackrade.** Follow signs for **Ahrensbök,** and continue south through hilly wheatfields on quiet secondary roads. From Ahrensbök, trace the route to Lübeck through **Neuhof, Curau,** and **Stockelsdorf,** turning left onto **Road 206** in Stockelsdorf.

We had planned to use the campground in Stockelsdorf as our base for Lübeck sightseeing, but a grumpy camp attendant informed us that the site was open only to auto campers, and our protests couldn't change his mind. If you're intent on camping, you'll have to ride to one of the sites northeast of Lübeck on the Travemünde Delta. If you want to alter your approach route to Lübeck to bring you by the campgrounds, swing east after **Ahrensbök** for **Schwochel** and **Pansdorf.** There are lots of inexpensive beds in Lübeck itself, including a youth hostel and a YMCA sleep-in.

From Stockelsdorf (basically a suburb of Lübeck), cycle along **Road 206** into the heart of town. Cross the train tracks and go past the main **train station** (on the left), then swing left to arrive at the Holstentor. This massive gateway with twin fortified towers is the trademark of Lübeck, a mighty city that once ruled most of Northern Germany and Holland.

There are three information offices with room-finding services — at the train station, next to the Rathaus, and at 95 Beckergrube. And there's a large auto club office on Holstenstrasse on the right (just past the Holstentor), if you're still hunting for maps.

Lübeck is a delightful city with lots to see and dozens of captivating byways. Traffic is heavy, so you may prefer to do your sightseeing on foot. Don't miss the Hospice of the Holy Spirit or the dark and beautiful Rathaus with its flower-filled square. You won't forget the moving evidence of war's destruction hidden within the vast Gothic shell of St. Mary's Church (Marienkirche). The shattered bell, the crumbling plaster, and the broken statues provide a poignant testimony to the devastation this city endured during World War II.

Lübeck to Lüneburg: 90 kilometers

From Lübeck's Rathaus, go south on **Sandstrasse** to **Mühlenstrasse,** and continue away from the city center, crossing the **canal.** Angle right onto **Kronsforder Allee** at the roundabout and cycle through Lübeck's tentacle-like suburbs, working to free yourself of the heavy city traffic.

Once out of Lübeck's grasp, enter quiet countryside as you cycle along the **old salt route** between Lübeck and **Lüneburg.** This route was once a major artery of trade to Scandinavia. Ride through **Niederbüssau.** A roadside **bike path** will escort you on to **Krummesse.**

Swing right onto the road for **Kastorf,** cross the **Elbe-Lübeck Canal,** then go left for **Rondeshagen** soon after. Pedal through Rondeshagen and merge right onto **Road 208** toward **Kastorf.** Then go left for **Niendorf** and **Kühsen.** Enjoy quiet, scenic riding with the canal on your left as you pass through Kühsen and continue to **Nusse.** Turn right at the **T** in Nusse, then go left for **Poggensee.** Cycle on to **Borstorf** and veer left for **Breitenfelde.**

From Breitenfelde, follow signs for **Lauenburg** to cycle the final 30 km along the easy canal-side route to town. Climb a long, gradual hill just before Lauenburg to reach the ridgetop and the city overlooking the Elbe River. Turn left onto **Road 5** toward **Lüneburg,** then angle right for **Lauenburg's center** (*Zentrum*). Plan to spend an hour exploring this picturesque town. There's a garden area and a viewpoint on the ridge above the Elbe, and you can make your way west to the hilltop clock tower that is the lone remnant of the city castle.

From the **clock tower,** wheel your bicycle down the small lane into the lower town. A riverside street of quaint sailors' homes hung with fascinating metal signs will entertain you with its variety as you rattle along on the cobblestones. Watch for the dates inscribed on the housefronts as you bounce down the hill toward the river.

Join **Road 209** to cross the **Elbe,** then go left at the intersection for **Bullendorf** and veer right 2 km later for **Lüneburg.** Quiet but bumpy secondary roads lead on through **Echen.** About 7 km before Lüneburg, pass a massive elevator where barges are lifted 125 ft from one canal level to another. There's a visitors' center, if you want to investigate. Cycle

under the canal and across the **freeway bypass** of Lüneburg, then go left onto the busy **Road 209** into town.

Lüneburg's campground is inconveniently located on the south side of town. If you need a room, you'll probably want to head directly for the tourist office, located in the Rathaus. Cross the **Ilmenau River** on Road 209, then branch right for the **city center** and the Rathaus. To continue on for the campground, stay on Road 209 through the city (swing left after crossing the river), and stay on the **bike path** as it takes you **under Road 209** to a route along the left edge of Road 209. Ignore a second bike underpass, and continue straight to cycle beside **Road 4,** pedaling about 4½ km from Lüneburg's center. You'll spot campground signs along the road. Turn left on a small road for **Deutsch Evern** to reach the pleasant, wooded site.

Lüneburg is a charming West German city with a wealth of old brick buildings, leaning housefronts, flower-filled windowboxes, and maze-like streets. Don't miss Am Sande, Lüneburg's impressive town square. And be sure to visit St. John's Church and St. Nicholas's Church, as well.

Lüneburg to Celle: 89 kilometers

Leave **Lüneburg** to the south, following the route toward the campground and taking the **bike route** along **Road 4.** Angle right for **Ebstorf** when the road branches. Pass through Bardenhagen and **Velgen,** and cycle through rolling forestland with several long, gradual climbs. Swing right for **Hanstedt I** at Velgen, then continue on through flatter terrain for Arendorf and Wriedel.

Turn right 2 km beyond **Wriedel,** then go left on the **first paved road** to cycle through a vast **military area** where dozens of signs threaten instant annihilation to those who wander off the road. You'll see very few cars (and only a handful of tanks) as you pedal through the area. Veer left after **8 km** and pedal past the British Forces Golf Course and a tank practice field before **crossing Road 71.** Continue following signs for **Celle.**

Military maneuvers do close the base to outside traffic at certain times. If that happens, you'll need to take the route from **Wriedel** to **W. Brockhöfe** to **W. Lintzel,** and pedal 9 km on the busy Road 71 before rejoining this route.

Cycle south to **Müden,** a busy tourist town with lovely farm buildings and lots of booted hikers carrying stout walking sticks. Continue toward **Hermannsburg,** a more modern-looking tourist spot with two large churches and a host of shops and stores. A final 25 km will take you to the large campground north of Celle. At **Sülze,** 9 km south of Hermannsburg, you can swing left onto a 2-km **parallel road.** It has a rotten surface, but the fine assortment of homes and farm buildings is worth the rattles.

From **Sülze,** it's possible to make the short sidetrip west to the **Bergen-Belsen Memorial,** where a monument honors the victims of the concentration camp that was here during World War II.

Rejoin the road for **Celle** and pedal to an intersection with **Road 3** on the northern edge of the city. Turn left on Road 3 and, if you're camping, go left one block later for **Vorwerk.** Follow the Vorwerk road for 2 km to a **T,** and turn left again. You'll see signs for the campground soon after. Camping Silbersee is an expensive spot with a pretty setting and clean, modern facilities, including on-site washer and dryer.

To reach Celle, return to **Road 3** and follow signs marked *Zentrum.* Cross the **Aller River** and go straight on **Hehlentorstrasse,** then turn right on **Kanzleistrasse.** Celle's lovely garden-encircled palace will appear before you, and the tourist information office is on the left, on Schlossplatz. There's a youth hostel in Celle, as well as a limited number of pensions.

Allow yourself at least a day to explore the city's enchanting streets, where painted houses line the way with a kaleidoscope of colors, their timbers carved and curved and their windows overflowing with brilliant petunias. Wander over to the palace grounds for a picnic lunch of dark rye bread piled high with pepper salami and Emmenthal cheese, then tour the palace and marvel at the ornate chapel and the beautiful theater inside.

Be sure to visit Celle's Rathaus and church, too. Then reward your tired legs with a double scoop of ice cream from one of the city's countless cafes.

Celle to Hildesheim: 70 kilometers

The ride from Celle to Hildesheim is a flat blend of fields, forests, and bleak industrial areas. Except for the final 17 km, you'll be on quiet secondary roads for much of the way. From Celle's tourist office, follow **Schlossplatz** south to **Südwall.** Turn left on Südwall and ride along the southern edge of the city center. Angle left with the road, then veer right to gain **Road 214** for **Braunschweig.**

At the outer edge of Celle, turn right off Road 214 to pedal toward **Nienhagen.** Go left in **Nienhagen** to reach **Wathlingen,** and continue south for 8 km to **Hänigsen,** where you'll angle left for **Uetze.** Continue straight for **Sievershausen** a short distance later. **Cross Road 188** and cycle lonely, flat roads through Schwüblingsen and on to Sievershausen. In **Sievershausen,** follow signs for **E8** to cross **over the freeway** and enter **Hämelerwald.**

Turn right by a large **power plant** about 5 km past Hämelerwald (just before crossing the canal), then turn left across the **canal** a short distance later, and gain a small road to **Mehrum.** Go right on **Road 65,** then turn left for **Hohenhameln** immediately after. At Hohenhameln, a pleasant town with handsome homes and barns, say goodbye to solitude as you turn right onto **Road 494** for the final 17 km to **Hildesheim.** There's a **bike path** along the road for much of the way, but it dumps you unceremoniously at the edge of Hildesheim and vanishes without a trace.

Pedal along the street paralleling Road 494 and look for *Zentrum* signs to take you **under Road 494** and the **train tracks.** Take the first road to the left, and you'll find a **bike path** to lead you toward the **center** of the city.

Hildesheim took a terrible beating during World War II and much of the city core was leveled. The dumpy-looking industrial suburbs you'll pass

A windmill stands above a wind-blown field of grain in northern Germany.

through as you enter town won't encourage you to linger, but the city does have some worthwhile spots to visit.

Hildesheim's tourist office is opposite the Rathaus, and the staff can provide you with literature and lodging information. Be sure to visit St. Andrew's Church (Andreaskirche) a few blocks away, if only to look at the sobering photo exhibit that shows the church's ornate Gothic walls standing like blackened bones against a war-darkened sky. The interior is stark and bare — still deathlike after 40 years. St. Michael's Church and the Dom are also worth a visit.

Our plans to camp in Hildesheim met a disappointing end when we discovered that the hilltop site near the city's overcrowded youth hostel had been closed for several years. The harried hostel keeper wanted nothing to do with us, so we had no choice but to push our bicycles into the surrounding forest and put up our tent.

Hildesheim to Bad Pyrmont: 65 kilometers

Leave Hildesheim's center by following the **bike path west** along **Road 1** for **Hameln,** and keep to Road 1 for the 28 km to **Hemmendorf.** You'll have bike path for much of the way. If you decide to stay on Road 1 all the way to Hameln, you'll add about 8 km and a bit more main-road riding to your day. But if a visit to the town of the Pied Piper sounds tempting, you may want to go this way.

Otherwise, turn left in **Hemmendorf** toward **Bad Pyrmont** and

Lauenstein. Lauenstein is a wonderfully situated town with many fine old buildings. Climb steeply through forest for about 1½ km, then descend even more steeply to the valley beyond. Climb gently a short distance later, crossing a ridge before coasting down to a lush green valley of checkerboard fields. Ride through **Bessinghausen** and continue on through Börry and E. Latferde.

At **Latferde,** turn right for **Bad Pyrmont** and **Hagenohsen.** Reach **Hagenohsen** and turn left over the **Weser River** for **Bad Pyrmont.** Then swing right on **Road 83** for **Hameln.** Follow Road 83 across the **Emmer River,** then go left for **Bad Pyrmont.** Traffic increases for the final 13 km into town, but you'll have bike paths for much of the way.

Hämelschenburg Castle overlooks the road a few km beyond Hagenohsen. With a handsome facade, tree-shaded grounds, and a small walled city kneeling at its feet, the castle makes a nice spot to rest or enjoy a picnic lunch. Guided tours of the castle's furniture and weapons collections are available at hourly intervals.

Continue pedaling to **Thal** and turn right for **Löwensen** and a well-marked campground. Climb a moderate hill outside Löwensen, and reach the campground after about 2 km. The rustic site is cheap, has so-so facilities, and is administered by a gruff, clog-wearing manager who cryptically informed us to plan on "rolls at 7:00." Unsure whether this breakfast was included in our small camping fee, we slept in instead.

If you're not camping, continue into **Bad Pyrmont** from Löwensen and hunt for a bed in the small spa town. Take an evening walk in the Spa Park (Kurpark) if you feel like a stroll, but save some energy for the tough days of riding ahead.

Bad Pyrmont to Paderborn: 55 kilometers

From Bad Pyrmont, regain the road **southwest** for **Lügde,** a 1200-year-old town scrambling hard for tourists. About **5 km past Lügde,** turn right off the main road onto a bike path (signed for **Glashütte**). Veer left about a block later to follow a **bike path** along the lake and onto a small road through the trees.

Pedal on this quiet route until you emerge from the woods, then angle left to rejoin the traffic on the **main road** into **Schieder.** The hub of a lively tourist area, Schieder is busy with cars and strolling West German vacationers. Turn right at the **T** in town onto **Road 239** for **Bad Meinberg.** In **Wöbbel,** turn left in front of the **church** and cycle through town. Go left at the **T** for **Steinheim.** At an **intersection** before Steinheim, turn right for **Horn-Bad Meinberg.** You'll encounter moderate hills and light traffic along the way.

Cycle the 9 km to Horn-Bad Meinberg, and turn left onto **Road 1** in town, following it through the business district, then angle right at the **Y** for **Detmold.** A 1-km jaunt will take you to the turnoff for **Externsteine.** Go left here and ride on pedestrian and bicycle paths to the limestone rocks of Extersteine. Carved into pulpits, chapels, and religious scenes by 11th-century Christians, the rocks are quite interesting. Eat a picnic in the grass and do some people watching while hordes of camera-carrying tourists file by, then pedal back toward Horn-Bad Meinberg.

At the edge of **Horn-Bad Meinberg,** turn right onto **Road 1** for **Paderborn.** You'll have a long, steady climb through forest, then a leisurely descent to reach the flatlands surrounding Paderborn. Veer left for **Schlangen** just past **Kohlstädt.** Take a left onto the **first main street** (unmarked) as you enter Schlangen, and pedal the 8 km to **Benhausen.** You'll have a **steep hill** to tackle just before the town.

In Benhausen, go right for **Paderborn** and follow the road straight into the jaws of the city. When you reach a **T** in Paderborn, continue straight onto a **bike path** and then back onto a **street** going the same direction. Keep pedaling to a **second T.** This time a rock wall bars forward progress. Go left, then right as you follow signs for the **Dom.**

Paderborn's cathedral is on the right as you arrive at a long pedestrian mall. Stop to stare at its complex exterior, then venture inside for a look at some dazzling modern stained glass. Walk your bicycle through the pedestrian mall. The 17th-century Rathaus is on the left and there's a tourist information office nearby. Ask for directions to the campgrounds north of town, or check on Paderborn's youth hostel or hotels.

Paderborn to Möhne: 55 kilometers

From Paderborn's pedestrian mall, continue west to regain the traffic and **Road 1** for **Soest.** We succumbed to a brief attack of "main-road-itis" between Paderborn and Soest, riding about 40 km along the wide shoulder of Road 1 as we pushed for a 100-km day and a campground on the Möhnsee. Although traffic wasn't bad during the early evening hours when we pedaled this straight shot, trucks and cars will be an irritating presence most of the day.

A slight detour north through Lippstadt (turn at Salzkotten) or south toward Büren (turn left off Road 1 about 9 km from Paderborn's center) will add kilometers and quietness to your day.

If you follow our route, you'll need to angle right to stay with **Road 1** about **9 km** outside Paderborn. The riding is mostly flat, with some slight hills and virtually no curves. Pass through **Geseke** and **Erwitte.** Continue on into **Soest,** the home of German pumpernickel bread, if you'd like to visit its two noteworthy churches or take advantage of its lodging opportunities.

Otherwise, turn left for **Opmünden** about **5 km before Soest.** Ride through Opmünden, turn right for **Soest,** and then go left for **Elfsen** and **Mullingsen.** After Mullingsen, cycle left to **Lendringson** and on to Möhne. Descend to **Möhne** and turn right on **Road 516** along the north shore of the Möhnsee. You'll see campground signs along Road 516 just past Möhne. Be forewarned, though, the Möhnsee is a favorite haunt of vacationing West Germans, and the campgrounds we saw had the look of overpriced and overcrowded mobile-home parks.

The Möhnsee is a 10-km-long artificial lake formed by the Möhne Dam. It's on the northern fringe of a hill-studded region known as the Sauerland.

You'll suffer through long, exhausting days and restless nights in noisy, crowded campgrounds as you pedal through this area. But the deep river valleys, steep wooded hillsides, and pastoral panoramas will do much to ease your pain. And the alternate cycling route to Köln — a trek through the flatter but infinitely more industrialized Ruhr Basin to the north — is not an option you'll care to choose.

Möhne to Hückeswagen: 97 kilometers

Pedal along **Road 516** past a handful of lakeside campgrounds and the 131-ft **Möhnsee Dam,** and continue on to **Ense.** Go left for **Neheimhüsten** and turn left into the town to cross **under the A445** freeway, following signs for **Arnsberg.** Cross the **Ruhr River,** go under the train tracks, and turn right for **Holzen.**

Climb a long, punishing hill, following signs for **Iserlohn.** Descend steeply to **Road 515** and go left on it to cycle through a narrow river **canyon.** Then swing right for **Iserlohn** once more. Climb another tough hill, and keep to the left for **Hemer** and **Iserlohn** at the top. A steep descent will take you to a left turn for **Stephanopel** (small sign near the bottom of the hill), and you'll gain a narrow side road through a cool, tree-shaded valley.

You'll have the song of the stream for company as you make a leisurely ascent beside the water. Follow the sign for **Heidermülle** and then reach a **T,** where the road ahead turns to dirt. Turn right and pedal hard for about 1 km to gain the ridgetop, then coast down a steep, roughly-paved lane to join the road for **Altena.**

An exhilarating descent that seems to last forever leads through a depressing industrial suburb into Altena. Turn left for the **Zentrum** at the bottom of the hill, then go left along the **Lenne River** on **Road 236.** Cross the river and follow signs for **Lüdenscheid.** A gentle climb (by Sauerland standards) leads to **Lüdenscheid,** where the road dives into a cars-only tunnel and disappears. Swing left into the **city center** and reach a large pedestrian mall. There's a city map on the right side of the plaza to help you get your bearings. If the hills and kilometers are beginning to take their toll, you may want to look for lodgings in the midsized city.

To pedal on for the campground (28 km), follow the street along the **ridgetop,** and turn left just past the **church.** Go straight at the stop sign, and begin a steep descent soon after. At the bottom of the hill, go left onto **Road 54,** then turn right onto **Road 229** for **Halver.** Stay on Road 229 as you climb, descend, and climb again to Halver. From Halver, follow signs for **Radevormwald** for 7 km, then turn left onto **Road 483** toward **Hückeswagen** and ride a **bike path** beside the road overlooking the Beverstausee.

Descend a **hill** toward Hückeswagen on Road 483, then veer left near the bottom for the **Beverstausee.** Your weary legs will grumble as you pedal up a final hill to a **junction** where campground signs point straight ahead and to the right. Cycle right to reach a sprawling lakeside site with upper tiers of trailers and a lower "slum" for tents and short-term guests. You'll be asked to hand over a 20-DM security deposit for the night. The facilities are

A summer music festival around the Köln Cathedral.

adequate but overworked, and the tent area is noisy with partying teens. But the view of the lake is pleasant and the escape from the saddle euphoric after a grueling riding day.

Hückeswagen to Köln: 65 kilometers

From the campground, continue southeast along the lake and ride **across the dam** at the tip. Turn right at the **T** and cycle along the creek to regain **Road 483**. Go left onto Road 483 for **Wipperfürth**. There's a bike path most of the way to the town. In Wipperfürth, turn right onto **Road 506** for **Köln**, then angle left for **Kürten** a short distance later. Pedal up and over a final hill, then treat your legs to a level, winding day of following rivers and quiet roads toward Köln.

Follow the creek to Kürten and on to **Hommerich**. Swing right for **Köln** in Hommerich. Cycle beside water to **Obersteg** and a **T**, and veer right once more for Köln. Cross **under the A4 freeway** and continue to **Rösrath**. Go right for **Köln** onto a busier road. There's a **bike path** along the left side. After about **6 km**, turn left off this road, following signs for the **freeway** and **airport**.

Go under the freeway and pedal for **Porz**, cycling a roadside **bike path**. Pass a large, walled **castle** on the right, and veer right for **Porz** just past the wall. Cross another freeway (**A59**) and turn left at the **T**, then take the **next right**. This road will lead you to the riverside route into Köln (Kölner Strasse). Turn right on **Kölner Strasse** to cycle toward the city.

Look for the massive freeway bridge spanning the **Rhine River** off to the left. Cross **A4** and turn left just past it onto **Im Wasserfeld**, following campground signs toward the river and left onto **Weidenweg**. Köln's riverside campground has an unbeatable location on the east bank of the Rhine. It's quiet, well kept, convenient to the city and the airport, and full of tourists from all over the world — a good spot to strike up evening conversations over steaming cups of coffee.

From the campground, cycle along the road paralleling the Rhine (**Alfred Schütte Allee**), cross under the train bridge and over a small **canal**, then go left on the **bike path** along **Siegburger Strasse**. Continue straight **under the first auto bridge**, and turn left to cross the Rhine on the second (**Deutzer Brücke**). The unmistakable silhouette of Köln Cathedral will tower over the city center to your right as you coast off the bridge.

Weave your way through the city streets to reach the Dom, the central train station, and the tourist-information office (it's across from the cathedral's west door). Ask at the tourist office for a free guide to hotels and pensions. (Köln has two youth hostels and loads of pensions, if you're looking for a room.) The guide is also an excellent street map of the city. And pick up the pamphlet on Köln's churches before you head out for a wonderful afternoon of sightseeing. Köln Cathedral is one of the most fantastic Gothic churches in West Germany, and the city possesses a host of other fine churches, as well.

If the city marks the end of your cycling, you'll be able to put your bicycle on a train at the Hauptbahnhof or return to the airport southeast of town to catch a plane. If you're pedaling on from Köln, read on into Tour No. 7.

TOUR NO. 7

TO BELGIUM, LUXEMBOURG, AND BACK
Köln to Trier, West Germany

Distance:	358 kilometers (222 miles)
Estimated time:	5 riding days
Best time to go:	June, July, or September
Terrain:	Some rugged areas with lots of long hills
Connecting tours:	Tours No. 6 and 8

This tour provides a pleasant blend of three European countries — West Germany, Belgium, and Luxembourg. You'll hear lots of German spoken throughout your ride, and you'll see a strong French influence as well in Belgium and Luxembourg.

Luxembourg is tucked comfortably in between its much larger neighbors to the east and west, and you'll need to observe carefully to fully appreciate its individuality. Much of the population is bilingual. French is the official language, Luxembourgeois is the common tongue, and German runs a close third.

Your sensitivity to the tiny country's hard-won independence will be appreciated by the locals, but the cosmopolitan Luxembourgers are unnervingly adept at dealing with the sometimes inept tourists who continually overrun their land. We were reminded of this native skill while ordering dinner in a restaurant in Luxembourg City. Struggling to use what we thought was the preferred language, we carefully ordered *"Zwei Bier, bitte,"* in faltering German. "Two beers? Here you go," was the young waitress's deflating reply. So much for blending in.

CONNECTIONS. You can reach Köln and the start of this tour by bicycle — simply follow Tour No. 6 from Kiel to Köln. If you're looking for other options, Köln has both an airport and a busy train station. If you plan to link this tour with Tours 8 and 9 for a leisurely ride to Munich, you may want to purchase roundtrip airfare to Munich, then take the train to Köln to begin.

INFORMATION. Write to the Luxembourg National Tourist Office, 801 Second Avenue, New York, New York 10017, for preparatory information on Luxembourg. *Baedeker's Netherlands, Belgium and Luxembourg* or the *Blue Guide Belgium and Luxembourg* are two excellent guidebook options for your trip.

MAPS. You can buy Michelin maps at 1:200,000 for your ride in Belgium, or use the 1:300,000 N.V. Falkplan/CIB *België-Belgique, Luxemburg-Luxembourg* to get an overall look at the route from Aachen to the Luxembourg/West German border. The latter map shows a multitude of campgrounds and youth hostels.

ACCOMMODATIONS. The general information for West Germany given in the introduction to Tour No. 6 applies to this ride. You'll find additional background on Belgium in the introduction to Tour No. 2.

SUPPLIES. Shopping hours in Luxembourg are similar to those followed by West German shopkeepers (see Tour No. 6), and cuisine is a happy blend of French, Belgian, and German dishes, with a few regional specialties thrown in. You may not even see any Luxembourg currency during your tour, as Belgian *francs* are abundant in the country's tills.

Köln to Aachen: 70 kilometers

From the west end of the **Deutzer Brücke** in Köln (see last entry of Tour No. 6 for Köln data), follow the bike path along the left side of **Pipinstrasse** as you cycle west. The bike path ends a short distance later, and you'll need to cross to the right side to ride with traffic from there. Continue on Pipinstrasse west as it goes through a series of name changes to become Aachener Strasse ("the street to Aachen"). You'll see signs for **Road 55** along the way, and you'll pick up a **bike path** for the remainder of the ride out of Köln's sprawling suburbs.

Cross the E42 freeway and continue straight on Road 55 for **Bergheim** and **Jülich**. The bike path ends at an **intersection before Königsdorf.** Turn left here, and take the second right onto a **poorly marked bike path** paralleling the flat and busy Road 55. Come to a **T** and turn right onto another bike path along the left side of the road, then angle left with the path onto a **city street.** Follow the street straight, then right to return to **Road 55.**

Cycle the bike path along Road 55 to **Bergheim** and continue on through **Elsdorf** and then toward **Jülich.** The flat ride between Köln and Aachen is relatively uninspiring, with lots of industrial scars to mar the countryside. Save your strength and your senses — the hills of the Belgian Ardennes await. Pass a massive mining operation with a viewpoint over a deep pit and a huge mountain of excavated soil beside the road. An ideal picnic spot it's not.

Continue on to Jülich and follow signs for **Road 55/Road 1** into **Aachen.** You'll have bike paths part of the way. Road 264 from Düren joins Road 1 about 8 km before Aachen's center, contributing additional traffic to your day. Continue pedaling and pass **under the freeway,** then enter Aachen's suburbs. Watch for signs for Aachen's municipal campground off to the right as you approach the city center. It's about 1 km from the cathedral, has a small camp store, good facilities, and free hot showers. The site fills up fast, however, so claim your spot before heading into the city for sightseeing. There's also a youth hostel in Aachen, if you're looking for an inexpensive bed.

Follow **Zentrum** signs to Aachen's cathedral, a wonderful conglomera-

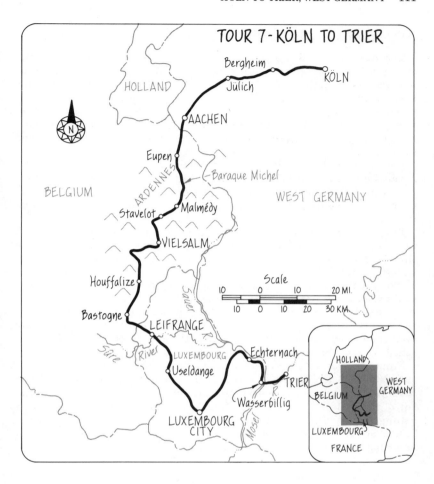

tion of architectural styles built around the nucleus of Charlemagne's ninth-century church. Visit the octagonal sanctuary with its tile-encrusted ceiling, stare at sturdy columns and a Gothic choir lit by rainbows of modern stained glass, and imagine the dreams of an emperor who once ruled most of Europe.

Aachen's Rathaus is a beautiful 14th-century building that looks out over the busy Market Square. Buy an ice cream cone in the square, watch the locals streaming into McDonald's, or invade the nearby tourist office for information on the city.

Aachen to Vielsalm: 79 kilometers

Leave Aachen on **Road 264** southwest toward **Belgium**. Climb a long, steady hill outside of town (the road has a **bike path**) as you begin your assault on the foothills of the Ardennes. Pass the West German **border station** and then turn left onto a secondary road for **Hergenrath**. Pedal through rolling green farmland on the route to Hergenrath and **Walhorn**, then join **Road N28** at **Kettenis**. Angle right on N28 for **Eupen**, and swing through Eupen's center to admire the town church and the cafe-lined streets.

Continue on N28 for **Malmédy**. You'll have a 13-km climb as you pedal steadily upward toward **Baraque Michel**, at 675 meters one of the highest points in the Belgian Ardennes. The road attracts heavy tourist traffic, so hug the shoulder while you enjoy the views of lush hillsides and distant fields.

From Baraque Michel, revel in a glorious 16-km descent to Malmédy. A **bike lane** provides added breathing space for several kilometers. Cruise through Malmédy, an attractive Belgian town, and pedal on for **Stavelot**. Climb a small hill, then descend into **Stavelot**. Leave N28 to cycle into the **city center**. You'll be jostled into wakefulness by the cobblestones of Stavelot's main street. You can celebrate your first victory over the Ardennes with a cool beverage at a streetside cafe. If you need a room for the night, Stavelot is the last town of any size until Houffalize, 50 km farther on. Campgrounds are abundant in the area, so you can set your own schedule if you have a tent.

From Stavelot, return to **N28** and ride about 6 km before turning left onto **N28/N33** for **Vielsalm** and **Luxembourg**. Cycle beside the Salm River to Vielsalm, a small town with a tidy one-star campground (it's to the left of the road). There's also a three-star campground, complete with fishing pond/swimming pool and refreshment bar, about 3 km from Salmchâteau, if the Vielsalm campground is full. Turn right onto N28 from Salmchâteau to reach the site.

Vielsalm to Leifrange: 67 kilometers

Pedal south on **N28/N33** to **Salmchâteau**. You can get to Houffalize two ways from here. Continue on **N28/N33** for 6 km and turn right for **Houffalize**, then cycle 7 km to a junction with **Road N26** and continue on to Houffalize (total of 20½ km). Or turn right onto **N28** in Salmchâteau, pass the campground 3 km later, and continue up a long, gradual hill to a junction with **Road N15**. Go left for **Houffalize** and descend a steep hill into town (total of 24 km). We chose the latter route because we camped outside Salmchâteau.

Houffalize is an attractive town with many shops and lots of summer tourists. As you continue toward Bastogne, you'll begin to see roadside reminders of the battles that were fought in this part of Belgium during World War II. Leave Houffalize on **N15** for **Bastogne**, passing an ancient tank on your way out of town. Climb a hefty hill and pedal through a challenging 17 km of dips and rolls to reach Bastogne.

Descend to the edge of the city and turn left for the **Mardasson War Memorial.** This striking modernistic monument and the slick on-site museum relate the story of the Battle of the Bulge. Your understanding of the region and its history will be greatly increased by the hours you spend here.

Bastogne itself is a touristy mix of traffic, hotels, and bars — a disappointing contrast to the simplicity and grace of the memorial. The city has a campground and a youth hostel if you need a bed.

Cycle through Bastogne's center and follow signs for **Arlon** onto the harrowing **Road N4.** Breathe easier as you swing left a few kilometers later to gain a quiet road for **Lutrebois.** Angle left to descend into Lutrebois, then pedal up a **hill** and keep to the right as you leave the tiny town. Descend to another **village** and keep left, then climb a steep hill to reach a **small stone marker** announcing your entry into Luxembourg.

Continue on to **Harlange,** with fine views of the fertile countryside, and pedal up another large hill before reaching a **junction** marked for **Luxembourg** (left 53 km) and Boulaide (right). Go left and descend a long, steep hill to a large reservoir formed by a dam on the Sûre River. Cycle along the reservoir's hilly northern shore. Cross a **small dam,** then climb a final hill to **Leifrange,** a pleasant village with a busy hillside campground. The campground is inexpensive, crowded, and full of friendly Dutch vacationers.

Leifrange to Luxembourg City: 65 kilometers

Continue along the main **waterside road** from Leifrange, climbing a **long hill** with vistas of the surrounding countryside. Turn right at the **T** for **Esch-sur-Sûre.** Reach the crest of the hill, then descend quickly to cross the reservoir on **another dam.** Go right beside the water for **Eschdorf,** then veer left to leave the reservoir on a **smaller road,** also signed for **Eschdorf.** Climb steeply, descend to an intersection, then climb steeply once more to reach the town.

In Eschdorf, turn right onto **Road N12** for **Luxembourg** and **Grosbous.** Pant through more rolling terrain as you stay left (still on N12) to reach Grosbous, then continue on through **Bettborn.** Angle left along the Attert River to **Useldange,** an interesting town with the remains of an old walled fortress. Turn right onto **Road N24** for **Noerdange,** then go left to rejoin **N12** toward **Luxembourg City.** Stay on N12 for the rest of the way as you negotiate an exhausting series of hills and ride through the heavy forests surrounding Luxembourg's capital.

Enjoy a long descent to the edge of the city. If you want to camp at the closest site to town, go left for **Echternach** onto a busy and exceedingly unpleasant bypass road. Follow signs for Echternach for about 3 km. You'll spot the hillside campground to the right off **Road E42.** It's crowded, noisy, and grim, but its closeness to the city and a crazy late-night card game with two Dutch bicyclists made it endurable for us.

Reach the **city center** by retracing your route along **E42** toward town and veering left to climb a **long hill** into the city core. Luxembourg City's fortified walls and stout turrets will mark your progress from the hillsides

Fellow cyclists are eager to talk of touring.

above. Arrive at a long pedestrian street (Grand rue) and go left past scores of glittering store windows. Walk to the rue du Capucins, then go left to reach the busy Place d'Armes and the city tourist information office. There's a national tourist office for Luxembourg at the main train station on the south end of town. The city has a youth hostel and dozens of hotels.

Get a walking map from the tourist office, and let your urge to wander have free rein in this fascinating capital of fortifications, towers, and tourists. Then stop to quench your thirst at a cafe in the Place d'Armes. You can even order in English!

Luxembourg City to Trier: 77 kilometers

Leave Luxembourg's center on the **Côte d'Eich**, and pedal **E42** toward **Echternach**, passing the campground and climbing a long, gradual hill. You'll have 15 km of main-road riding with intermittent hills and steady traffic to **Junglinster**. Turn left for **Grundhof** just past Junglinster, leaving traffic and hills behind. Descend to ride beside a small river through a beautiful, cliff-enclosed valley, and share the scenery with dozens of energetic walkers wandering pathways through the trees.

Continue following signs to Grundhof, and turn right at the **T** just past Grundhof to cycle beside the **Sauer River** and begin your ride through countless acres of vineyards. A **bike path** will take you beside the main road for most of the 10 km to **Echternach**. Plan to stop for a picnic lunch and enjoy the sights and sounds in Echternach, a busy town of cobblestone streets and colorful buildings. Echternach's tourist office is near the Basilica. If you'd like to spend a few more days in Luxembourg before crossing back into West Germany, this small city makes an excellent stopping place.

There are campgrounds and a youth hostel in Echternach, and you can forsake your bicycle for day hikes in the surrounding forests. The tourist office will supply information on trails.

Continue along the **west bank** of the Sauer River for the 19 km to **Wasserbillig**. Cross the bridge spanning the Sauer to make the **border crossing** into West Germany. The beautiful terraced vineyards of the Mosel River will soothe your senses as you ride along the north shore on **Road 49** for **Trier**. Pass a sign that says *Trier - 9 km* and hop onto a small bike path to the right of the road. Stay along the river as Road 49 goes up and over the train tracks. Endure a short stretch of rough going on the bike path, then regain smooth, easy riding along the river.

You'll pass three campgrounds on your way into Trier. The last site is about 2 km from Trier's center. It's usually crowded, but the good facilities and pleasant setting are worth the close quarters. And you'll find lots of cyclists to share stories with in this popular cycling area.

To continue into Trier on foot, follow the riverside bike path to **Römer Brücke** and climb the stairs to walk across the bridge into the city. If you're pedaling into town, return to **Road 49** and turn right for Trier's **center** to cycle across the bridge. Once the capital of the Western Roman Empire, Trier is Germany's oldest city. It offers Roman monuments such as the Emperor's baths and the dark gateway called the Porta Nigra, and it boasts Germany's earliest Christian church, Trier Cathedral.

The tourist information office is near the Porta Nigra. Take Karl Marx Strasse toward the Hauptmarkt from Römer Brücke. Ask at the office for information on the Mosel Valley, cycling, camping, wine tasting, or anything else you're interested in. A youth hostel and several pensions provide inexpensive lodging options in the city.

If you have time, put this tour together with Tour No. 8 and enjoy another five days of delightful West German cycling on the Mosel and the Rhine.

Vineyards, castles and picturesque towns line the Mosel River beyond Trier.

TOUR NO. 8

RHINE, WINE, AND TOURISTS
Trier to Bingen, West Germany

Distance:	253 kilometers (157 miles)
Estimated time:	5 riding days
Best time to go:	June, July, or September
Terrain:	Mostly flat with some gently rolling hills
Connecting tours:	Tours No. 7 and 9

On this tour, you'll pedal from the ancient Roman city of Trier along the vine-lined Mosel River to Koblenz and the legendary Rhine. Then you'll cycle past castles and vineyards galore as you continue on to Bingen through the beautiful Valley of the Rhine.

CONNECTIONS. You can reach Trier and the start of this tour by cycling Tour No. 7 and pedaling in, or you can arrive by train instead. If you plan to link this tour with Tour No. 9 for the ride to Munich, you may want to purchase roundtrip airfare to Munich, then take the train to Trier to begin.

Read the introductory section of Tour No. 6 for general information on cycling in West Germany.

MAPS. Refer to maps information in the introduction to Tour No. 6.

ACCOMMODATIONS. Check the accommodations section in the introduction to Tour No. 6.

SUPPLIES. Look for details on shopping hours and food purchases in the introduction to Tour No. 6.

Trier to Traben-Trarbach: 85 kilometers

From Trier, you'll have three lovely, leisurely days of cycling as you trace the winding route of the Mosel on its journey to the Rhine. Set your own pace and stop often to explore the dozens of picturesque towns along the way. We've suggested cycling days and listed some of our favorite spots, but the region is so full of charm, you'll undoubtedly have your own list of favorites when you're through. Campgrounds are plentiful on both the Mosel and the Rhine, so you'll have lots of flexibility if you have a tent.

There's a riverside **bike route** on the **Mosel's north bank** between Trier and Schweich, but it will take lots of patience to follow it, as there are gaps and many confusing sections along the way. The route was being worked on when we cycled it, so perhaps it's better marked by now. Set out along the riverside bike path, and watch for small green **Mosel Radweg**

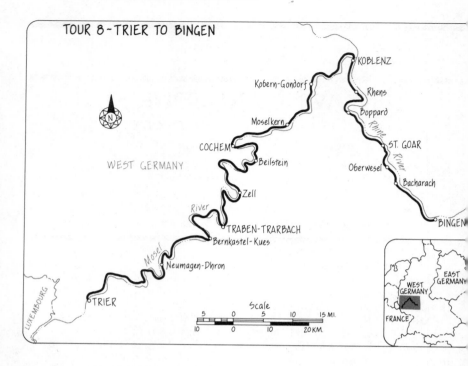

signs or the standard blue bicycle signs as you ride. If you get stuck along the way, don't hesitate to ask the locals for help. They're used to dealing with confused cyclists.

Your main reference point as you travel along the river will be **Road 53**. There are **bike lanes** on some sections of the road and the riding is not too bad, despite heavy tourist traffic. We lost the bike path just before **Trier Ehrang** (about 7 km before Schweich) and rejoined **Road 53** to cycle into town. A **bicycle sign** for **Schweich** leads to the right off the main road in Trier Ehrang. Follow it onto a **side street** and pedal to the river's edge.

Ride in solitude beside the river, passing under **two bridges** before returning to **Road 53** and cycling on through **Ensch.** Just past Ensch, veer right to cross the **Mosel,** then go left for **Köwerich** along a wonderful secondary road on the river's southern shore. Stay on the south side of the Mosel as you pass through Köwerich, round a long bend, and cycle on to **Neumagen-Dhron.** Road 53 crosses the Mosel to join you in this pretty town of flowers and wine presses.

Continue on Road 53 through **Nieder-Emmel,** then go left for **Minheim** across the **bridge** spanning the Mosel. You'll lose the traffic again as you play hide-and-seek with Road 53, pedaling through **Kesten** and on to **Lieser.** Stroll through Lieser and pass beautiful stone houses with flower-dripping window boxes on your way to the town square. A cheery fountain, a trim church, and the friendly smiles of women on their morning shopping rounds will greet you in the town.

Continue along the river to **Bernkastel-Kues,** and change sides with **Road 53** once more. Take an hour to explore the fairy-tale town of Bernkastel-Kues. Tucked beneath a castle ruin, it's full of tantalizing streets, enchanting houses, and unique metal signs — all of them sure to drastically deplete your film supply. Save some shots for the overwhelming Hauptplatz. With its sparkling central fountain and ornate Rathaus, the Hauptplatz's charm transcends the milling crowds that prowl its shops for postcards.

There's a tourist office in Bernkastel-Kues at Gestade 5, along the river, and there's a hilltop youth hostel if you want to spend the night.

Cycle along the Mosel toward **Zeltingen** and continue on to **K.-Kindel.** Cross on the **north bank** and rejoin **Road 53.** Ride through **Kröv** and pedal on to **Traben-Trarbach.** The city tourist office is on the right, inside the Rathaus at 22 Bahnstrasse. Look for it just before you turn right to cross the **Mosel** on Road 53. There are several pensions and a youth hostel in this twin town that sits astride the Mosel. The surrounding vineyards and the ruined Grevenburg Castle increase its appeal as a stopping spot.

Traben-Trarbach to Cochem: 49 kilometers

Cycle along **Road 53** to **Enkirch** and take a few minutes to walk your bicycle through the center of town. Picturesque houses, mazelike streets, and air filled with the fragrance of freshly baked bread will make you want to linger. Continue along the Mosel's winding shoreline for the 11 km to **Zell,** another small town with streets that beg for exploration. Abandon the main road just before Zell, staying on the **south bank** as the road recrosses to the north. There's a campground on the north bank of the river about 1 km from Zell's center.

From Zell, cycle on a quiet **secondary road** to **Neef.** Cross the **Mosel** to join the main road (now **Road 49**) just past Neef. Ride through **Ediger,** a lively tourist town with a busy waterfront, then pedal on to **Nehren** and forsake Road 49 again as you cross the **Mosel** and ride toward **Beilstein.** You'll be delighted by this miniature town, squeezed in between the river and its hillside church. Burg Metternich, a picturesque castle ruin, dominates the valley from the ridge above.

Beilstein's tourist office is near the stairs to the Karmelitenkirche. Climb the city's steep, narrow streets for a peek inside the church. There's a fine view from the courtyard in front, and the interior offers handsome woodwork and decorative painting.

From Beilstein, continue on the Mosel's **south shore,** and lose much of the traffic as you pedal the final 8 km to **Cochem.** Recross the river when you reach the city. Cochem is one of the loveliest of the Mosel towns. The view of the city from the **bridge** into town is the stuff that travel posters are made of. A colorful riverside park, a central core of jumbled houses and church towers, a near-perfect castle perched on one hill, a ruined fortress on another — Cochem is a gem.

Walk your bicycle through the crowded streets to the chaotic town square, where a bright pink Rathaus is one of the more reserved buildings overlooking the festive scene. Cochem's tourist office can help you locate a room in a pension or hotel. There's a youth hostel across the bridge in Cond, and several campgrounds dot the shoreline beyond the city.

Cochem to Koblenz: 50 kilometers

Take **Road 49** out of Cochem, with the Mosel on your right, and pedal to **Karden,** where Road 49 crosses the river to the south shore. Stay on the north bank, following **Road 416** to **Moselkern.** There's a large riverside campground in Moselkern where you can spend the night if you'd like to make the 4.8-km hike into the hills above town to visit Burg Eltz. It's a pleasant climb on a well-marked trail to reach the secluded castle. Burg Eltz is a rare example of an unspoiled Mosel fortress — because of its isolated position, it was never taken in a siege.

Continue along **Road 416** to **Kobern-Gondorf** and turn **into town** to parallel the main road and the train tracks. The ridgetop ruins and green vineyards above the city add to its charm. At the **end of town,** hop onto a **small road** between the tracks and the vines, and enjoy quiet riding until rejoining **Road 416** at **Winningen.** There's an excellent **bike lane** along Road 416 for much of the remaining 8 km to **Koblenz.**

Come to a **T** with **Road 258** and turn right. The road picks up heavy traffic as it crosses the Mosel River. Follow signs for **Road 9** and **Mainz** as you pedal toward Koblenz's core. You can ride with the traffic as you cross the **Mosel bridge,** but it's safer to get up on the sidewalk instead. A **roundabout** on the far side will direct you to a **city center** exit. Take it and then turn right at the first big intersection onto **Hohenfelder Strasse.**

Continue straight on Hohenfelder Strasse and ride beside the train tracks to reach the main **train station** (*Hauptbahnhof*). The city tourist office is just across the street from the station. Koblenz has a popular youth hostel (in Ehrenbreitstein Fortress) and a campground. Ask at the tourist office for help with lodgings and information on the city and the Rhine Valley.

Pick up a street map at the office, too, and plan to spend a few hours exploring the city. Although it's too big and too modern to be called quaint, Koblenz has several interesting sights and its setting at the confluence of the Mosel and the Rhine adds to its appeal.

Koblenz to St. Goar: 38 kilometers

From the main **train station,** work your way **east** to the bank of the **Rhine.** There's a pedestrian and **bike way** through the park along the river's edge, and you can pedal through the long greenway before joining **Road 9** south toward **St. Goar.** Road 9 has heavy traffic during the tourist season (one of the reasons August wasn't recommended as a time to ride this tour), so mingle your castle gazing with caution. This stretch of the Rhine River is one of the premium tourist areas in all West Germany. The scenery will show you why, but the constant traffic makes bicycling tense at times.

There are marked **bike lanes** for much of the route to **Bingen.** They range in quality from pleasant, wide strips painted along the shoulder of the main road to narrow, bumpy asphalt paths fighting losing battles with the weeds. Often, the bike lanes are on the river side of the road, so you'll sometimes be facing oncoming traffic as you ride.

A tidy German campground rolls out the "welcome wagon."

Watch for the Lahneck Tower on the opposite shore as you leave Koblenz on Road 9. Ahead, you'll spot Stolzenfels Castle ruling the west bank of the Rhine. Pedal about 1½ km up a very steep hill to reach **Stolzenfels Castle** by turning right at **Kapellen** onto a small, curving road. There's a great view from the castle terrace, and tours of the refurbished interior are available for a fee.

Continue south on **Road 9** to **Rhens,** a small town with wonderful half-timbered houses. You'll see the grandiose Marksburg Castle on the ridgetop across the Rhine as you pedal on. Marksburg is unique among Rhine castles because it has never been taken in a siege — quite an accomplishment in this war-torn region.

There's a **bike path** for much of the way from **Rhens** to **Spay.** Cross under the **main road** on the bike path as you enter Spay, and cycle down to the river's edge to gain a quiet promenade and a fine view of Marksburg across the water.

Stay on the **bike path** through Spay and keep pedaling until the path comes to an abrupt end. Then take a rough **asphalt track** to a **small road** and ride on to regain **Road 9.** Follow the bike lane along Road 9 to the edge of **Boppard,** and turn left at the first opportunity, to head for the **river's edge** once more. Walk your bike along Boppard's crowded, colorful Rhine Promenade and absorb the atmosphere of this perky riverside town. Hundreds of strolling tourists will join the parade, as Boppard is a major stopping point for Rhine tour boats.

Regain **Road 9** from Boppard. You'll lose the bike lane for awhile as you enter one of the most scenic stretches of the Rhine Valley. The Hostile Brothers Castles, the Mouse Castle (Burg Maus) and St. Goarshausen beneath its castle called the Cat (Burg Katz) will delight you from the opposite shore. Stay on Road 9 until the town of **St. Goar,** where the square, flag-bedecked ruin of Burg Rheinfels is rooted in the ridgetop.

If you're camping, turn right at the **campground turnoff** just before St. Goar, and climb gently for about 1 km to reach the secluded, streamside site. There's a small restaurant at the campground, and the facilities, though limited, are adequate. From the campground, you can take off on a small trail up the hill to make the 20-minute assault on Burg Rheinfels. For a modest entry fee, you can explore the castle's ruined walls and turrets, visit the small castle museum, and enjoy a fantastic view of the castle-rich Rhine Valley.

If you're looking for a bed for the night, continue into St. Goar and choose between the city's youth hostel and hotels.

St. Goar to Bingen: 31 kilometers

Continue south on **Road 9** from St. Goar, and turn off after about 5 km to ride through **Oberwesel,** a midsized town with two large churches, 18 watchtowers, and a castle. There's a youth hostel in town, as well. Stop to explore the Church of Our Lady on the south end of Oberwesel. A lovely painted ceiling and several handsome stone carvings make the stop worthwhile.

Pedal **south** from Oberwesel on **Road 9.** The way is narrow and busy, and you'll find few sections of bike path for relief. Look for the town of Kaub on the opposite shore, with the ruin of Gutenfels Castle guarding the hill above it. A little farther on, Pfalz Castle sits squarely in the center of the river, its once-mighty turreted walls now claiming tribute only from the tour boats that stop to drop off visitors.

Turn off Road 9 at **Bacharach** and pedal through the town, stopping to admire the half-timbered houses on the main square. Climb a rough path to Burg Stahleck, visit the city church, or stop to marvel at the Gothic Chapel of St. Werner. There are a campground and a youth hostel in Bacharach. The tourist office is in the Rathaus, and the helpful staff will load your packs with free English-language literature on the town and its surroundings.

Rejoin **Road 9** and pass beneath three castles as you pedal on toward **Bingen** on the busy road. Sooneck, Reichenstein, and Rheinstein are all open to tours. The Mouse Tower (Mäuseturm) on a small island in the Rhine marks your arrival at Bingen, and you'll see the Ehrenfels ruin on the opposite shore, surrounded by the vineyard-covered hillsides stretching down to Rüdesheim.

Enter Bingen on Road 9 and turn left at a sign for the **tourist office.** Coast down a short hill and cross the **bridge** spanning the **Nahe River.** The tourist office is to the left of the road, next to a hotel. Ask for information on lodgings there.

To ride to Bingen's campground, continue straight along a road paralleling the **train tracks** for about 3 km. The site is well marked and has a pleasant riverside setting and excellent facilities.

If you'd like to visit Rüdesheim, the popular wine town just across the Rhine, you can take one of the frequent ferries crossing the river from Bingen. Rüdesheim has a campground, a youth hostel, and several hotels.

If you'll be cycling from Bingen to Heidelberg to continue riding on Tour No. 9, we suggest you pedal **south** through **Wörrstadt,** Westhofen, Worms, Freinsheim, and **Speyer,** then swing northeast for **Heidelberg.** Or you can simply hop a train in Bingen and ride the rails to Heidelberg. If Bingen marks the end of your European cycling trip, Frankfurt's busy international airport is a short train trip east.

TOUR NO. 9

ROMANTIC ROAMING
Heidelberg to Munich, West Germany

Distance:	449 kilometers (279 miles)
Estimated time:	7 riding days
Best time to go:	June, July, or September
Terrain:	Lots of easy river riding sprinkled with gentle hills
Connecting tours:	Tours No. 8 and 10

If you're looking for an intensive, two-week introduction to West Germany, with gentle terrain, lovely scenery, and enchanting cities, this tour is hard to beat. You'll see three of West Germany's best-loved cities on this tour — Heidelberg, Rothenburg ob der Tauber, and Munich. Sure, you'll also see lots of fellow tourists along the way, but you'll share their delight in the sights, the sounds, and the tastes of the Neckar Valley, the Romantic Road (*Romantische Strasse*), and beautiful Bavaria.

Combine this ride with the one described in Tour No. 8, and you'll get a better look at West Germany than most short-term travelers ever dream of.

Read the introductory material for Tour No. 6 to prepare for your ride in West Germany.

CONNECTIONS. Heidelberg doesn't have an airport, but it's easily accessible by train from Frankfurt, Munich, and other cities with international air connections. Refer to the final paragraph of Tour No. 8 for information on cycling to Heidelberg from Bingen.

MAPS. Refer to maps information in the introduction to Tour No. 6.

ACCOMMODATIONS. Check the accommodations section in the introduction to Tour No. 6.

SUPPLIES. Look for details on shopping hours and food purchases in the introduction to Tour No. 6.

Heidelberg to Bad Wimpfen: 75 kilometers

Heidelberg, on the banks of the Neckar River, is a city for the lover of learning and history. Huddled beneath a mighty hilltop fortress, honored with the oldest university in Germany, Heidelberg has both an exquisite setting and irresistible charm. As you explore the city's streets and museums or climb to the ramparts of its magnificent castle, your admiration will continue to grow. Try to block out the chatter of the tourist crowds you'll rub shoulders with, and don't lose heart over the torrents of English and Japanese you'll hear — Heidelberg is special — and the word is out.

123

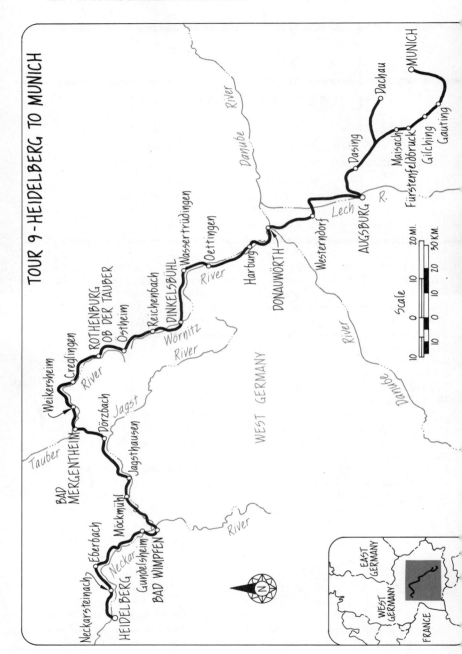

TOUR 9 – HEIDELBERG TO MUNICH

Heidelberg, awash in charm and tour groups, stands beside the Neckar River.

As a tourist, you'll be well looked after in Heidelberg. Stock up on English-language literature and get a city map at the tourist office next to the train station. There are dozens of hotels near the station, and you can get a list of addresses and prices from the tourist-office staff. Heidelberg has a youth hostel, and there's a campground at Heidelberg-Schlierbach, 6 km east of the city on the south bank of the Neckar.

Plan to spend a day to two exploring Heidelberg. Climb to the castle and enjoy the view of red tile roofs around the Gothic Church of the Holy Spirit, and then stroll along the Philosopher's Way (Philosophenweg) on the Neckar's opposite shore to get a postcard look at the river city beneath its fortress. If the crowds begin to get you down, look forward to the riding days ahead, for Heidelberg is not an end but a beginning — a gateway to the Neckar Valley and the Romantic Road.

Leave Heidelberg's center by crossing one of the **Neckar bridges** to gain the river's **north shore.** Cycle **east** on the main road, paralleling the river toward **Neckarsteinach.** You'll have flat riding and fairly heavy traffic for most of the ride to **Bad Wimpfen** as you follow the river's winding course. There's a mediocre bike path for the first few kilometers away from Heidelberg. Pass a riverside campground about 7 km from the city and continue on to where **Road 37** crosses the Neckar to add more cars to your route.

Soon after, look for a **bike path** sign for **Neckarsteinach.** Turn right off the main road and follow the bike path to a paved riverside lane that provides a pleasant break from traffic. Rejoin the **main road** just before **Neckarsteinach,** a small river town that boasts four castles and an attractive city center. There's a good bike lane along **Road 37** for most of the ride to **Hirschhorn.**

Go right and swing **under Road 37** just **before Hirschhorn.** The main road crosses the river and shoots into a tunnel here, lopping off one of the Neckar's many loops, but you'll take the **secondary route** and cycle **through Hirschhorn,** a midsized town with a tourist office and the obligatory castle. Follow a well-signed **bike route** for **Eberbach** from Hirschhorn, crossing a **bridge** above the Neckar and turning left along the **south shore.** Ride on a small road to the end of town, then gain an unpaved walking/biking path toward Eberbach.

You'll have a bit of rough going on the gravel surface, but the solitude and scenery are worth the rattles. If you'd prefer faster, smoother cycling on **Road 37,** you can **recross the river** when the shortcut road pops out of its tunnel. There's a wide **bike lane** along Road 37 for most of the remaining kilometers to Eberbach.

From Eberbach, follow **Road 37** through **Lindach, Neckargerach,** and **Binau,** passing Zwingenberg Castle along the way. Go right to cross the Neckar into **Obrigheim,** then pedal along the **secondary road** toward **Hassmersheim** and **Bad Wimpfen.** On the opposite shore, its tall round tower standing proudly atop a vine-covered hillside, is Hornberg Castle, one of the oldest and most striking of the Neckar castles.

Ride through Hassmersheim, staying with the signs for Bad Wimpfen, and continue on to **Neckarmühlbach.** You can make the short sidetrip to tour the medieval museum in Guttenberg Castle if you have the time. The keep offers a fine view of the Neckar Valley. To reach **Gundelsheim** (across the Neckar on Road 27) and a pleasant riverside campground, continue on from Neckarmühlbach and turn left to **cross the river** and gain **Road 27.** Go left again to find the **campground.** It has nice facilities and a friendly manager.

Gundelsheim is worth a visit, and it's just a short walk from the campground to the city center. With its old walls and towers, its renovated castle (now an old folks' home), its humble church, and its half-timbered houses hung with flowerboxes, this small city is one of the hidden delights of the Neckar Valley.

You may want to cycle on to **Bad Wimpfen** if you're hunting for a room. The city offers a youth hostel and a handful of pensions. Return to the south side of the Neckar on the **Gundelsheim bridge** and ride the 7 km along **Road L588** to the ridgetop town. The brief uphill push won't be fun if you're riding this at the end of a long cycling day. But Bad Wimpfen will charm you out of your weariness with its colorful houses, enchanting streets, and ruined palace.

Be sure to stop at the tourist office in the Rathaus (across from Stadtkirche) to get a map and an English walking tour for the city. The talkative gentleman behind the desk will load you down with more literature than you can carry.

Bad Wimpfen to Bad Mergentheim: 75 kilometers

We camped at Gundelsheim, made a day trip into Bad Wimpfen, then rode on toward our rendezvous with Rothenburg by heading south along **Road 27** from **Gundelsheim.** At **Offenau,** turn left for **Duttenburg.** Ride through Duttenburg and go right at the **T** just past town. Cross the **Jagst River** and climb a small hill past a tumbledown **castle**. Veer left for **Jagsthausen** at the next intersection.

If you're riding from Bad Wimpfen, reach the same spot in the following way. Leave the city center by descending on **Road L530** to the banks of the **Neckar**. Turn left to cross the river and gain **Road 27**. Go right on **Road 27** for **Bad Friedrichshall** and **Heilbronn**, cross the **Jagst River** and the train tracks, then go left onto a **secondary road** toward **Möckmühl** and **Jagsthausen**.

You'll be riding in the quiet Jagst Valley, enjoying peaceful roads and moderate hills as you follow a snakelike path northeast toward Bad Mergentheim and a junction with the Romantic Road. Pedal through **Untergriesheim** and **Herbolzheim**. Play hopscotch with the river and train tracks as you follow signs for Jagsthausen.

Make the short sidetrip to cycle through the center of **Neudenau** (turn left after crossing the **bridge** below town). The attractive old houses on the Marktplatz and the friendly smiles of the men who linger in the square make the detour worthwhile. Return to the **main road** and continue past **Siglingen** and on to the handsome belfry and tower at **Möckmühl**.

In Möckmühl, turn right for **Jagsthausen** and follow the river's contortions to Götzenburg Castle, just outside Jagsthausen. If you feel like a splurge, spend the night at this restored castle/hotel or catch an open-air play in its courtyard on a summer night. Ride on along the river to **Schöntal** (6 km from Jagsthausen). An immense Cistercian abbey engulfs the town. Be sure to visit the abbey church for a closeup look at baroque gone wild. If the alabaster carvings, glittering gilts, and painted ceilings don't give you indigestion, stop for a picnic lunch on the abbey grounds.

From Schöntal, ride another 16 km to **Dörzbach,** then go left on **Road 19** and bid the Jagst Valley goodbye. Make the long, gradual climb to the plateau above. Traffic is heavier on Road 19, but it's not unpleasant. You'll have about 8 km of uphill before the 6-km descent into **Bad Mergentheim.** There's a marked **campground** to the right, 4 km down the road for **Wachbach,** if you want to camp before Bad Mergentheim.

Sprawling on the banks of the Tauber River, Bad Mergentheim marks your arrival on the Romantic Road. The city has a castle dating back to 1565, a beautiful surrounding park, and several pensions and hotels. Check at the tourist office at Marktplatz 3 for help with lodgings.

Bad Mergentheim to Rothenburg ob der Tauber: 50 kilometers

The main road between Bad Mergentheim and Rothenburg follows the vineyard-dotted course of the **Tauber River**. The scenery is pleasant and the small towns are a treat, but the heavy traffic on the narrow Romantische Strasse is enough to make the romantic spirit of any cyclist run for cover. Luckily, the bike route known as the Liebliches Taubertal runs beside the Tauber River from Wertheim in the north all the way to Rothenburg. Unless you're in a great hurry to cover ground, this is the route you'll want to follow

The streets of Rothenburg ob der Tauber delight from every angle.

from Bad Mergentheim. The path is well marked by **signs with bike logos** and *Liebliches Taubertal* printed underneath (green print on white background), and the local populace is accustomed to helping disoriented cyclists find their way. Tourist offices in the area stock an excellent map of the route, as well. You'll stick fairly close to the main road the entire way, sometimes riding beside it, other times pedaling in solitude beside the river.

Look for the bike route signs as you leave **Bad Mergentheim** along **Road B19,** then angle right at **Igersheim** to follow the **Tauber River** south. **Weikersheim** is a colorful town built around a 16th-century castle. If you're lucky enough to arrive during a weekend festival, you can spend a delightful afternoon listening to an "oompah" band and wrestling with enormous pretzels while ruddy-cheeked West Germans sing and dance around you.

Continue along the **south bank** of the Tauber to **Bieberehren,** then join the **main road** for a short distance. The gently rolling terrain is sprinkled with orchards, vineyards, and thin forests. **Creglingen** is an attractive Tauber town. You can make a short sidetrip (about 3½ km) from Creglingen to visit the **Chapel of Our Lord** (Herrgottskirche). An amazing altarpiece by the greatest of West German woodcarvers, Tilman Riemenschneider, is housed in the chapel.

Pedal beside the **river,** then cross it to join the **main road** once again at **Tauberzell** before pedaling the final 9 km to **Rothenburg.** You'll see fuzzy splotches of white grazing on the verdant hillsides as you cycle through a deep, rolling valley toward the city. The closest camping to Rothenburg is at **Detwang,** about 2 km from the city center. It's a pleasant walk into the city from the large riverside site, and you'll share your tent space with travelers from dozens of countries throughout the world. The campground has a well-stocked store and good facilities, and it's a two-minute walk to Detwang's church, where another carved altarpiece by Riemenschneider awaits.

If you're looking for a room, continue into Rothenburg, climbing a hill to reach the matchless city on a ridge above the Tauber. Head for the tourist office near the Rathaus to gather maps and pamphlets for your sightseeing in the town. There are two hostels and several pensions in Rothenburg. Like Heidelberg, Rothenburg must contend with the side effects of fame. Thousands of tourists fill its streets on every summer day. But who can blame them? Rothenburg, too, is one of a kind.

Invest an entire day in wandering the city streets, marveling at the carved altarpiece in St. James's Church (a Riemenschneider, of course) or making the harrowing climb to the top of the Rathaus tower. Wait in the Marktplatz for the clock to strike 12:00, and watch the figures in the Ratstrinkstube clock perform their famous ritual. Shop at one of the stores outside the old town, and walk to the Burggarten beside the city walls to enjoy a picnic lunch of crackers, cheese, and sliced salami while you watch the Tauber wind through the valley below.

Rothenburg ob der Tauber to Dinkelsbühl: 45 kilometers

From the **campground,** follow the small road through **Detwang** along the river's edge. Avoid the climb to Rothenburg by turning right just outside

Detwang to **cross the Tauber** and taking the first left beside the water. You'll have a terrific view of the city's famous skyline as you pass Topplerschlösschen, an old tower/house. Continue on to cross the river on **Doppelbrücke,** an old two-tiered bridge. Turn right after the bridge, then **recross the Tauber** a short distance later. Veer left onto a **small road** beside the river. You'll have a short stretch of gravel along the way.

Reach an **intersection** with Road 25 for Dinkelsbühl. If you're coming from Rothenburg's center, you'll join the route here. **Cross Road 25** and gain the road toward **Gebsattel.** Cycle through Gebsattel and **Bockenfeld,** passing through quiet farmland on silent roads. Go left at the **T** in **Diebach,** then take the **next right** (it's unmarked). You'll see signs for **Östheim** as you cycle out of town.

Veer left onto **Road 25** in Östheim and endure about 5 km of unpleasant riding as you climb the day's only hill on a narrow, winding stretch of main road. Cross the **freeway** and turn right for **Wörnitz,** forsaking Road 25 once more. In **Wörnitz,** go right for **Schnelldorf,** then veer left **one block** later for **Ulrichshausen.** Reach a **T** and go right for **Ulrichshausen,** then swing left for **Waldhausen.**

Cycle through Waldhausen and ride on to **Zischendorf.** Go right for **Zumhaus,** then turn left at the **T** for **Ungetsheim.** Cross **under the A6 freeway** and pedal to **Reichenbach. Cross Road 14,** continuing straight for **Mosbach.** From Mosbach, follow signs for **Schopfloch** and ride past the midsized town (on the left across the Wörnitz River). Go straight at the **junction** to stay on a **small road** along the west bank of the Wörnitz for the final 6 km into **Dinkelsbühl.**

Enter at the north gate (Rothenburger Tor) of the small walled city, and immerse yourself in tantalizing streets filled with half-timbered houses, amusing metal signs, and kaleidoscopic colors. Dinkelsbühl is a scaled-down Rothenburg — with a few less tourists and a less impressive silhouette, but a healthy dose of small-town charm. Go straight on **Martin Luther Strasse** from the Rothenburger Tor to reach the tourist office (it's on the right, across from the church). There's a youth hostel in Dinkelsbühl, and there are several pensions and hotels.

To reach the campground on the edge of town, leave Dinkelsbühl via the **Wörnitz Tor** (go left off **Martin Luther Strasse** just past the **church**), **cross the river** and turn left on **Road 25** toward **Feuchtwangen.** Go right just past the **train tracks,** and follow signs to the campground (about 3 km from the city center). Dinkelsbühl's campground is one of the cleanest, most modern sites you'll find in West Germany, with free hot showers, heated bathrooms, and hot water for dishwashing. Check in at the office before you put up your tent, as some areas are reserved for trailers. From the campground's upper slopes, there's a fine view of the spotlighted city walls at night.

Dinkelsbühl to Donauwörth: 70 kilometers

Leave Dinkelsbühl on **Road 25** toward **Nördlingen.** You can pedal the Romantic Road a little while longer by following Road 25 south for the 31 km to Nördlingen, another walled city of ancient gateways and stout towers. We opted for a quiet ride toward Donauwörth instead, enjoying the Bavarian countryside along the way.

Swing left off **Road 25** just outside Dinkelsbühl, following signs for **Wassertrüdingen.** Pass through gentle hills and descend to **Wittelshofen.** Continue on through farmland and small villages toward **Wasser-trüdingen,** then follow signs for **Oettingen.** With its riverside setting, old buildings, and traces of a city wall, Oettingen is a town worth diving into. Swing right onto **Road 466** just before town, and go left for **Munningen** as you pedal away.

Cycle the quiet secondary road through Munningen, We-Fessenheim, and on to Ha-Heroldingen. Veer left on the far edge of **Ha-Heroldingen,** and climb a hill past **Ronheim.** You'll have a fine view of Harburg's castle from here. Follow the road along the **Wörnitz River** into **Harburg,** and take the old **bridge** into the heart of town. Turn left to cycle through the **city center,** then recross the Wörnitz at the **second bridge.**

Go right and pedal toward **Brünsee.** Climb a slight hill to ride through Brünsee, and continue along the Wörnitz Valley to **Ha-Ebermergen, crossing Road 25** along the way. Turn left in **Ha-Ebermergen,** then go left again for **Wörmitzstein.** Turn right at the T in Wörmitzstein, cross the **train tracks,** and go left for **Riedlingen** and **Donauwörth.**

Climb a steep hill, then descend into Riedlingen, with Donauwörth spreading up the hillside beyond. Pedal through town, keeping the **train tracks** on your right. Then cross under the tracks and join **Road 16** to ride into Donauwörth's center. You'll get your first look at the Danube (Donau) River in this midsized city overlooked by its Holy Cross Church.

Be sure to make the short trek up the hillside to this wonderful baroque church. Its interior is a visual extravaganza of colorful ceiling murals, elaborate stuccoes, and ornate gilt altars. Don't miss the richly attired skeletons resting peacefully in their glass coffins around the sanctuary.

Donauwörth has a youth hostel and pensions if you're looking for a less permanent spot to rest your bones. Check at the city tourist office in the Rathaus.

Donauwörth to Augsburg: 48 kilometers

Leave Donauwörth on **Road 16** toward **Neuburg,** crossing the **Danube River** and going right for **Wertingen** and **Mertingen** soon after. Ride through Mertingen and continue on to **Nordendorf.** Then turn right for **Blankenburg.** When the road **branches,** take the **small road** to the left to ride along a pretty valley toward **Westerndorf.** Angle left to enter Westerndorf, and cross **under Road 2.** Cycle on to **Ostendorf.**

Go right for **Thierhaupten,** then swing left beyond **Waltershofen** at a **second sign** for Thierhaupten. Cross the **Lech River** and take a **small road** to the right when the main road angles left. Cycle into **Thierhaupten** and go right, riding through **Bach** and **Sand** on the way to **Mühlhausen.**

As you continue south throughout the day, pedaling deeper into the heart of Bavaria, you'll notice the gradually changing architecture — bulb-towered churches and finely crafted homes — and you'll be greeted with the traditional Bavarian *"Grüss Gott"* as you pass women in bright embroidered blouses and men in supple *Lederhosen*.

In **Mühlhausen**, veer right for **Augsburg.** You'll pass three campgrounds in quick succession. We stayed at the second one (on the right), and we were delighted by its grassy setting and well-kept facilities. Use this spot as your base and make the 8-km ride into Augsburg without your bags.

To pedal into Augsburg, ride along the busy main road from the **second campground** and turn right at the **bike path sign** a short distance later. Cycle along a small road that veers southwest and leads onto a **second road** running west toward **Gersthofen.** Go right on this road, then turn left onto **Neuburger Strasse.** Cross **over the A8 freeway,** pedal through busy suburbs, and cross the **Lech River.**

Enter Augsburg's core at the **Jakobertor Gate.** Augsburg's tourist office is on the opposite side of town at Bahnhofstrasse 7, near the main train station. Go straight on **Jakoberstrasse** from the gate, and continue onto **Pilgerhausstrasse** past the Rathaus (on the left) and the Dom (on the right) to **Schaezlerstrasse,** where you'll turn left.

There are several pensions and a youth hostel in Augsburg, and this ancient yet very modern city offers much for the sightseer. The beautiful medieval Rathaus, the Dom, and the city's many churches will take you hours to explore. Wander the alleyways of the Fuggerei or stroll Maximilianstrasse as you make your way from place to place.

Augsburg to Munich: 86 kilometers

You may want to consider loading your bike and baggage aboard a train in Augsburg to make the short rail trip into West Germany's mighty Bavarian city, Munich. If you don't like dealing with big-city traffic, a train ride could save you some stomach-churning miles. But Munich is crisscrossed with excellent bike paths, and you can hook onto the network from many points outside the city, so riding in really shouldn't be too harrowing.

We were lucky enough to have a friend who lived in a small community south of Munich, so we didn't have to brave the city center with our bicycles. We'll describe our end-around route, with some suggestions for direct riding routes into the city core.

If you're departing **Augsburg** from the **campground** outside town, turn right on the **main road** as you leave the campground entrance. Take the left for **Dickelsmoore** at the **first street light** past the **airport.** Parallel the **A8 freeway,** riding through **Derching** and angling right for **Haberskirchen** and **Dasing.** Go by a freeway underpass, climb a short, steep hill, and go right to cross **over the freeway** and enter **Haberskirchen.**

If you're leaving from **Augsburg's center,** retrace your route out of the city via the **Jakobertor Gate** and turn right off **Neuburger Strasse** for **Friedberg** after crossing the **Lech River.** Veer left for **Stätzling** soon after, and continue on to **Haberskirchen** from there.

Follow signs for **Dasing** from Haberskirchen. In Dasing, go left onto **Road 300,** cross the **train tracks,** and then turn right for **Harthausen.**

Play "connect the dots" from one Bavarian village to another, staying on small roads through rolling forests and farmland. Watch for the onion-bulbed churches, the beautifully carved balconies, and the painted walls of homes and churches as you ride.

If you want to approach Munich **from the north** rather than the south, turn left just outside of **Dasing**. Ride through **St. Franziskus, Burga-delzhausen,** and **Ebertshausen,** pedaling southeast. Veer east at **Eins-bach** to pedal the final 12 km to **Dachau.** You can visit the concentration camp memorial and museum at Dachau, then work your way south to the outskirts of Munich. There are excellent **bike paths** around the **Olympic Park** in the northwest quarter of Munich, and they'll lead you into the city center on preferred bike routes. The total distance for this ride into Munich is about 75 km.

To follow the **southerly approach** to Munich, ride for **Harthausen** from Dasing. Turn right for **Rinnenthal** in Harthausen, and pedal on to Euras-burg, Hergertswiesen, Weyhern, Aufkirchen, and **Maisach.** Reach a **T** just before **Maisach** and turn right for **Fürstenfeldbruck.** In Fürstenfeld-bruck, a busy Bavarian town on the Amper River, go left onto **Road 2** for Munich (München). Cross the **Amper River** and continue out of the city on Road 2, climbing a long hill.

Veer right for **Starnberg** 5 km past Fürstenfeldbruck, and follow signs for Starnberg through **Alling** and **Gilching.** Pass the **A96 freeway** and go left 4 km later for **Gauting.** From Gauting, follow signs for **Buchendorf** and continue on to a **T,** then go left to parallel the **A95 freeway.** Cross **under the freeway** and go right at a **second T.** Then reach a junction with **Road 11** for Munich.

When you join Road 11, you'll be within a few kilometers of both the youth hostel in Pullach (to the south) and the campground in Thalkirchen (to the north). Both have good train connections for sightseeing in Munich. There is also a **bike route** into the city along **Road 11.**

Munich is big and beautiful and as captivating as Bavaria itself. Pick up a guidebook for the city or collect an armload of literature and a city map at the tourist office in the main train station. Then join the crowds who linger in "Munich's livingroom," the Marienplatz, and plan your sightseeing strategy while you await the fanciful Glockenspiel.

Be forewarned — Munich goes wild during the two weeks of *Oktoberfest* from late September to early October, so plan to avoid (or seek out) the mayhem, according to your personal pleasure. Even without the added spirit that *Oktoberfest* brings, Munich will surely capture your heart with its world-class museums, its overwhelming churches, its rich culture, and its irresistible charm.

If you're game for more pedaling from here, pick up the start of Tour No. 10 in Salzburg, Austria, by cycling east from Munich with a stop at the beautiful Bavarian Chiemsee along the way. The ride is hilly and scenic, and provides a wonderful opportunity to bid a leisurely *"Grüss Gott"* to the friendly folk of Bavaria.

TOUR 10 - SALZBURG TO VIENNA

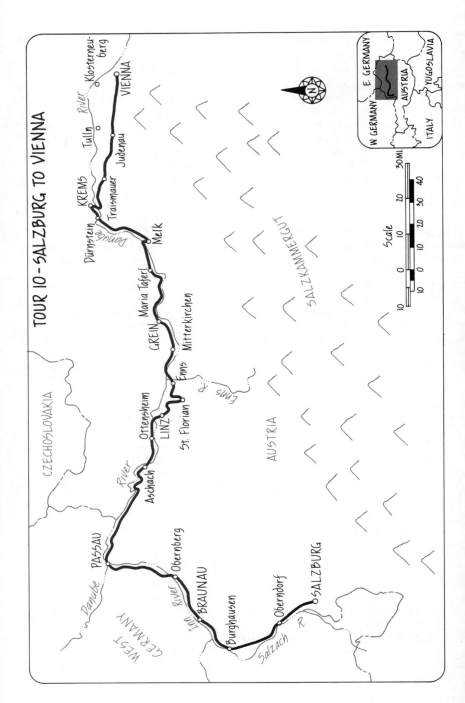

TOUR NO. 10

IN TUNE WITH THE DANUBE
Salzburg to Vienna, Austria

Distance: 462 kilometers (287 miles)
Estimated time: 6 riding days
Best time to go: June, July, or September
Terrain: Relatively easy, with a few tough hills
Connecting tours: Tours No. 9 and 11

If you're looking for a superb week and a half of riding, with lovely scenery, gentle terrain, and visits to two of the most stimulating cities Northern Europe has to offer, consider this ride between Salzburg and Vienna. You'll follow the Salzach River north to Passau, West Germany, then ride along the banks of the Danube, viewing vineyards, castles, and monasteries along the way. And you'll finish the tour in Vienna, an extraordinary city rich in architecture, history, and culture.

Austria offers much to the cyclist — friendly people, beautiful buildings, delicious food, and pleasant scenery. Roads are well maintained and Austrian drivers temper their standard European fondness for blazing speed with a welcome courtesy toward cyclists. Marked bicycle routes provide occasional opportunities to leave traffic and roads behind.

Work on your German civilities while you're riding each day — a *"Grüss Gott"* and a *"Danke"* will take you far in this Catholic and somewhat formal land.

CONNECTIONS. Salzburg is served by the Vienna-Salzburg railway line (a good option if you'll be flying in and out of Vienna, where this tour ends). You can also get to Salzburg by train or bicycle from Munich (end of Tour No. 9). Salzburg has an international airport, as well.

INFORMATION. Write in advance to the Austrian National Tourist Office, 500 Fifth Avenue, New York, New York 10110, for information on cycling, camping, hotels, shopping, and so forth. If you want an *intellectual* taste of Austria, save some pastry money for a guidebook. Michelin's *Green Guide Austria* provides extensive coverage of Salzburg, Vienna, and the Danube Valley. *Baedeker's Austria* or the *Blue Guide Austria* are other options. Take advantage of the tourist offices in Austria, too. They have plenty of free English-language literature.

MAPS. For route finding in Austria, you can use the 1:300,000 *Gross Strassenkarte Österreich No. 1,* published by Freytag and Berndt. It covers the entire Salzburg-Vienna ride, shows campgrounds, and is easy to read. Look for it in bookstores. For more detail, the 1:200,000 series published by the Austrian Automobile Club (ÖAMTC) covers the entire country with eight maps (three for this tour). It's also available in bookstores.

ACCOMMODATIONS. Living costs in Austria fit neatly between the high prices of Scandinavia and the wonderful economy of Greece and Portugal.

We enjoyed using Austria's well-run and generally inexpensive campgrounds, making the most of some stunning early-September weather along our way. *Always* ask permission before freelance camping in Austria.

Hotel rooms can be expensive. If you're not camping, hunt for small pensions or student-oriented lodgings instead, and your budget will survive.

SUPPLIES. Shops in Austria close on Saturday afternoons and Sundays, and you may have trouble finding groceries during the lunch break (12:30-1:30 p.m.) in the smaller towns.

Be sure to sample the local specialties — hearty meals of Viennese filet of veal (*Wiener Schnitzel*) or Hungarian stew (*Gulasch*) washed down by delicious Austrian beverages and followed by the country's famous *Tortes* or *Strudels*.

Cycling is popular in Austria, and you'll see good bicycle shops in Salzburg, Linz, and Vienna. Specialized touring gear is rare, however.

Salzburg to Braunau: 72 kilometers

Salzburg has several strategically placed tourist-information offices (train station, airport, Mozartplatz, and main roads into town). They'll provide you with a handy city map and lots of literature. There's a campground near the airport on the west side of the city — a good option for jet-lagged cyclists. Or try the convenient Stadtcamping Fallenegger on Bayerhamerstrasse near the train station (*Bahnhof*). It's the closest campground to the downtown core, but it has strong potential for bedlam during the height of tourist season. Several other campgrounds to the east and north, a handful of youth hostels, and lots of hotels fill out the selection.

Make your way to Salzburg's center, fortifying yourself with a nibble or two of Mozart chocolate along the way, and dive inside the massive Salzburg Cathedral (*Dom*). Make yourself dizzy staring at the fantastic central dome, then go outside to watch a giant-sized chess game in the busy Kapitelplatz nearby. Climb the hill to Hohensalzburg, a massive fort that runs a close second to Mozart as the city's most recognized trademark.

If you'd like to take a short day trip on your bicycle while you're visiting Salzburg, pedal around the east flank of Hohensalzburg's hill on **Mühlbacherhofweg**. Then follow **Freisaalweg** to **Hellbruner Allee**, a quiet pedestrian and bicycle way lined by pompous mansions. Cycle south from the city on Hellbruner Allee for the 20-minute ride to Schloss Hellbrunn, an irreverent bishop's palace with fountain-filled gardens.

After you've satisfied your tourist appetite on Salzburg's sights and specialties, it'll be time to abandon the city for your ride toward Vienna. From Salzburg's **train station,** take **Kaiserschutzenstrasse** to **Plainstrasse.** Turn right and follow Plainstrasse across the **train tracks,** then

A Salzburg street artist draws a crowd.

take the first left onto **Schillerstrasse.** Go left at the **T** onto **Road 156** for **Oberndorf** and **Braunau.** The road is wide, but busy with city traffic.

Ascend a short, steep hill in **Oberndorf,** and veer left for **Ostermiething** to gain a smaller road. Follow the gently rolling route through Ostermiething and **Tarsdorf,** cycling the most direct line for **Burghausen.** Cross the **Salzach River** and enter **West Germany** at Burghausen. Follow the road along the river to Burghausen's attractive main square (Hauptplatz). The tourist office is on the right in the Town Hall (Rathaus).

Burghausen's castle stretches along the ridge above the city, its long walls overlooking the thousand-year-old town where Napoleon crossed the Salzach in 1809. You can push up the hill to the fortress for a fine view of the city, the Salzach, and the Wöhrsee, but it's probably worth the climb only if you're hunting for a special picnic spot.

Leave the Hauptplatz and ride toward the river. Cross a **bridge** spanning the Salzach and reenter **Austria** (Österreich). At the **main road** beyond the bridge, turn left for **Braunau** and climb a steep hill. Continue following signs for Braunau through gentle terrain on a well-surfaced road. Pedal through **Ranshofen, cross Road 309,** and go straight for **Osternburg.**

A salesman shows his wares on the busy streets of Salzburg.

Two women watch the Danube and the days flow by in Passau.

Watch for signs for the Braunau campground, a pleasant, grassy site near the city center.

With its lively main street, its handsome church, and its grocery stores stocked with pretzels, wieners, mustard, and beer, Braunau will ensure your visit is a pleasant one. If you need a bed, you'll be able to find a pension in the small city core.

Braunau to Passau: 65 kilometers

This day's ride ends in the West German town of Passau, so don't forget to exchange some of your money for *Deutschmarks* to prepare for your evening expenditures. Leave the Braunau campground, cycling toward the **city center,** and turn right just past the large **sports complex.** Follow this street through town, cross the **train tracks,** and turn right on a main road leading toward **Road 309** for **Altheim.** Avoid the busy Road 309 by swinging off onto a **small road** to the left just before the **junction.** Pedal this quiet road until a turn marked for **Mining,** and veer left.

Continue through Mining and **Mühlheim,** angling left for **Kirchdorf.** Climb a short, steep hill and gain **Road 142** toward **Obernberg,** a small town with a colorful main square, a chortling fountain, and a bulb-domed church. Admire Obernberg's square, then **retrace your route** out of town and turn right just past a **roadside view spot** to descend steeply to the **Inn River** and a second crossing into **West Germany.**

Pedal across the **bridge,** then turn right for **Mittich** and follow a flat route through quiet countryside. Cycle through Mittich and continue on for **Sulzbach.** In Sulzbach, swing left toward **Eglsee** and Fürstenzell. Cross the main road for Fürstenzell and follow signs for **Passau** (16 km), passing through Eglsee. Pedal steadily uphill for about 10 km, and turn left onto the busy **Road 12** for the last part of your ride. Enjoy an easy descent into Passau.

Near the bottom of the hill, watch for signs for the **Passau tourist office.**
It's on the right-hand side of the road. Passau offers hotels and a hilltop youth
hostel for those in search of a bed. If you're camping, don't miss the city's
delightful "tents only" campground. It's hard to find but well worth the
search, tucked away on a grassy riverbank near the city center.

To reach the campground, cross the **Danube** (Donau) River and turn right
on **Angerstrasse.** Cycle through a **tunnel** just before the **Ilz River,** cross
the river, then turn left and go left again, recrossing the Ilz. To the right, on
Halser Strasse, a **tiny campground sign** will beckon you along the river
and up a residential street to a secluded tent spot beside the water.

Passau has attractive streets, personable buildings, and the pretty waterfront setting of a town where three rivers come together. The richly decorated Dom is a sparkling jewel set among the city's many glittering churches.
The ladder of flood marks on the Rathaus tower tells a 400-year story of
river-city woes. And the castle-topped hill above the city invites a pleasant
climb to an impressive view.

If you want to cut out a portion of this ride along the Danube, you can check
on sailing times at the ferry office on the south bank of the Danube. However,
the 5½-hour float to Linz covers one of the river's less scenic stretches, and
the cost is about $12 with a bicycle.

Passau to Linz: 95 kilometers

Leave Passau along the **southern shore** of the Danube River, following
signs toward **Linz** on **Road 130.** From the **campground,** retrace your route
down **Halser Strasse,** go through the short **tunnel** to the right, and turn
left to cross the **bridge** over the Danube. Pedal to the right along the river's
edge for several blocks, then turn left where a **second bridge** crosses the
Danube. Ride across the narrow peninsula of land between the Danube and
the Inn, and turn left again on the shore of the **Inn.** Cross a **final bridge**
over the Inn and begin following signs for **Linz.**

Pedal **Road 130** along the river. It's busy but wide enough to allow a
comfortable coexistence with the traffic. Pass through a relaxed **customs
post** and say *"auf Wiedersehen"* to West Germany. Race beside the meandering Danube with easy terrain and pleasant scenery to delight you.
There are several campgrounds along the way. Swing through the city
center in **Wesenufer** for a brief break from main-road traffic.

If you want to leave Road 130 for even longer, do as we did and explore the
Donau Radweg, a secluded bicycle route clinging to the river's edge. The
path follows the snaking river instead of cutting straight across (and up
and over) the surrounding hills with Road 130. It adds kilometers to your
ride, but it's worth it for the peaceful cycling and lovely scenery you'll have
along the way. To find the bike route, look for a **small sign** on the left side of
Road 130 as you abandon the winding river and begin to climb the hillside.

The *Donau Radweg* sign will beckon you onto a small paved road, then a
rideable dirt route along the river's edge. Watch the ridges for the many
castles overlooking the river as you ride. Regain pavement at a **ferry
crossing** point (don't take the ferry!), but angle left onto dirt again when the

paved road climbs away from the river. Just before **Aschach,** reach pavement once more.

Turn right in **Aschach** before the **bridge** across the Danube, and go left on **Road 131** to pedal across the river. You can stay on Road 131 along with lots of traffic, or weave your way through the cornfields on quiet country roads. Unfortunately, these small roads are unsigned, so sorting them out can be confusing. If you're willing to give it a try, take the **first right** off the bridge, then go left to parallel the river, and veer left again to ride toward **Feldkirchen** on a small, unsigned road.

Enter Feldkirchen and angle right onto a **larger road.** Then go left toward **Goldwörth.** Pedal through Goldwörth, reach **Road 131,** and follow Road 131 to a junction with **Road 127.** Turn right for **Linz.** Pass through **Ottensheim** and come to a **"no bicycles" sign** indicating a tunnel ahead. Swing left across the main road, go over the **train tracks,** and follow a **smaller road** parallel to Road 127. Cross under Road 127 and ride around the tunnel-causing hill.

Regain **Road 127** and keep to the **bike path** along the left edge for the rest of the ride into Linz. At Linz, cross the Danube and cycle straight ahead to the attractive Hauptplatz in the city core. There's a tourist information office on **Klosterstrasse** (to the right off the Hauptplatz), and you can pick up a map of the city and lodging information there. Linz has a youth hostel, a campground, and several hotels.

Linz to Grein (via St. Florian Abbey): 70 kilometers

From Linz's Hauptplatz, continue along **Landstrasse,** a pedestrian street lined with lots of shops and more ice-cream stands than you'll be able to resist. Continue onto **Wienerstrasse** and go under the **train tracks,** then swing to the right onto **Wankmüilerhofstrasse** to pass under the **freeway.** Continue on to **Kremplstrasse** and gain a bike path along **Wienerstrasse** to pedal out of Linz.

Cross the **Traun River** and continue along the main road (now **Road 1**) toward the Pichlingersee. You can use the pleasant Pichlingersee campground as a base for visiting St. Florian Abbey, but if you push on past Linz to the campground on the ride from Passau, you'll have a long riding day of about 110 km. It's a 10-km trip to the abbey and back from the campground.

St. Florian Abbey, the largest monastery in upper Austria, is the burial place of St. Florian, a Roman soldier who became a Christian and was martyred by being tossed into the Enns River with a millstone tied around his neck. You'll probably want to visit the monastery just to satisfy your curiosity about poor St. Florian, for he seems to claim a wall on every church and barn in Austria in his role of patron saint of fire and flood.

To reach the abbey, continue on Road 1 past the Pichlingersee **campground,** and take the first right turn. Cross under the **freeway** and angle right at the **Y.** Continue straight past a road branching off to the right, then take the next left. It's marked with a **small sign** for St. Florian (under the tree). Pedal up a steep hill to **Gemering** and keep to the right, then follow **Bruckner Strasse** down the hill to the abbey The entrance is on the right. Take the 90-minute tour of the abbey complex, and marvel at the library with its thousands of leather-bound books or the abbey church with its wild baroque interior of gilt and wood.

Return to **Road 1** and pedal on toward **Enns,** said to be the oldest town in upper Austria. Records show that it was a Roman settlement with a city code at least as early as A.D. 212. Visit Enns's attractive Hauptplatz on the north side of Road 1 to take a look at the impressive 16th-century city tower (*Stadtturm*). From the Hauptplatz, descend steeply to cross the **Enns River** on Road 1.

Turn left on **Road 123** and pedal across the **Danube River,** then circle left to gain **Road 3** toward **Grein.** Abandon Road 3 after about **2 km,** swinging right toward **Mitterkirchen.** Pass through **Naarn** and continue on quiet, level roads through agricultural land, keeping to the left toward **Grein** as you ride through **Mitterkirchen.** Cross the **Naarn River** and follow signs for Grein. Turn right when you reach **Road 3** again.

If you want to stay off the narrow and busy Road 3 a little longer, watch for small **green bike path signs** about **1 km** after you cross the Naarn River. The route zigzags through the countryside, merging with the **main road** about 9 km before Grein. Grein offers a quiet and inexpensive municipal campground, as well as a handful of pensions. Set off on foot to view the small town's church and hilltop castle. Be sure to venture outside after dark to catch the floodlighted castle at its best.

Grein to Krems: 80 kilometers

Leave Grein on **Road 3** and follow the narrow, winding **Danube Valley,** its steep hillsides tumbling down to the river's edge. Traffic can be surprisingly light through this section, and you'll be able to enjoy views of the wooded green hillsides in silence. The valley widens after **Persenbeug.** Small asphalt **bike paths** parallel the main road at times, but most come to sudden and unpredictable ends. They're worth the trouble only if you feel like dawdling.

Enjoy a striking view of the Church of Maria Taferl on the ridge above **Marbach,** then turn onto a wide **asphalt path** to the right of the main road just past the city. You can follow this quiet route all the way to a **large dam** across the Danube, passing the languishing castle ruins above Weitenegg and catching glimpses of **Melk Abbey** commanding a hill ahead.

A lucky break at the dam saved us a return to Road 3 and the ride down the river to the bridge for Melk. We tagged along with an Austrian family out for a bicycle ride in the sun, and we listened as the father spoke rapid German into an intercom near the gate barring access to the dam. An unseen guard "buzzed" us through the wire gate, and we were soon riding across the river on top of the dam. This shortcut saves several kilometers of riding to the abbey, and you can follow signs for **Melk** after you gain the main road on the other side of the Danube. Try the dam if you feel lucky, but remember that it isn't simply "open to the public."

If you trust neither your German nor your luck, abandon the bike path before you reach the **dam,** turning left to regain **Road 3.** Follow Road 3 along the river and veer south to cross at the **bridge** for **Melk.** Ride to the lower town, dwarfed by the amazing yellow facade of the abbey complex crowded on the hill above. You can walk up a **steep pathway** to reach the ridgetop buildings from the lower town, or you can pedal up, following signs for *Parking — Stift Melk.*

Marvel at the fantastic baroque interior of the abbey church and wander the extensive grounds of the complex before continuing on for Krems. From Melk, you can take the busy Road 3 along the north bank of the Danube (with close-up looks at the attractive towns of Spitz and Weissenkirchen), or you can abandon the tourist hustle and bustle of Melk and its surroundings to pedal peaceful, almost traffic-free roads along the Danube's southern shore.

For the **north bank** ride, leave the abbey parking lot and cross the Danube on the lofty **concrete bridge** to gain **Road 3.** Then go right and follow signs for **Krems.** For the **south bank** ride descend to Melk's downtown along the steep footpath from the abbey to get a fine view of the Hauptstrasse and the south facade of the abbey before leaving the city on the road toward the abbey parking lot. Veer to the left on **Road 33** toward **Krems** before starting up the hill.

You'll have wonderful views of the vineyards and towns on the opposite shore on this route, and you'll get a close look at Schönbühel Château on its rocky perch above the Danube. At several points along the way, water ferry (*Wasserfahre*) signs will invite you to visit towns across the Danube. Bicycle route signs (*Rad Wanderweg*) trace a circuitous course through orchards, vineyards, and small towns along the river's southern shore. We left the road to explore the bike routes on occasion, but try them only if you feel like lingering.

At **Rossatz,** you can swing down off the road to reach a campground and a small **ferry** that crosses to the charming town of **Dürnstein,** just across the river. The campground is rather dumpy, though, so it's better to pedal on for Krems and backtrack to Dürnstein along the northern shore.

Pedal across the Danube **bridge** at **Mautern,** cross **Road 3,** and turn right for **Krems** on a small road paralleling this "no bikes" section of the main road. Cycle on to Camping Donau, an excellent, well-situated campground just to the right off Road 3 as you enter Krems. A grassy setting, clean facilities, and steaming showers make the campground a pleasant spot to spend the night. Krems has hotels and a youth hostel, if you're looking for a bed.

Make the short 7-km ride **back along the Danube** to visit **Dürnstein.** The main road between Krems and Dürnstein is off limits to bicycles, so follow the **side road** on the north flank of Road 3 toward Dürnstein, then take a well-marked **bike path** paralleling the main road, and finish up on signposted **small roads** as you pedal into town.

Despite busloads of tourists, Dürnstein is worth a trip for its pretty Hauptstrasse hung with wrought-iron signs, for its parish church, and for the climb to the ruined castle above the city. Sit on a tumbled stone and dream of Richard Lionheart languishing in prison in this castle, waylaid on his journey homeward from the Third Crusade. Or look out over Dürnstein and the spreading Danube Valley, staring at hills green with vineyards and dreaming of Vienna.

Krems to Vienna: 80 kilometers

If you don't have a good street map of Vienna, buy one in Krems before you begin your riding day. Vienna is one European city where you'll need more than instincts and luck to find your way. From Krems, return to the **south shore** of the Danube by retracing your route to the **bridge** a few kilometers to the west and crossing to **Mautern.** Coast through Mautern, following signs for **St. Pölten,** and angle left for **Palt.** Pedal the quiet secondary road to **Wagram** and turn left for **Traismauer,** crossing the **freeway.** From Traismauer, take **Road 43** toward Vienna (Wien). Cycle on to **Mitterndorf** and turn left toward **Tulln** and **Judenau.**

At **Judenau,** follow signs for Tulln onto a main road (**Road 19**), then turn right toward **Klosterneuburg** after crossing a small **river.** You can alter this route if you'd like to visit Tulln or Klosterneuburg. The former has a 13th-century funerary chapel and the latter boasts an abbey church. We were eager to reach Vienna, so we simply pedaled on.

Continue along the quiet road toward Klosterneuburg until just past **Königstetten,** then turn right for **Wien-Neuwaldegg.** The day's ride is fairly easy to here, with only moderate hills, but now the climb through the Vienna Wood (Wienerwald) to the ridge above Vienna begins. Follow signs for Wien-Neuwaldegg throughout the long, steady ascent (about 12 km), cycling through quiet forests of thin-trunked trees.

Descend steeply through sharp switchbacks to a junction with **Neu-waldeggerstrasse.** Swing left onto this busy street and prepare to do battle with the city. Vienna is not a city for cyclists. You'll see only a handful of brave bike riders during your stay in Vienna, and the cobblestone streets, treacherous trolley tracks, and harrowing traffic of the city core will show you why. Stay with Neuwaldeggerstrasse (it goes through several **name changes**), eventually emerging onto **Hernalser Hauptstrasse.** This street will take you deep into the city.

You may decide to get off your bicycle and walk once you get into the city core. It's safer (and saner) and it gives you a chance to admire Vienna's majestic buildings at a slower pace. If you don't have room reservations in town, pull out your street map and work your way to the tourist information office across from the State Opera House at 1 Opernpassage. Their accommodation service can save you lots of legwork in this sprawling town. There are several campgrounds in Vienna and there's a youth hostel, too, but they're inconveniently located far from the city core.

Once settled into a room, hit the streets without your bicycle and fall in love with a lovely city. Forget you're a cyclist, ignore the cobblestones, the trolley tracks, and the traffic, and discover Vienna. Sip a cup of coffee at a streetside café and choose a delicious-looking torte or sweet roll (büchteln) from display cases that make indecision a delight. Walk to the Dom and stare in fascination at its incredible Gothic exterior, or wander for hours in the palace complex of the Hofburg.

Grandeur, beauty, culture, and wealth weave a spell throughout Vienna that will tie you to the city with a timeless bond.

TOUR NO. 11

TIP-TO-TIP ALONG A STUNNING COAST
Koper to Bar, Yugoslavia

Distance:	872 kilometers (541 miles)
Estimated time:	14 riding days
Best time to go:	April, May, June, or September
Terrain:	Punishing hills and spectacular scenery
Connecting tours:	Tours No. 10, 12, and 14

Yugoslavia. Although the country has been a familiar vacation destination to Northern Europeans for years, to North Americans the land is still a mystery — an undeveloped country balanced precariously on a tightrope between communism and capitalism. The 1984 Winter Olympics in Sarajevo did much to clear up the mystery, but Yugoslavia still remains an undiscovered land for many Western travelers.

If you're willing to take on the physical challenge of Yugoslavia's rugged Adriatic Coast, you'll be in for an unforgettable three weeks of incredible scenery, unique seaside towns, and some of the most inexpensive tourist living to be found anywhere in Western Europe.

If at all possible, avoid cycling here in July and August. Yugoslavia is a landing spot for vacationing Germans, Italians, Austrians, English, and French by the thousands, and the main coastal road can be downright hazardous with all the cars. Large sections of the main coast road are closed to cyclists between 3:00 and 8:00 p.m. from June 15 to September 15. We've noted those sections in the text when possible.

You'll find more solitude and still have a chance at warm, dry weather if you ride in April, May, early June, or September. Wind can be a bothersome element along the coast. Local residents told us that wind from the north brings clear skies, and rain comes with wind from the south, so cycling this tour as written should give you a tailwind and dry skies — if you're lucky. But bring along some good wet-weather gear in case you're not.

Generally, Yugoslavs are friendly, gracious people. You'll get lots of blank-faced stares as you pedal through small towns and rural areas, but you'll also be treated to schoolyards full of laughing, waving children and cheerful shouts of greeting from women working in the fields. You'll find fewer English speakers here than in other European countries, although many people along the coast do speak Italian or German. Carry a Serbo-Croatian phrase book to help you with the unfamiliar words and alphabet. With a few greetings, a ready smile, and good manners, you should get along fine.

Yugoslavia is poor. Its economy totters on the edge of collapse, and food

145

prices here are so low you'll wonder how to spend the *new dinars* in your pocket. Tourism, especially on the Adriatic Coast, pumps much-needed vitality into the local economy, so tourists are coddled and catered to all along the coast. The contrasts of unmatched natural beauty with dismaying pollution; extensive tourist development with glaring poverty; and Western modernism with Eastern orthodoxy are just a few of the complexities that make Yugoslavia a challenging, stimulating, and rewarding country to choose for your cycle tour.

CONNECTIONS. To reach Koper, about 10 km south of the Yugoslav/Italian border on Yugoslavia's Adriatic Coast, you can travel by train or bicycle from Trieste, Italy (21 km north). Trieste has good rail connections with other cities in Europe. There are roundabout rail lines to Koper from major cities in Yugoslavia, but riding to the coast on a Yugoslav train can be slow torture. We pedaled to Koper from Vienna, Austria (end of Tour No. 10), cycling through Graz, Maribor, and Ljubljana before turning west for the Adriatic.

Ferry service is plentiful along the coast, with connections between major cities (Rijeka, Rab, Zadar, Split, Hvar, Korčula, Dubrovnik, and Bar) and with long-distance lines to Greece and Italy. Jadrolinija is the major Yugoslav ferry line, and you'll find offices in all the cities above. For short hops between the mainland and offshore islands, local ferry lines are less expensive than the sleek Jadrolinija ships. With all these ferry options along the coast, you'll be able to shorten this tour at will if you find you can't ride the entire route.

INFORMATION. Write to the Yugoslav National Tourist Office, 630 Fifth Avenue, Rockefeller Center, Suite 210, New York, New York 10020, for preparatory information. Ask for the brochure *Camping in Yugoslavia* if you'll be bringing along a tent.

You won't need an advance visa to enter the country, but you will have to get a visa at the border when you cross. You'll be given a free 30-day entry permit for your stay.

Larger towns along the Adriatic Coast usually have dozens of tourist offices, and it's sometimes hard to tell which are official and which are merely travel agencies. Almost all of them have staffs that are helpful and polite, and you'll be able to check on lodgings and get city maps and literature in the better ones. These offices usually exchange money, too, but beware of occasional high commission fees. The exchange rate is set by the Yugoslav government, so rates shouldn't vary from place to place, though it never hurts to check around.

There's an excellent five-book series of English-language guidebooks called *The Yugoslav Coast* that will enrich your cycling immeasurably. The books are available in bookstores and tourist offices in Yugoslavia, and they cost about $1.50 each. Each book covers a section of the coast, with notes on cities (including city maps), local history, and climate; and each contains a small fold-out map of the section (1:300,000) that can be used in a pinch for route finding. The *Blue Guide Yugoslavia* and *Baedeker's Yugoslavia* are other guidebook options for your trip.

MAPS. Yugoslavia is one country where it's a good idea to have a detailed

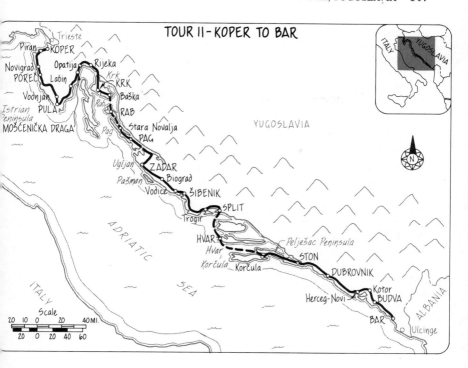

map before you arrive, as good maps are hard to find. If you come from Austria, pick up the Austrian Auto Club's *Die Generalkarte,* a three-map series on the Yugoslav Coast. Once in the country, look for the *Jadran Auto Karta* in the larger bookstores. It covers the entire coast at a scale of 1:400,000. Another option is *Autokarta Slovenije,* a 1:350,000 map that shows campgrounds and sights of interest.

ACCOMMODATIONS. Camping in Yugoslavia offers mixed rewards. It's cheaper than staying in rooms, and nothing can beat an Adriatic sunset from your own tent door. But the price difference between a *sobe* (see below) and a campground can be quite small, especially if you're forced to use the sprawling coastal sites that thrive on the Northern European tourist trade. These camp sites not only cost a lot — they're often quite unpleasant, with overcrowded facilities, cold water, and toilets that are simply "the pits." Instead, look for small campgrounds and the occasional family-owned site tucked away in somebody's backyard, and avoid the monster campgrounds whenever possible. But be prepared to be turned down if you ask to camp on someone's land, as the government doesn't encourage freelance camping.

Indoor accommodations in Yugoslavia are inexpensive, but steer clear of the hotels. Most have inflated prices and zero appeal. Look for rooms in private homes instead. They're called *sobes,* and they're available almost everywhere along the coast. Your Yugoslav hosts will delight you with their hospitality and with the cleanliness of their rooms. Even in Dubrovnik, the undisputed tourist capital of Yugoslavia, we paid only $6 for a small room in the home of an elderly couple — and that was with homemade refreshments thrown in!

And don't be surprised by the Yugoslavs' penchant for paperwork. There's no such thing as a "first-name basis" when you camp or get a room here. You'll be asked to turn over your passport for vital statistics whenever you seek lodgings.

SUPPLIES. Grocery stores keep convenient hours in Yugoslavia, but you'll need to watch out for Saturday afternoon and Sunday closures. Food selection is limited and the quality is poor in comparison with products in the United States or Western Europe. Most Yugoslav stores have an entire aisle dedicated to cookies and another reserved for wine and liquor. You'll be amused by the dreary packaging and the dusty supermarket shelves, and you'll search long and hard to find products that aren't manufactured in either Belgrade, Zagreb, or Ljubljana. Cheeses and breads don't match the superior products of other European countries, and you'll do better to buy your fruits and vegetables in the numerous outdoor markets in the towns along your route.

Groceries are incredibly cheap. Sometimes that makes up for the crumbled cookies, dust-covered canned goods, and mold-flecked cheese. Sometimes it doesn't.

One important note on camping supplies in Yugoslavia. If you're cooking with a Gaz stove and small butane cartridges, stock up *before* you cross the border. You won't find the cartridges in Yugoslav stores.

Restaurant meals are a good bargain in Yugoslavia, especially if you shop around. Watch out for the beverage prices, though, as they can be disproportionately high. Cafes are great places for quick snacks. Be sure to try the *burek,* a tasty cheese or meat pie made of layered pastry.

Don't expect to find much in the way of bike parts in Yugoslavia. Imported goods are practically nonexistent here. Arrive equipped with replacement spokes, a foldup tire, spare tubes, and lots of patches. We got more flats during our month of cycling here than in our other 11 months of European cycling combined. The country is half submerged in litter, and the roadsides glitter with broken glass.

Koper to Poreč: 74 kilometers

Koper sits on the northern edge of the Istrian Peninsula, a great bulge of land thrusting out into the Adriatic. Ancient Venetian and modern Italian influence is still strong on the peninsula, and you'll see examples of Venetian architecture and hear the chatter of Italian tourists throughout your visit. Koper's tourist office is at the bus station on Istrska Cesta, southeast of the city center.

Venture into the old city from the bus station and take a look at the 15th-century Praetor's Palace or wander the narrow, tourist-packed streets. Then walk down to the harbor to see the real attraction — the sparkling Adriatic that will be your companion for the next three weeks. Koper has

A rush of unfamiliar images overtakes a cyclist in Koper.

several hotels and *sobes*. Visit the large bookstore at Tomažičev Square (*trg*) to search for guidebooks and maps.

Leave the city center by cycling on the pedestrian way along the harbor to the **main road.** Continue on a path beside the road until it ends in sand, then join the trucks and tourists on **Road E751,** bound for **Izola.** There's a long, skinny campground beside the bay at Izola, 6 km from Koper, if you're looking for a spot to pitch your tent.

From Izola, climb a long hill and descend to **Strunjan,** sharing the main coast road with heavy traffic. Climb again after Strunjan, laboring up a tough **hill** before turning right for **Piran.** Approach the gemlike city of

Piran from above, passing by the old town wall. One look at the spectacular vista of Piran snuggled against the sea, with the Church of St. George perched on a hilltop above it, and you'll be sure you made the right choice in cycling the Yugoslav coast.

Descend a precipitous cobblestone street to the Church of St. George with its 17th-century baptistry. Peek inside the church, then continue down the hill to Piran's main square, bordered by the Town Hall, the Court Palace, and the Church of St. Peter. Push your bicycle through Piran's narrow streets as houses crowd you on both sides and freshly-washed laundry flutters overhead. Piran's waterfront is lined with scores of fancy hotels and overrun with tourists. Cycle beside the water on the seaside promenade before rejoining the road outside of town.

Climb away from the sea through vineyards and farmland, passing through **Portorož** and regaining **E751,** the main road south for **Pula.** Go up and over a small hill, then pedal up another **long incline.** At the top, veer right toward **Umag** and go left about **3 km** later to forsake the fierce main-road traffic for the rest of the ride to Poreč. Pass through **Marija na Krasu** and continue on for **Umag,** another Adriatic town of fascinating alleyways and flapping sheets. The small city is built on the tip of a promontory, and you'll see the sea on either side as you walk the streets.

Stop for a *burek* and a glass of lemonade at one of the small cafes along the water, then continue south to cycle the remaining 31 km to **Poreč.** Pass through Novigrad, another medieval town with remnants of the old fortification system.

If you're planning to camp near Poreč, you'll have to ride past the town to reach the huge campground at **Zelena Laguna.** It's about 5 km from the city center (well marked from the road), but it's overpriced, crowded, and dirty. If you can get a *sobe* in Poreč instead, do it.

Despite a hefty dose of tourists, Poreč is a nice Yugoslav city, and the 6th-century Euphrasian Basilica is resplendent with well-preserved mosaics that glow in gold and blue. Climb the rickety steps of the tower for a view of the town, but watch out for the two-hour noon break when the entire basilica complex is locked up tight. There are several tourist offices in Poreč, most pushing specific tours and hotels, but you should be able to ask questions or exchange money at any of them.

Poreč to Pula: 51 kilometers

Leave Poreč's **center** and cycle south toward **Vrsar.** Veer left **3 km** from Poreč onto a secondary road for **Fuškulin.** This is a pleasant, paved route with light traffic and rolling hills. Pass through Fuškulin and angle right for **Flengi.** Pick up more traffic as you swing left toward **Gradina.** Ride through quiet countryside of vineyards and vegetable gardens, passing crumbling stone towns and rounded haystacks that look like brown gumdrops scattered in the fields. Keep to the right through **Gradina** and join **E751** for **Pula** about 4 km later.

You'll have an impressive view of the Limski Canal as the road drops almost to sea level, then climbs to the ridge beyond. This section of E751 is restricted to cyclists (as noted in tour introduction). Pedal past **Brajkovići,** then take a break 9 km later to explore the ancient streets of **Bale.** A friendly resident offered us an honest appraisal of his town in piecemeal German: *"Stadt kaput,"* he said with a smile as he gestured toward the city's beaten walls.

From Bale, continue south on **E751** to **Vodnjan,** a larger town with a handsome tower and church. Cycle the final 10 km to **Pula.** Follow signs for Pula's **center** as you enter town, and look for the massive Roman Amphitheater springing out of the midst of the modern city. There are an archaeological museum, a triumphal arch, and several churches in Pula, as well. The tourist office at Trg Bratstva-Jedinstva 4 can help you find a room if lounging around the bus station and waiting for offers of a *sobe* does not do the trick.

To reach the campground on the edge of town, follow the street **Obala Maršala Tita** along the harbor and around the shipyards, and turn right onto **Bulevar Borisa Kidriča.** Follow signs for **Veruda** to camp at Ribarska, a 600-site campground with hot showers (if you're persistent). The campground is on the left on the bay.

Pula to Mošcenička Drage: 73 kilometers

From Pula, turn northeast across the Istrian Peninsula, bound for Rijeka. Leave Pula by cycling along the sea side of the **Roman Amphitheater** and turning right a few blocks later toward **Rijeka.** Gain **E751** and climb through rolling hills for the 28 km to **Barban,** a tumbledown town with an 18th-century church and a decrepit palace. Cruise down a long, steep hill to the Raša River, then endure a grueling ascent toward **Labin.**

Labin is a fascinating city perched atop a precipitous hill, but unless you're into self-inflicted pain or panoramic views, you'll probably want to skip the added climb to the town and stay on the **main road** for **Rijeka.** Continue **north,** ascending gently for about 4 km, then descend to **Vozilići.** Pedal uphill to reach Plomin, a beautifully situated city of grey stone, then continue cycling along the cliff-lined Adriatic with stunning views of the sea.

You'll have easy, scenic riding along the undulating coast to **Mošcenička Draga,** descending gradually as you go. Brseč is worth a stop for an exploratory stroll. There's a pleasant campground at Mošcenička Draga, and the coast between the city and Rijeka is a hotel- and *sobe*-studded circus of tourists and traffic where lodging options abound.

Mošcenička Drage to Krk: 84 kilometers

Continue on **E751** to **Lovran,** a pleasant resort town with handsome old hotels. Pass Ika and Icići, then enter **Opatija,** the resort capital of this stretch of coast. The town is overrun with luxuriant vegetation, deluxe hotels, and beach-happy tourists. To get a close-up look at the entertaining opulence of Opatija, swing down off the main road to walk through the city center (one-way traffic runs against you). The road returns to two-way traffic after about 1 km.

Follow signs for **Rijeka** and Preluk Campground to gain a **secondary road** and swing east around the bay. Rejoin the main road for the unpleasant ride into Rijeka, a sprawling, dirty port city with few attractions for the cyclist. Yugoslavia's largest Adriatic port, Rijeka is immense and industrialized. Cycle the main road through the city, paralleling the sea. The fine bell tower on the edge of the old town (Stari Grad) is worth a look, and there are a few other attractive buildings in town, such as the Capuchin Church (on the left past the main train station).

You can swing left off the main road to see the church, then go right to cycle past the Jadran Palace and reach the bell tower. Return to the **main road** and follow signs for **Senj** as you continue along the bay. Climb a hill out of town, descend to the water, and climb again. Camping Kostrena is on the right, next to an all-night (and very loud) cafe/disco, about 6 km from Rijeka's center.

Continue on **E65** toward **Senj** and loop around the Bay of Bakar, enduring hills and heavy traffic. **Bakarac** has a campground and a hotel. The road clings to the shore above the water, and the vistas are impressive. Watch for **Kraljevica** and its castle below. Your day will take a marked turn for the better as you veer right **off E65**, bound for **Krk.**

Cross a long **bridge** onto the rock-strewn island. The terrain is harsh, with treeless, uncultivated soil in the north. Pedal south the remaining 25 km to **Krk,** and pass through old towns of mortarless stone houses that crowd beside the narrow road. Stay on the curving, lightly traveled road as you follow a hill-filled route to Krk. Make the long descent into the island's compact capital city, following signs for the **center.**

Krk is a handsome port town with a cathedral dating back to the 5th century and streets that beg for exploration. There are dozens of *sobes* in and around Krk, and there's a campground on the edge of town.

Krk to Rab: 32 kilometers

Leave Krk on the road for **Baska** (19 km) and climb a steep hill out of town. You'll have a postcard view of the huddled buildings of the city and the blue Adriatic from the bluff above. Descend to the sea and watch for the unique 9th-century Church of St. Dunat near the turnoff for Kornić. Continue on for Baska, pedaling up a long, **punishing incline** as you cross the high backbone of the island. Stop to admire the vistas around you — the city of Krk beside its wind-whipped bay; the bitter, stone-walled fields of straggling vines; the endless empty hillsides.

Reach the crest after about 5 km. The final 200 yards will have you begging for mercy. Enjoy a steep downhill, then make a long, gradual descent into the Baska Valley with awesome views of the emerald sea beyond. Pedal along the valley and pass through the roadside town of **Baska Draga,** made picturesque by a sprinkling of hilltop churches.

Baska itself has a stunning setting on a green, cliff-edged bay. The town is a perfect size for exploring, and there's an attractive seaside campground and numerous *sobes* if you decide to stay. Walk down to the harbor and continue to the east edge of the docks to reach the small ferry office. Crossings to Lopar on the island of Rab and to Senj on the mainland are offered daily during tourist season. We decided to continue our island hopping, trading the heavy traffic and bitter hills of the mainland for quieter but equally tough island cycling.

Make the one-hour crossing to **Lopar** (cost about $2), enjoying the scenery from a new vantage point. The mountainous profile of Krk will slowly fade as you pass numerous small islands, barren humps of stone pounded by the waves and inhabited by handfuls of hearty sheep. Arrive at **Lopar** and follow signs for **Rab** (13 km), winding along the shore of the island, then climbing a gentle hill before descending into the valley leading to the island's capital.

Rab Island is gentler than Krk, and you'll arrive at Rab Town refreshed and ready for sightseeing. Rab Town is one of the loveliest cities you'll see in Yugoslavia, with a near-perfect profile of walls and churches, towers and tile, against a background of sparkling sea. You may want to take an extra day to enjoy the town at leisure. Check at the waterfront tourist office for information.

Rab has dozens of *sobes,* and there's a large but pleasant campground just around the bay from the city. Take the harborside road from the city center, and loop around the bay to Camping Banjol. The hillside sites on the outer edge of the campground are particularly nice, and you can walk back into the city for sightseeing. Don't miss the Tower of St. Christopher, where you can get a fine view of Rab from the wall, and stop for a look at the carved choir stalls in the bell-tower-topped cathedral. Rab has dozens of cafes and restaurants, mobs of tourists, and truckloads of charm.

Rab to Pag: 41 kilometers

From Rab Town, take the **main road** toward **Banjol** and **Barbat.** Pass the old ferry dock at Pudarica and continue on to **Misnjak,** climbing a short hill before descending to the **ferry landing.** We caught the 11:30 a.m. ferry (several crossings daily in high season) to **Jablanac,** cruising past a long line of foreign license plates to roll aboard. The cost for the 30-minute ride to the mainland is about $1.

You can pedal south along the mainland coast from Jablanac, but a 45-minute **ferry** ride will carry you to **Stara Novalja** on the island of **Pag** instead. The small ferry is well worth the investment for Pag's scenery and solitude, and you'll be able to catch the ferry to Pag at the same spot you land as you arrive from Rab.

Watch the coastline for a glimpse of Zavratnica Gorge, a deep inlet cut into the cliffs, as the ferry pulls away from Jablanac. Arrive at **Stara Novalja** and pedal the easy 5 km to the midsized fishing town of **Novalja,** coasting down a small hill into town. The old core is along the bay. Continue out of Novalja, following signs for **Pag.**

The scenery is exquisite as you slowly ascend the backbone of Pag Island. Fantastic walled fields of rocky, barren soil stretch out on both sides of the road, and you'll see the peaks of the mainland mountains to the east. The glowing white rock of the fences parceling up desolate patches of green scrub provides a haunting foreground to the scene. Of course, beauty can do only so much to alleviate pain, and you'll struggle through a series of punishing hills before making a welcome descent to the island's western shore.

One warning for your cycling on Pag — some road maps don't show the roads here accurately. The road continues on past Simuni along the western shore of the island.

Climb from the western shore of Pag to cross another **ridge**, then fly down an 8-percent grade to the island's capital city. There's a campground on the bay, and the Pag tourist office can help you locate an inexpensive *sobe*. The waiter at the restaurant we chose for dinner said we were only the second American couple he'd served that year, and the curious stares of the locals as we wandered the tiny city verified his report.

A delicious dinner of grilled meat, fried potatoes, onions, cabbage, *goulash,* and hunks of bread ($7), a quiet night in the upstairs bedroom of two ancient Pag matrons ($3.50), and a stimulating morning walk in the sun-drenched city of stone assured us we'd found yet another Yugoslav treasure.

Pag to Zadar: 70 kilometers

From Pag, follow signs toward **Zadar** and cycle south along the bay with the silhouettes of the mainland mountains glimmering on the left. Follow a gentle valley route past Gorica and on to **Dinjiska,** then climb to a ridge above the sea as you pedal the 10 km to the **Pag mainland bridge.**

Continue on to **Rtina** and climb again to another **ridge.** We had hoped to shorten our ride to Zadar by angling right at Ražanac onto a secondary road, but the way wasn't paved so we pedaled on. Continue following signs for Zadar on the **main road** and descend to **Posedarje,** then veer right to ride the final 24 km to **Zadar** on the primary coast road. Climb to the tableland above Posedarje with steady traffic, then pedal through gentler terrain to Zadar, passing dozens of farms and scores of roadside produce stands where black-garbed women offer fruit, vegetables, and home-bottled wine.

Zadar is a big city, but it's easy to cycle into. Follow signs for the **center,** entering town along the edge of the bay. There are a tourist bureau and ferry office on the left side of the road (at the harbor). Zadar offers ferry connections to Ancona, Italy, and to the island of Ugljan. For accommodations in the city, track down a *sobe* or ride about 3 km from the city center to the sprawling Autocamp Borik (open May through September). It's huge, clean, and modern. To reach the campground, cross the bay on the **footbridge** and turn left to cycle along the **marina.** Reach a **main street** and follow signs for **Borik** to reach the campground.

Zadar has a wealth of churches and palaces. The ninth-century Church of St. Donatus (Sveti Donat) and the adjoining Roman Forum are particularly noteworthy, as are the cathedral and the City Loggia. You'll want to investigate the entire city core on foot, as there are dozens of fine buildings sprinkled throughout.

Zadar to Šibenik: 75 kilometers

From Zadar, you can continue south along the coast to Split, as we did, or do more island cycling by taking a ferry to Ugljan and Pašman before returning to the mainland at Biograd. To follow our route, leave Zadar's core

*A woman samples
her wares in a
Zadar street
market.*

through the **Mainland Gate** and ride beside the water, following signs toward **Split.** Retrace part of your ride out of town before veering right onto the **main road** south toward **Biograd.**

Traffic isn't too bad along this section, and the terrain is flat all the way to Biograd. Turn down off the main road to get a close-up look at **Turanj,** a friendly small town with a neat bell tower. Gain a quiet **secondary road** along the sea to **Filipjakov.** Then follow signs for **Split** back onto the **main road.** There are several small campgrounds along this stretch, if you're looking for a tent spot.

Biograd is worth a detour if you need to shop or camp. Otherwise, continue on the **main road** toward **Sibĕnik** and **Split.** Pedal a ridge between the sea and a large inland lake, with gentle hills for company. There are pleasant views of the Adriatic Islands along the way. Descend to the sea just before **Pirovac,** then climb again. Coast downhill to **Vodice,** ascend a small ridge, and descend to the **bridge** for **Sibĕnik.**

The main road bypasses Sibĕnik, so you'll need to turn off for the **city center** to reach the cathedral and the old core. Although the streets of Sibĕnik are fascinating and the cathedral is outstanding, the city is a headache for cyclists. It's riddled with stairs and cobblestones, and it's definitely better seen on foot. You can try for a *sobe* and stash your bicycle, or pedal about 5 km past town to **Camping Solaris.** It's well marked from the road for Split.

Be sure to visit Sibĕnik's cathedral. The elaborate stone carvings on the exterior, particularly a bashful Adam and Eve, will help you forgive the tangled streets that brought you there. And the dark stone interior with its incredible carved baptistry is also a delight. There's a tourist office at the opposite end of the old town from the cathedral. Follow the road **south** along the harbor and watch for information signs as you swing left away from the bay.

Sibēnik to Split: 88 kilometers

Pedal the road for Split out of Sibenik and parallel the curving coast to **Primoŝten,** an alluring town clustered on the tip of a promontory. You'll have hilly riding past the turnoff for Rogoznica (don't turn), then climb a long, gradual hill before **Marina,** where a fortified tower pokes above the housetops. Stay along the sea toward **Vranjica.** There's a modern hillside campground beyond Vranjica (Camping Medema). It has an excellent campground store if you're hunting for groceries.

Continue through gentle terrain to **Trogir,** a compact city that's worth exploring. Trogir's cathedral is one of the finest in Yugoslavia, with fanciful stone carvings and a beautiful baptistry. The plaza beside the cathedral is lined with handsome buildings, and the streets leading off the square are full of visual delights.

Soak in the pleasures Trogir has to offer, because the remaining 30 km to Split start at mundane and sink to downright disagreeable. Pedal through Split's gritty industrial suburbs as you struggle toward the city. The main auto route is **closed to bicycles,** so you'll need to swing right onto the **airport road** about **5 km** beyond Trogir. Pass through several small towns, then enter an area blighted with belching factories. Rejoin the **main road** just before **Split** and follow signs to the right for Split's **center** as the main road makes its bypass curve.

Walk your bicycle along the **main harbor road** (Titova Obala) to reach Obala Bratstva Jedinstva, the bus station, and the ferry terminal. Unless the city is stuffed with tourists, a few minutes spent at the bus station or ferry dock should get you several offers for *sobes.* The Split tourist office is at Titova Obala 12 and the staff will supply you with maps and literature on the city. If you want to camp, the closest site is 5 km east of town on Trstenik Bay.

Despite its rude industrial welcome, Split is actually an interesting host. The old town built in and around the third-century Palace of Diocletian is a mazelike treasure of ancient buildings, underground passageways, and shadows of the past that will keep you wandering for hours.

Split to Hvar: 4 kilometers

Split has ferry connections with Italy (Pescara, Ancona, Bari), as well as cities up and down the Yugoslav coast. Our route goes to Hvar, the beautiful capital city of **Hvar Island.** Walk along Split's busy harbor road to reach the **ferry terminal.** The two-hour crossing to **Vira,** on the northern shore of Hvar, costs about $2.50. You'll enjoy views of the Yugoslav islands and mainland along the way.

From **Vira,** a small port city with a ferry dock, a campground, and little else, climb steeply across the tip of the island to the **ridge** above Hvar. Wind through hills covered with lavender bushes, producers of the essenses for the lavender perfumes that are important products of the island. Stop to admire the view, then descend to the picture-perfect town of Hvar, its pale stone buildings curving around the blue-green harbor.

Hvar is a wonderful spot to spend some relaxing hours in pursuit of sun and sand. There are excellent swimming beaches on both sides of the city. Go north to find the more sheltered coves, and head south for the less crowded waters. Don't neglect the captivating streets of the compact city, either. A climb up the stairs to Fort Spänjol will reward you with an impressive view.

You should be able to claim a reasonably priced *sobe* in Hvar without difficulty. Try hanging around the Jadrolinija ferry office at the harbor if you're hoping for offers. The tourist office is right next door. The nearest camping is back at Vira (4 km and a hill). From Hvar, you can cycle the 20 km down the ridge of the island to **Stari Grad,** another lovely Adriatic city. Make the trip to Stari Grad by bus if you want to avoid a battle with the island's hilly terrain.

Hvar to Ston: 62 kilometers

A Jadrolinija **ferry** connects Hvar to **Korčula** (capital of Korčula Island) and Dubrovnik. We got off at Korčula for sightseeing, took a short ferry trip across to the Peljesac Peninsula, then cycled on to Dubrovnik. If you're pressed for time, however, you may want to ride the ferry all the way from Hvar to Dubrovnik. You'll be passing up some spectacular scenery, but you'll also avoid one of the most gruesome hills on the entire coast.

Leave the ferry in **Korčula City** and walk up into the old town (some stairs — you may want to lock your bicycle below) to visit the cathedral, the Arneri Palace, and the other handsome buildings within the city walls. Korčula has the unmistakable stamp of the seafaring Venetians, and its massive walls give testimony to the warlike history of the area. There are three campgrounds near Korčula, and you'll probably be accosted by *sobe* sellers as soon as you roll off the ferry. Korčula claims to be the birthplace of Marco Polo, and the staff of the tourist bureau in town ("Marko Polo") will tell you why.

Leave Korčula on the **main road** east toward **Lumbarda.** Climb steadily to a **ridge** above the city, and swing left for the **ferry** (*trajekt*). Follow *trajekt* signs as you descend to the sea. The ferry landing is about 4 km from Korčula's center. The 30-minute ride to **Orebić** on the southwest coast of the Peljesac Peninsula costs less than $1, and there are about seven crossings per day.

Leave the ferry dock at Orebić and go south to parallel the coast on a small road, then join the **main road** signed for **Ston** and **Dubrovnik.** Stay along the sea for a short distance. The torture soon begins as the road shoots up an **8-percent grade** that seems to last forever (actually about 8 km — but we're sure the bike computer lied). The scenery is spectacular as you climb away from the sea with the steep mountains of the peninsula behind and the cliffs tumbling into the water below.

Curve away from the shore and turn into the heart of the peninsula. There's more climbing left to do as the road winds between bitter hills, snaking up and up. Arrive in the vineyard-green heartland of the peninsula at last, and continue on the quiet road through gently rolling terrain. Follow signs toward Dubrovnik to **Zupanje,** then go up and over a hill at **Pijavičino.** Descend a long, steep incline **above Trstenik.** The rough road surface makes for a bumpy ride.

Then climb again to cross a mercifully low ridge and gain the north side of the peninsula. Coast past **Janjina,** an attractive stone town set among vineyards. Ride past **Drače** and admire the coastline across the water, following the sea for a time, then ascending a long, gentle hill to the peninsula's vine-covered core. If you sample the red Peljesac wine that comes from these hills, you'll wonder how anything so flavorful could be produced by such a rugged piece of land.

The road rises gradually past **Dubrava,** then descends a long hill to the sea. There's a campground (open June through September) on Prapratna Bay, just before **Ston.** Ston is a unique Yugoslav city linked by a long fortified wall to **Mali Ston,** just across the narrow peninsula. Look for a *sobe* in the town if you need a bed.

Ston to Dubrovnik: 61 kilometers

From Ston, continue beside the wall to **Mali Ston,** then swing right for **Dubrovnik,** the mainland, and a reunion with the main coast road. Climb gradually to the **main road** and turn right. The section from here to Dubrovnik is restricted to bicycles (see tour introduction), and you'll notice a marked increase in buses, trucks, and foreign plates as you pedal on.

Ascend a long hill, then descend to the sea once more. From **Dunta-Doli,** cycle near the sea with pleasant views of the rolling coastal terrain. After **Loznica,** begin a long jaunt **inland** beside the Rijeka Dubrovačka Inlet, passing hillsides of high-rises and hotels — the heralds of Dubrovnik's wealth. Return to the sea with the main road, and arrive at **Gruž** and Dubrovnik's busy modern harbor. The Jadrolinija **ferry office** is on the left, across from the ferry dock.

Dubrovnik offers ferries to Greece, Italy, and major Yugoslav cities to the north (Split, Zadar, Rijeka). If you're hoping to land a *sobe,* hang around the ferry dock and look homeless.

To reach Dubrovnik's **center,** continue along the water and go straight at the **intersection** at the far end of the harbor. Climb up and over the **ridge,** continuing straight to descend into the city. Despite the raves Dubrovnik receives from the many travelers who have never taken the time to compare it with the rest of Yugoslavia's lovely Adriatic towns, the city is truly not overrated. It is a gem.

Climb to the bluff on the north side of town and watch the sunset play across the city walls while the Adriatic beats against the rocks below. Or walk the circuit of the walls and marvel at the beauty of Dubrovnik on its perch above the sea. The colorful patches of tile, the fluttering bits of laundry, the sentinellike forms of bell towers — all combine to produce an unforgettable panorama against the blue-green backdrop of the Adriatic.

Dubrovnik's tourist office (inside the west gate) can help you with accommodations or ferry information, and the staff has piles of excellent English-language literature on hand. You'll hear more English spoken in Dubrovnik than anywhere else in the country, and though you'll be glad you've seen more of Yugoslavia than the tourist-filled Placa (Dubrovnik's shop-lined main street), you'll still be glad you came.

Dubrovnik to Budva: 115 kilometers

Climb a long, steady hill away from Dubrovnik, following the **main road** south toward **Kotor.** Look back for a final glimpse of the lovely city before you cross the ridge and descend along the bay toward **Cavtat.** Stay on the main road and pedal uphill from **Zvekovica** to enter a long basin of gentle hills. Cross a final ridge, then descend into **Herceg-Novi,** a sprawling, modern town on the Gulf of Kotor.

Continue inland along the gulf to **Kamenari** and catch one of the frequent **ferries** across the water (cost with bicycle is about 15 cents). There are signs for Kotor and Budva at the ferry. Leave the **ferry dock** and swing left to pedal the final 14 km along the water to **Kotor,** a haunting city of half-collapsed houses and uncleared piles of rubble. Kotor was the victim of a 1979 earthquake that devastated much of this part of Yugoslavia. There's a campground near the town if you decide to stay.

From Kotor, you can either cut up and over a steep inland ridge past **Skaljari** to join the road to Budva (this route adds a lot of hill) or backtrack the 14 km along the water and continue around toward **Tivat** and **Budva** (this route adds 20 km to the day's total).

Negotiate a short, steep hill and a brief **tunnel** before descending to **Budva** and the sea. Like Kotor, Budva was ravaged by the 1979 earthquake, but modern tourist hotels have capitalized on the rubble and invested in the sand on the surrounding beaches to make Budva a busy tourist spot once more. There are several campgrounds in the area, and you can visit one of the tourist offices on the waterfront if you're looking for a *sobe.*

Budva to Bar: 42 kilometers

Climb away from Budva on the main road and cycle a scenic hillside above **Sveti Stefan,** a picturesque city planted on a tiny mound of rock encircled by the sea. A narrow causeway leads to the village on the rock, but the view from above is probably the best part of the popular tourist town.

Continue south toward **Bar,** staying on the hills above the Adriatic, then follow the road inland and climb steadily past **Katun** and **Misići.** Descend a long hill to regain the sea, and pedal the remaining 8 km to **Bar,** passing a handful of beachside campgrounds along the way.

Bar offers your last chance at **ferry connections** to Bari, Italy; Corfu and Patras, Greece; and the northern coast of Yugoslavia. Ferries to Greece stop running in mid-October, but the Bar-Bari ferries run all year. Pedal to the harborside ferry offices to check on schedules and buy your ticket.

Albania presents a forbidding border to the south. You can cycle the 25 km to Ulcinj along a scenic stretch of coast, then continue on increasingly quiet roads toward the Albanian border, 16 km farther south. There are scores of resorts and several campgrounds on the long sandy beaches south of Ulcinj.

An ancient olive grove south of Bar.

There are also lots of touchy military personnel along the border, so don't pedal too far!

It's possible to swing inland and pedal through rugged, mountainous terrain to bypass Albania and enter northern Greece. Roads are primitive and people are less accustomed to, and therefore less friendly toward, strangers once you venture away from the coast. A ferry ride is probably a better choice.

TOUR NO. 12

PEDALING ON THE PELOPONNESE
Patras to Athens, Greece

Distance:	899 kilometers (559 miles)
Estimated time:	14 riding days
Best time to go:	April, May, June, September, or October
Terrain:	Murderous hills and magnificent scenery
Connecting tours:	Tours No. 11, 13, and 14

Greece. Just the word evokes visions of sparkling blue sea and brilliant beaches, haunting ruins and pulsating sun. But Greece for the cyclist is so much more — endless hillsides of shimmering olive trees trembling in the afternoon breeze, the quiet smiles of black-garbed women sitting atop dusty donkeys, a welcome pause to watch as a flowing melody of bell-collared goats crosses a lonely road.

But Greece, despite its incredible richness in scenery, climate, and culture, is not a land that bestows its treasures without charge. And the Peloponnese Peninsula is one of the most generous and yet most miserly of all Greek hosts. So lighten your load and train your body for a hill-studded ride that will challenge, exhaust, and test you. Then let the harsh and aching beauty of this ancient land wash away your weariness with the warm massage of gentle Mediterranean waves and with the tintillating scent of oleander on the evening breeze.

CONNECTIONS. The Greeks have had a maritime civilization for thousands of years, and one of the best ways to reach the country is by sea. You can get to Patras and the start of this tour via ferries from Bar, Yugoslavia (end of Tour No. 11), or Ancona or Brindisi, Italy. If you'll be entering and leaving Greece from the international airport near Athens, you can load your bicycle on a train or pedal the Piraeus-to-Patras portion of Tour No. 13 to reach this tour's beginning.

INFORMATION. Write in advance to the Greek National Tourist Office, 645 Fifth Avenue, Olympic Tower, New York, New York 10022, and be sure to ask for the excellent Athens map they provide. Once in Greece, consult offices of the Greek National Tourist Organization (GNTO) for free English-language literature. Rand McNally's *Blue Guide Greece, Baedeker's Greece* or *Let's Go: Greece* are guidebook options for your visit. If you're particularly interested in archaeological sites, the *Blue Guide* provides comprehensive coverage. Of course, if you feel like one Swiss cyclist we met, who admitted he

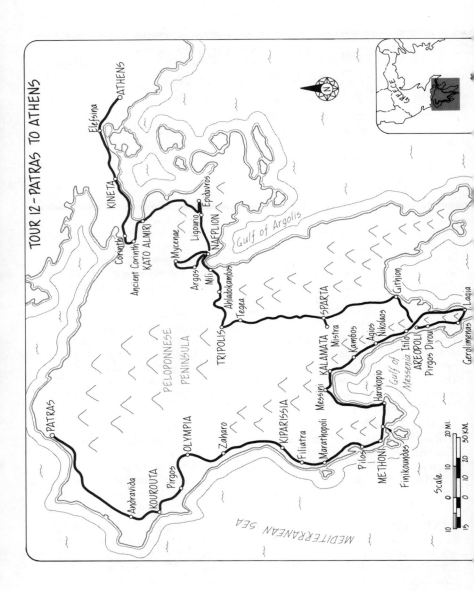

was "tired of looking at a bunch of toppled stones," there's always the luxurious Mediterranean to welcome you at the end of your cycling day.

MAPS. For route finding, Map No. 5, *Peloponneso-Peloponnese,* published by Efstathiadis Group, is available in bookstores in Greece. It has a scale of 1:300,000 and gives place names in both Greek and Latinized forms. (The Latinized forms may differ slightly from map to map, so be prepared to do some creative interpreting.) An alternative map, *Peloponnese,* by Clyde Surveys Ltd., has a scale of 1:400,000, but Greek spellings are not provided.

ACCOMMODATIONS. Greece is a camper's paradise. Imagine a hillside, a spreading panorama of sea and olives before you, a tent tucked beneath the silver and green branches of a twisted olive tree. This dream is reality on the Peloponnese. Organized campgrounds in Greece are plentiful, inexpensive, and well equipped. The hot-water supply is often based on solar power, so showering at night will usually produce more steam than a morning "waker upper."

Although freelance camping is not officially allowed in any part of the country, ask permission from the friendly Greek landowners and be amazed by their unhesitating hospitality. We were able to camp in olive groves and on beaches, and were constantly delighted by the beauty that greeted us through the open doorway of our tent.

Lodgings in hotels are affordable, especially in the off season, when prices range from $5 to $12 per night for two people. Greek hosts are relaxed about bicycles, and they'll usually provide a secure shed or a lobby corner for night lockups.

SUPPLIES. Shopping in Greece is an exercise in ingenuity and endurance. Products are often scattered among dozens of shops, each specializing in vegetables, fruit, cheese, beverages, or bread. Just let go of your Western "one-stop-shopping" mentality, and you'll be delighted by the results of your excursions. Instead of meeting one shopkeeper, you'll meet five; instead of emerging with a plastic-coated hunk of tasteless cheese, you'll carry a paper-wrapped lump of tangy *feta;* instead of acquiring a hard, cold loaf of bread, you'll cradle a hot bundle that begs for immediate consumption.

"The climate is always right" is the rule Greek shopkeepers live by when establishing their store hours. Shops open about 8:00 a.m. and close in the evening at 7:00 or 7:30 p.m., with a midday respite from the heat that lasts from 1:30 to 5:00 p.m. Saturday morning is the last sure bet for weekend shopping, and the majority of stores are closed Saturday afternoon and Sunday.

If you need bike parts in Greece, only the large cities offer a selection. There are several good bicycle shops in Athens, clustered near Omonia Square on Eolou Street.

Patras to Kourouta: 85 kilometers

The tour begins in Patras, Greece's third-largest city and a major port for ferry traffic with Yugoslavia and Italy. Check at the **GNTO office** near the ferry terminal to pick up armfuls of free literature on the country. Patras has several campgrounds 5 to 10 km east of the city. Pedal east from the ferry terminal on the harbor road, and you'll see camping signs within a few kilometers. There are several hotels in Patras, as well.

To begin the tour, leave Patras on the **main road west,** following signs for **Pirgos.** (Most main road signs give names in both Greek and Latinized forms.) The flat, four-lane road skirts the sea. Traffic lessens as you draw away from the city, and the road narrows. For a brief escape from the cars, turn off toward **Rogitika** onto a **small road** beside the sea. The road deteriorates to dirt after about 5 km. Swing inland to regain the **main road** just before the road turns to dirt.

The nicely surfaced main road has a wide shoulder most of the way to **Kourouta.** The New National Road and the Old National Road intertwine along this section, sometimes going their separate ways, sometimes merging into one. Both are signed for Pirgos. Only the Old National Road is shown on all but the most recent maps. The New Road is smooth and fast, but the Old Road is more interesting, winding through the small towns along the route.

Try this combination. Follow the **Old Road** to **Kato Ahaia,** the **New Road** to **Andravida,** then the **Old Road** once more through **Gastouni** and on to where it loses itself in the **New Road.** At the **main turnoff** for **Kourouta** (ignore the first Kourouta sign pointing down a gravel road to the sea), follow a paved road to the right to reach a pleasant campground just before the small town. Take time for an afternoon swim on the excellent beach near the campground.

Kourouta to Olympia: 40 kilometers

Return to the **main road** and follow signs for **Pirgos.** Pause to practice your multistop shopping in Pirgos's frenetic downtown. You'll emerge with a good appetite and the makings of a great picnic lunch. Walk your bicycle through the city hubbub, then remount to follow signs for **Olympia,** branching left after the **center** of town.

Hills increase during the 21 winding kilometers to Olympia, and the road narrows. We realized we were on a popular sightseeing route when a toddler waved and called to us from the roadside, "Hello tourist, hello tourist." In Olympia, choose among two campgrounds, several hotels, and a youth hostel. Camping Diana is the closest campground to the archaeological site. Tucked into a hillside above the city, it's well equipped, clean, and offers solar-heated hot showers.

Olympia rolls out the tourist carpet in a big way. Collect English-language reading material, maps, and postcards in the shop-infested downtown, then escape to the archaeological site on the edge of town to wander the extensive ruins, stirred by visions of those first Olympic athletes. If you can tear yourself away from the haunting beauty of the stones, visit the museum nearby.

Olympia to Kiparissia: 59 kilometers

Leave Olympia on the **Krestena** road and climb a short, steep hill before descending to the **Alfios River.** Turn left toward **Krestena** after crossing the river, and follow the valley to **Makrisia,** a fascinating little city on a hill.

Pedal through town, peeking in doorways to watch old women and black-robed priests on their morning shopping rounds. Then continue on the rolling road toward Krestena.

At the **unmarked junction** just **before Krestena,** turn right and pedal over a small **hill,** then go left on the **main coast road** signed for **Kiparissia.** Pass through pine forests and olive-covered hillsides with the sea beyond. Small ascents and descents break up the mostly level riding. Watch for the old fort on the hill above Kiparissia, a midsized town with lots of shops and a sprinkling of hotels.

Kiparissia to Methoni: 62 kilometers

Continue along the **coast road,** following signs for **Pilos. Filiatra** is a confusing jumble of streets and intersections, but stay with the labyrinthine route signed for Pilos and you'll make it through. Veer right onto a paved turnoff for **Ag. Kiriaki 4 km** beyond Filiatra. At the **T** intersection that follows, turn left to ride on a quiet asphalt road along the coast, passing discos and vacation homes along the way.

If you're looking for a secluded beach for camping, there are several opportunities in the area. We camped on a lovely beach behind a small cafe, enjoyed an evening of conversation with its friendly Greek-American owner, and woke at dawn to watch a shepherd lead his flock along the water's edge.

The **secondary road** continued along the flat coast to **Marathopoli.** Here, you can turn left to regain the main road at Gargaliani (8 km), thus guaranteeing a look at Nestor's Palace (and a steep climb, as well). Or you can continue on the quiet **secondary road,** trading the ascent to Nestor's Palace for about 5 km of unpaved road (area residents assured us the road will be paved in a few years, but...).

For the latter route, turn right at the **junction in Marathopoli,** then go left **one block before the sea.** This is a confusing section, and it's subject to changes because of ongoing roadwork. Muddle through the unpaved kilometers (don't try it after a heavy rain!), regain the **paved road,** and turn left to reach the **main thoroughfare** toward Pilos. Go right on the **main road** and pedal up a steep incline just before the **Kalamata junction.** Turn right at the junction and continue climbing for **Pilos,** then descend steeply to the sea.

From the compact harbor town of Pilos, follow signs for **Methoni** up a grueling 2-km ascent. Proceed past the turnoff for Mesohori and continue following signs for Methoni, sailing down a silver ribbon of road through whispering olives. Signs in Methoni lead to the impressive seaside fortress. There are lodging options in the small city, and there's a campground that stays open until mid-October.

Methoni to Kalamata: 80 kilometers

Leave Methoni and follow signs for **Harokopio.** Climb a long, steep hill to **Evangelismos** and let the beauty of the Greek landscape recompense you for your labor. A steep descent leads to the sea at **Finikoundas,** a town set on a curving white beach. Follow the sea for a short while, climb a short, steep hill, then descend again. Pass a pretty seaside campground and begin a long, punishing climb from the sea. The road turns to gravel for about 200 meters but returns to asphalt soon after.

Pedal through **Akritohori** and continue climbing toward Lamia. At the **junction** just before **Lamia,** ignore the road branching off to the left and continue straight into town. In customary Greek fashion, the road surface goes from good to awful in Lamia, then improves again after the city. You'll be rewarded for the day's toilsome climbs and bumpy passages by the smiling Greeks working beside their patient donkeys, by the laughing men who fly by in their Japanese pickups and honk enthusiastic greetings, and by the panorama of hill after hill of olives, somber green against the dancing blue of the sky.

Enjoy a long descent toward **Harokopio** and cruise up a short hill just before town. At the **junction** in the city, veer left for **Kalamata.** If you have the time and energy, you can make the 8-km round trip down the hill to Koroni. The seaside city has a large, dilapidated Venetian fortress and an attractive harbor. Unfortunately, it also has a 4-km climb back to Harokopio and the main road.

Follow the gently undulating coast along the brilliant blue Gulf of Messenia, drinking in views of the cliff-faced mountains across the water. Climb a slight hill before **Rizomilos,** then gain the main **Pilos-Kalamata road.** Traffic increases here, but it's not unpleasant and drivers are polite and friendly (friendly in Greece means lots of honks). There are several campgrounds along the coast in this area.

Cycle through **Messini** and join the **main road** approaching **Kalamata** from Megalopoli. Pass through **Asprohoma** and take the turnoff to the right marked for the **New Beach Road** (it's just past a large **factory**) to bypass the Kalamata congestion. Descend along this secondary road and turn left at the **junction** for **Kalamata,** then go right at a sign for **Areopoli.** The way is unmarked from here. Skirt along the edge of Kalamata's harbor, passing a large docking area and turning right to follow the road to the sea.

There are several campgrounds to choose from along the beach just past Kalamata, or you can swing up into the city if you need a room.

Kalamata to Areopoli: 79 kilometers

Follow the **coast road** along the Gulf of Messenia and turn right at the **T** intersection for **Areopoli.** The road begins to climb at Alniro. The grade is moderate to **Kambos,** a small town watched over by a ruined castle and by dozens of men in streetside cafes. Descend briefly to the rugged Koskaras Defile and stop on the bridge to enjoy the impressive view. Climb again, winding among dry golden hills and snaking across gorges, curving around steep, mounded hillsides covered with olives — climbing, climbing, climbing.

Reach the summit at last and look down on the sea and 8 km of **switchbacks to Kardamili,** a handsome resort town with campgrounds, shops, and a well-stocked grocery store. The descent is steep and loaded with sharp curves, so don't let the exhilaration of speed keep your fingers too far from your brakes.

Stay beside the sea between Kardamili and **Agios Nikolaos.** If it's late in the day, you might want to stop at one of the campgrounds or hotels along the way. A gruesome series of **switchbacks** that seems to last forever awaits you after Agios Nikolaos. Struggle up the punishing hill, and try not to watch the progress of the cars that pass you if you'd rather not see how far you have left to climb.

Reach **Platsa** after about 8 km, with the worst of the hill behind, and enjoy a ridgetop ride through tiny towns of tumbled stone — towns with unique dome-topped churches, men who cheer your courage, and women who laugh and wave from doorways. From **Itilo**, there's a striking view of the ruined fortress of Kelefa, its old walls tracing a massive rectangle on the hillside.

Plunge down a **steep descent** to the sea and follow the road along the beach to **Limeni,** a small town with a gemlike harbor and a toppled church. A 4-km ascent up another steep grade leads to **Areopoli,** hotel rooms, and a blissful release from your bike. There is no campground in Areopoli, but the olive groves outside town provide a wealth of quiet tent spots from which to choose (don't forget to ask permission to camp on private land).

Areopoli to Areopoli (via the Mani Peninsula): 78 kilometers

If you have the time and your legs still have the strength, don't skip a day trip around the unforgettable Mani Peninsula, using Areopoli as your base. Hauling your gear along this route would be a punishing affair, but you can manage the 78-km loop as a strenuous one-day trek if you get an early start — and if you don't stop to shoot every single roll of film you own on the scenery.

What an incredible day of riding you'll have on the Mani Peninsula! The hills are every bit as tough as the inhabitants — a people never conquered by the Turks, even when all their comrades fell around them. The terrain will exhaust you, but the scenery will repay you generously for all your labor. Make the elliptical loop in a clockwise direction, cashing in on the morning sun on the mountainous eastern side of the peninsula and tackling the challenging hills early, before heat and fatigue make them too cruel.

In our 78-km day of cycling in this lonely section of Greece, we were passed by fewer than 30 cars. However, we did have to deal with one very pokey flock of sheep and several "haawwnking" donkeys. Be sure to carry a pump, emergency repair tools, and lots of liquids, as towns are few and far between.

Pedal south through **Areopoli** and turn left at the **junction** for **Kotronas** 2 km beyond the city. The road climbs to **Himara,** then descends to **Loukadika,** a stone city guarding a ridge that overlooks the sea. Descend steeply to a turnoff for **Kotronas** and turn right for **Kokala.** Everywhere you look you'll see lonely square towers perched on the rugged heights and clustered in the somber towns, their stout walls giving testimony to the war-filled history of the area.

A series of short ups and downs leads to Kokala on the sea, then a **punishing climb** up a golden, tower-studded ridge leads to the lofty town of **Lagia.** From Lagia, continue around the hillside and up another short hill to

gain a fine vista of the sea. Descend steeply to **Alika,** and turn right at the **junction** for **Gerolimenas,** a more modern Mani town with a nice harbor and a grocery store. Climb a short hill and then enjoy the relaxing 22 km back to Areopoli along the peninsula's western shore.

If time allows, the 5-km descent to the caves near Pirgos Dirou makes a pleasant addition to the day. Turn left at the **junction** in **Pirgos Dirou** to reach the **well-signed caves.** A 45-minute boat ride through cool passageways glittering with frosted white formations provides a welcome break for hill-weary legs. Unfortunately, the steady climb back up the road for Areopoli is the unavoidable aftermath of the sidetrip.

Areopoli to Sparta: 70 kilometers

Leave **Areopoli** on the road for **Githion,** climbing a gentle hill, then following a creek bed down a long, gradual descent. The road follows valleys cut between mounded hills, providing easy riding and pleasant scenery. Just before Githion, follow the edge of the sea past bright citrus groves and several large campgrounds. Climb a small hill and swing down to the attractive harbor town of Githion. (You can make ferry connections to Piraeus and Crete from here.)

Follow the **waterside route** through town to an intersection where the road branches in a **Y.** Take the **left branch** (unmarked when we were there) and wind through a small business district before reaching the **edge of town** and a sign (in Greek) for **Sparta.** The narrow, twisting road climbs into the hills, ascending steeply away from Githion. Enter a gentle valley, then pedal up another long, steep hill.

Climb until just past the turnoff for Monemvassia, with spectacular views of terraced, olive-covered hillsides. Beyond the junction, descend steeply and follow a rolling route toward **Sparta.** The final 20 km of the ride offers impressive views of the rugged mountains to the west, but heavy traffic and lots of horn-happy drivers make the riding hectic.

Sparta is a modern-looking town that gives little evidence that it was once the home of the illustrious warriors who ruled this harsh and rugged corner of Greece. Explore the mounded hillock on the edge of town, and the past will come alive in its quiet sunken theater and the etchings on its timeworn stones.

Sparta has several affordable hotels, dozens of cafes and shops, and entertaining city streets. There is a luxurious campground (complete with swimming pool) 2 km outside town on the road toward Mistra. Be sure to follow the well-marked route to **Mistra** (7 km), a hauntingly beautiful Byzantine city on an olive-speckled hillside. The climb to Mistra is gradual, but the final 1½ km between the modern town and the archaeological site are steep. Set aside a morning to visit the spot. You won't be disappointed.

Sparta to Tripolis: 60 kilometers

Leave Sparta following signs for **Tripolis.** You'll discover what made the ancient Spartans so tough as you climb steadily for the next 20 km through

Climbing toward the Mani tower town of Lagia.

mounded hills, barren except for scattered olive trees and scores of beehives. A steep but disappointingly short downhill leads into another 10 km of climbing, then on into a splendid high valley rimmed by golden mountains. Reach a ridgetop 45 km beyond Sparta and savor the view of Tripolis on its green and yellow plain of apple orchards, vegetables, and olives.

Descend quickly to the flatlands below, but sneak a look at the trim, tile-roofed town of **Manthirea** along the way. We bypassed Tripolis and shortened our route by taking the turnoff to the right for Tegea. If you need to find a bed, continue toward Tripolis on the main road and follow signs for the city. Leave Tripolis on the route for Argos the next morning.

To take the **shortcut** route and avoid Tripolis' urban sprawl, turn right for **Tegea.** Follow the quiet road past the small Tegea museum, turn left at the **T,** then go right toward **Lithovounia.** Follow the road straight into **Lithovounia,** then angle left as you pass the small town. Cross some typically treacherous Greek **train tracks** and turn right on the road for **Argos.** You'll have acres of campsites to choose from, and you can spend the night, as we did, sheltered by a lone olive tree and happily trading the lights of the big city for the brilliant Mediterranean sky.

Tripolis to Nafplion: 60 kilometers

Pedal the **Argos road** through the long **Tripolis Plain.** Climb along a steep hillside, passing above Ahladokambos in the valley below. Cross a high ridge after 5 km of climbing and make a steep, switchback-studded descent to the sea. Be careful on this scenic but dangerous downhill. Gain the coastal road to **Nafplion** by turning right at **Mili** a few kilometers beyond **Lema.**

Approach Nafplion and enjoy fine views of the harbor town, shadowed by its massive fortress and fronted by a tiny fortified island in the bay. There's a city campground on the Argos-Nafplion road (open through September) and there are plenty of hotels in the lively, touristy downtown. Go for an early-morning walk along the harbor and watch sun-tanned fishermen working on their boats, or dive into the city streets and absorb the unique flavor of a midsized Greek town.

Nafplion to Nafplion (via Tiryns, Mycenae, and Argos): 47 kilometers

If your appreciation for toppled stones is still intact, consider a day trip to Tiryns, Mycenae, and Argos from your base in Nafplion. Leave **Nafplion** on the road toward **Argos** and turn off for the ruined fortress of **Tiryns 3 km** later. It's just off the road, to the right. The site is well marked by road signs.

Return to the **main road** and go right, then take the next **turnoff** marked for **Ag. Trias.** Follow signs for **Mikines** along the level secondary road, passing orchards and small towns. Climb a short hill just before Mikines, turn right into the touristy city, and follow signs for **Mycenae** (*Mycenea* on the signs). Climb sharply to reach the archaeological site 2 km from town.

Some of the most impressive archaeological discoveries in modern history have been made in Mycenae. Marvel at the engineering wonder of Agamemnon's tomb, linger over the beauty of the Lion's Gate, and sense the striking

A fisherman in Nafplion tenderizes his morning catch.

loneliness of this 3,000-year-old city of tombs and tumbled stones, tucked into a wild hillside above Argos and the Gulf of Argolis.

To return to Nafplion, you can simply retrace your route back to the city if you prefer quiet riding, or you can take the **main road** from **Mikines** toward **Argos** if you'd like a look at that fortress-guarded city. The main road has a smoother surface than the secondary road, but heavier traffic makes riding less pleasant. In Argos, follow signs for Nafplion to pedal the 13 level kilometers back to your base.

Nafplion to Kato Almiri: 79 kilometers

Leave Nafplion, following signs for **Epidavros**. Climb gradually for 25 km, passing through pleasant countryside and many small towns. In

Ligourio, go right at the junction for **Epidavros,** then turn left **3 km** later to reach the site. The amphitheater at Epidavros is like no other. Set among tree-dotted hills, the stone seats await their long-dead occupants, and the air within the structure trembles like a finely tuned instrument, amplifying the most delicate sounds with incredible clarity.

Some maps show a road from Epidavros directly to the sea, but the way is barricaded and road workers told us the route is no longer open. Retrace the ride **back to Ligourio,** then turn right in the city at the **junction** for **Nea Epidavros** and **Athens.** Throughout your ride from this point on, you'll see signs for Athens spelled in a variety of ways (*Athene, Athine, Athina*). All versions are recognizable.

Coast downhill, staying with signs for Athens. Descend almost to the sea, then pedal up a long, steady incline to cross a ridge. Descend steeply above a lovely bay, then climb once more up a gradual hill. There are fine views of the sea throughout the ride, and evergreen forests provide a welcome change from endless olives. From the final summit of the day, you'll get an enchanting look at the curving blue coastline stretching toward the Corinth Canal and mainland Greece.

Descend rapidly to the seaside town of **Kato Almiri.** There are several campgrounds on the beach. We shared our supper at Camp Poseidon with a friendly dog, two puppies, and a cheese-eating cat, then walked to the beach for a midnight swim under the stars.

Kato Almiri to Kineta: 52 kilometers

From Kato Almiri, follow the **coast road** through **Loutro Elenis.** Turn left and climb gradually toward **Xilokeriza** and **Examilia.** Enter **Examilia** and turn left at the small town's **main intersection** (it's unmarked from this direction). As the road traverses the tip of the peninsula, look for the fortress of Acrocorinth ahead, its walls like jagged teeth on the mountainside. Pedal the 3 km to the **main Corinth road** and turn left, following signs for **Ancient Corinth.**

While the archaeological sites of Greece are gripping in their stark simplicity and wild beauty, the tourist towns that squat beside them are often quite depressing in their tacky commercialism. Save your mood for the site, and cruise through Ancient Corinth as rapidly as possible to seek the sun-bleached ruins just beyond the town.

Lock your bicycle under the watchful gaze of the ticket-booth attendant and spend a quiet hour wandering the extensive grounds. The Temple of Apollo with its fantastic sky-piercing columns is a definite highlight of the visit, and the on-site museum has several nice exhibits.

Descend from Ancient Corinth, following signs for **Athens.** Reach a **T** and turn left, then swing right to gain the **main Athens road.** You can shun the main road and follow the **overpass** across and down to a secondary route along the sea. Unfortunately, this road leads through the snarl of modern Corinth, with pitfalls of its own. There's a campground on the sea, west of Corinth.

If you decide to brave the busy main road, you'll ride along its wide shoulder for 3 (possibly illegal) kilometers before spotting an "end of cars only" sign (a white car on a blue background with red diagonal slash), but strangely, there are no restrictions posted on the on-ramp for the road. Both routes **merge** into one busy road 3 km before the **Corinth Canal,** and riding is unpleasant along the way.

Cross the **bridge** spanning the narrow canal and turn right onto the **non-toll road** for **Athens.** Descend a short hill, then follow the flat coastline east along the sea. The narrow, quiet road winds between the busy freeway and the seashore. At first it's rather dull, with ugly refineries, but these soon give way to millionaire mansions patrolled by barking German Shepherds.

There are a few large campgrounds just **before Kineta,** or you can ask a friendly-looking local for permission to camp on the beach. An evening under the glowing stars and a late-night swim in the sparkling phosphorescent lights of the Mediterranean will do much to wash away the traffic-induced tenseness of the day.

Kineta to Athens (Campground): 48 kilometers

Beyond **Kineta,** the road climbs to wind along a cliffy section of coast, then descends before Megara. Follow signs for *Athens – Old Road* or *Athens – Non-Toll Road* to avoid the freeway route. Bypass Megara and climb a short hill before descending to the sea again. **Elefsina,** with a freighter-filled bay and truck-heavy streets, is an unpleasant interlude after the peace of the Peloponnese. As Athens draws nearer, noise, traffic, and big-city congestion follow.

Cruise through Elefsina and join the **main road** just beyond the city. There is a wide shoulder and lots of traffic. Skirt along the **edge of the bay,** then turn inland to climb a long, gradual hill with fleets of coughing cars and trucks. Reach the top and **Dafni,** with a Byzantine monastery church and a large, tree-shaded campground. The site is about 11 km from Athens's center.

You can continue on to **Camping Athena,** a few kilometers farther along the main road. The campground is on the north side of the road and it's fairly well marked. It's open all year, has hot showers, and provides easy access to Athens, with a bus stop just across the street. The campground at Dafni is also served by Athens buses. Be forewarned, though, that after a few nerve-rattling bus rides into Athens, you'll be convinced that all Greek bus drivers are former Indy 500 champs.

Another option for those who don't want to camp is to continue into Athens by bicycle. Proceed with care. The relaxed Greek drivers of the Peloponnese are nowhere to be found in the tire-squealing din of this enormous city. If you have to cycle in, do it on a weekend or during the midafternoon lull in traffic.

If you're ending your cycling trip in Athens with a flight for home, you can swing right for **Piraeus** after **Elefsina** to do an end run around the tangle of Athens and reach the **airport** south of the city. There are several hotels in Piraeus, and there's a campground on the coast just beyond the airport. Piraeus also offers ferry connections to Greece's sparkling islands, and you can hook up with Tour No. 13 from this busy port.

Dawn light at Delphi.

TOUR NO. 13

VISIONS OF THE ANCIENTS
Iraklion to Patras, Greece

Distance: 668 kilometers (414 miles)
Estimated time: 10 riding days
Best time to go: April, May, June, September, or October
Terrain: Mix of moderate flatlands and punishing hills
Connecting tours: Tours No. 12 and 14

Crete is just big enough, just far enough from the Greek mainland, and just diverse enough in terrain, culture, and history to hang onto a tough independence that sets it apart from the rest of Greece.

You'll sense a difference in the people here if you've spent much time on the mainland or in the Peloponnese. Perhaps it's due to their familiarity with the thousands of tourist "invaders from the sea" that arrive each spring. Perhaps it's due to their pride in a heritage that reaches back to the Minoan Period (2600 to 1100 B.C.) and the roots of European civilization. Or perhaps it's simply because they're from Crete. Whatever the reason, the warm spontaneity of the Peloponnese Greeks is not as evident on Crete. You won't be awash in floods of honks when you're on the roads, and you won't find as many ready smiles, especially in the heavy tourist areas. You might even get a few refusals when you ask permission to camp.

But delve beneath the surface hardness of the Cretans with persistence, politeness, and sincere expressions of appreciation for the riches the island offers, and you'll uncover the wonderful Greek generosity and warmth that make a visit here so special.

For a fantastic month of riding in some of Greece's loveliest and most challenging terrain, combine this tour of Crete and Delphi with the Peloponnese ride in Tour No. 12.

CONNECTIONS. You can get to Iraklion, Crete, and the start of this tour by taking a ferry from Piraeus, Athens's tumultuous port. If you fly into Athens, the airport is about 10 km from Piraeus's harbor. If you're cycling this tour as a continuation of Tour No. 12, pedal from Athens to Piraeus to catch the ferry. It's a 12-hour ride from Piraeus to Iraklion, and ferries run every evening. Check at the tourist office in Athens or the ferry office in Piraeus for timetables and prices.

INFORMATION. Review the introductory material for Greece on the Peloponnese (Tour 12) to prepare for your ride.

MAPS. There's an excellent 1:200,000 map of Crete available in book-

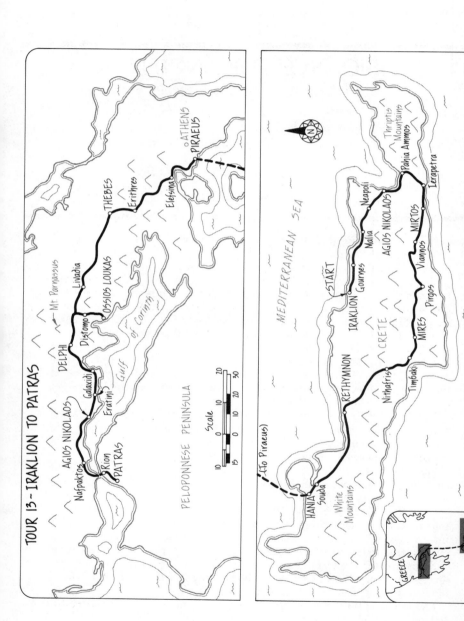

stores on the island. Published by Freytag and Berndt, it shows hostels, campgrounds, hotels, archaeological sites, and churches, and provides small street maps for the island's major cities.

ACCOMMODATIONS. Refer to the accommodations information provided in the introduction to Tour No. 12.

SUPPLIES. Look for details on shopping hours and food purchases in the introduction to Tour No. 12.

Iraklion to Agios Nikolaos: 68 kilometers

Arrive by ferry in Iraklion, Crete's main port and largest city. Despite its size and industry, Iraklion is an attractive spot. A Venetian fortress, arsenals, and other interesting remnants of Venetian rule make a walk through the city enjoyable. Don't skip a visit to the Archaeological Museum. It's a standout, even among its excellent Greek peers, and you'll begin to develop a concept of Crete's illustrious past from the hours you spend there.

From the ferry dock, follow signs for the **Archaeological Museum** to reach **Eleftherias Square** on the east side of the city. The GNTO office is across the street, and you can pick up literature on the city and the island there. Iraklion offers several affordable hotels, a youth hostel, and a large campground 5 km to the west, if you're planning an overnight stay. If you do stay in Iraklion, you can make the short day trip to Knossos, 6 km south of town, to visit the reconstructed palace of King Minos. It dates back to 1950 B.C.

To ride for Agios Nikolaos, leave **Eleftherias Square** on **Ikarou Street,** following signs for **Sitia.** Descend to ride through the city suburbs. Ignore the first right turn signed for **Agios Nikolaos,** and take the **second signed turn** to gain the **old road** beside the sea. The coastline is dotted with hotels and dirty beaches as you pedal east toward **Gournes,** where the old and new roads merge. Pass a large U.S. Air Force base and continue on to **Malia,** pedaling past hotels and roadside tourist towns.

Malia is a hopping tourist spot with a main street lined by cafes and postcard racks. There are a youth hostel and a campground in the city. Besides its popular beaches, Malia centers its tourist trade around the Palace of Malia, 3 km east of town. This is one of the three great Minoan palaces on Crete, along with those at Knossos and Phaestos. To reach the palace, cycle through Malia and swing left at a **sign for the archaeological site** beyond the town. Stroll among the prostrate stones and stretch your imagination with your legs.

Return to the **main road** and go left. The road **branches** soon after, with the new road swinging right to pass through the Gorge of Selinari and the **old road** going left to take a curving, climbing route through the hills above. The new road collects most of the traffic and avoids the climb by diving into a long tunnel. You'll have a safer, more enjoyable ride if you angle left to weave through the hills. Ascend in steep switchbacks to **Vrahasi,** and enjoy a look at an unspoiled Cretan town, then descend to ride for **Neapoli.**

Follow signs for Neapoli and coast down into the city. Veer left at the main square in town, then go right soon after to gain the **old road** toward **Agios Nikolaos.** Continue on toward **Nikithianos,** watching the hillsides for the stone windmills that overlook the olive groves. Keep right for Agios Nikolaos when the road **branches,** and pedal past thousands of olive trees as you ride through gentle terrain to **Houmeriakos.**

Pass under the new road and continue on to **Xirokambos.** Join the **new road** after Xirokambos, and go left soon after for the center of **Agios Nikolaos,** a pretty town set on a shining blue harbor. Shop-lined streets slope down to the boat-speckled bay, and outdoor cafes fill the waterfront. The city is one of Crete's most popular tourist spots. Listen to the clamor of languages being spoken by the tourists that swarm its streets, and you'll wonder how people from so many lands found such an out-of-the-way spot.

Agios Nikolaos's tourist office is on Omirou Street, above the harbor. They'll be able to direct you to the city's youth hostel or to one of its scores of hotels.

Agios Nikolaos to Mirtos: 50 kilometers

From Agios Nikolaos's **center,** climb away from the harbor and follow signs for **Ierapetra** to gain the **main road** southeast along the sea. Enjoy scenic riding as you cycle through undulating terrain, passing cliff-encircled bays of brilliant turquoise. Follow the up-and-down route to **Gournia,** the site of Crete's best-preserved Minoan town. You'll have a good view of the excavated city from the road.

Swing right for **Ierapetra** just past **Pahia Ammos,** and **turn inland** to cross to Crete's southern coast at the island's narrowest point. To the east, the sheer faces of the Thriptis Mountains spring from the valley floor, and you'll spot tiny white churches and scattered settlements as you climb gradually for about 6 km. Sail down the final stretch of road to Ierapetra while the valley winds whirr in the flying blades of modern windmills in the fields along the way.

Ride **through Ierapetra,** a resort town with hotels and a hostel, and turn west for **Mirtos.** You'll have flat seaside riding with some short hills as you pass dozens of greenhouses on the 15-km ride to Mirtos. This small town attracts scores of solitude-seeking travelers to its quiet beaches. There's no campground at Mirtos, but there are lots of rooms available in the town.

Mirtos to Mires: 100 kilometers

As you ride away from Mirtos, you'll be leaving "tourist Crete" behind and exchanging hotels and postcard racks for several hours of tough mountain riding, a few kilometers of rough dirt roads, and an abundance of magnificent scenery that will make your days a joy. The farther you pedal from the tourist towns, the warmer the greetings, the more enthusiastic the waves, and the readier the smiles from people you pass along the way.

Leave Mirtos on the road signed for **Viannos** and **Iraklion.** Climb gradually for 2 km, then leave the valley to ascend steeply into olive-sprinkled hills. The road surface is good, traffic is light, and the inclines are murderous. The views out over the surrounding countryside will soothe your soul, even as your legs beg for mercy. Scattered level stretches and an isolated downhill or two break up the 14-km climb.

Reach **Pefkos** and enjoy a short descent, then climb steeply to a ridge where a lone memorial guards the heights. The view from the point is almost worth the climb! You'll have mostly level riding beyond the ridge, then a quick 3-km descent into **Viannos,** a small hillside town with a church and a handful of cafes. Climb a final **ridge** from Viannos, then descend steeply for 4 km toward **Martha.**

Veer left toward **Skinias** just past a **turnoff** for Martha, and coast down gradually past Skinias and on toward **Demati** and the Anapodaris River. When we rode this section, roadwork had transformed the asphalt surface into mud and rock, but the road should be repaved by now. Cross the bridge above the **Anapodaris River.**

After the **bridge,** the road deteriorates abruptly. Swing to the right up a very steep hill into **Demati** and follow an unpaved road around the hill past Favriana and on toward **Kato Kastelliana.** Scattered signs mark the route toward **Pirgos.** Stay to the right at **Ano Kastelliana** to bypass the town and reach a **signed junction.** Continue straight for **Pirgos.** Evidence of roadwork in this area indicates this section might be paved by now. We regained asphalt 4 km beyond Ano Kastelliana and cruised into **Mesohori** with only scattered patches of gravel.

In Mesohori, veer right for **Pirgos** and cycle the 6 km to the midsized town. Several cafes and small food stores line the main street. From Pirgos, swing right for **Iraklion** and pedal into the level expanse of the broad, heavily cultivated **Mesara Plain.** You'll have stunning views of Crete's Mount Ida massif as you cycle along the valley floor. The snow-capped peaks seem out of place in the southern reaches of Greece, and their wild beauty contrasts sharply with the cultivated lands below.

Cycle easy terrain toward **Protoria** and go right toward **Iraklion,** then veer left just afterward for **Asimi.** Ride a gently rolling route along the northern edge of the plain, and pass through Asimi and Stoli on the way to **Ag. Deka** and the Roman ruins of **Gortys.** Gortys was the capital of Roman Crete and was the largest city on the island. Stop to look at the sixth-century church of Agios Titus (to the right of the road), said to be the site of the first bishopric of Crete. The tumbled stones of the Roman *Agora* lie beside the church, and beyond the Agora is the Roman *Odeum,* where a law code from 500 B.C. is inscribed in stone.

From Gortys, continue through level terrain with gradually increasing traffic to **Mires,** where the day's early hills will probably send you in search of a room. There are no campgrounds in the vicinity. Timbaki, 12 km farther on, also has hotels.

Mires to Rethymnon (Rethimno): 80 kilometers

Follow signs for **Timbaki** away from Mires. Reach the turnoff for **Phaestos** about **6 km** beyond Mires. The Minoan palace at Phaestos is comparable to those at Malia and Knossos. If you want to take a look, it's a 2-km climb from the main road to reach the hilltop site. Then continue on the main road to Timbaki, a midsized town with a busy main street.

Pedal straight through town and continue toward the sea. Bypass the turnoff for Kokkinos Pirgos and climb steeply to a **ridgetop junction.** Turn right to follow a quiet, 61-km route toward **Rethymnon.** Pass through countless tiny mountain towns as you labor up and over the backbone of Crete. You'll have spectacular views of mountains, sea, and twisted olive trees to make up for your muscles' screams. Climb steadily to Apodoulou, following signs for Rethymnon. The road ascends more gradually after Apodoulou, winding past hillsides where lone shepherds watch their flocks.

Ride through **Nithafris** and Kouroutes, cross a ridge to **Apostoli,** then coast down to the narrow canyon beyond. Follow the canyon to Filakio, then enjoy a short stretch of level riding before climbing once again. Cross a ridge and descend steeply to Prasies, then continue on to reach a final downhill to the sea. At **Perivolia,** turn left on the **old coast road** to pedal the final 3 km into **Rethymnon.** If you want to camp, go right at Perivolia to reach a campground soon after.

Rethymnon's tourist office, at 100 Kountouriotou Street, is on the right as you pedal into the city. Stop for information on the town or to get help with your search for lodgings. There's a youth hostel in Rethymnon, as well as several hotels.

Rethymnon is a wonderful city for strolling. It's big enough to be interesting, yet small enough to cover in a single afternoon. Walk along the old harbor to the Venetian fortress that rules a bluff above the sea. Turn into the city's narrow streets, overhung with balconies and lined with shops and cafes, and walk back toward your room, watching for minarets along the way.

Rethymnon to Hania: 61 kilometers

From Rethymnon, follow signs for **Hania** as you pedal out of town. The road branches at Atsipopoulo, with the **new road** going **straight** and the old road angling to the left. The new road is level, smooth and direct, but the old road is a better choice on heavy traffic days. We pedaled the new road.

Except for a short hill outside of Rethymnon, the riding is level for the first 20 km along the coast, and you'll have fine views of Crete's White Mountains as you pedal. There are scattered campgrounds along the way, and sandy beaches beckon beside the road. Swing inland to climb gradually for about 12 km, passing through fragrant pine forests and catching glimpses of the snow-capped mountains to the south. Old and new roads cross several times during the climb, so you'll have lots of opportunities to trade.

Angle toward the sea, descending to **Kalami** and continuing along the edge of **Souda Bay,** where dozens of ships rest at anchor. At **Tsikalaria,** about 5 km after you return to the sea, abandon the main road and swing right for **Souda.** Avoid a steep hill by pedaling through Souda, then follow the busy 6-km route into **Hania** from there.

Head for the GNTO office at Hania's Venetian harbor to get information on lodgings and ferry connections to Piraeus. You'll have to cycle back to Souda to catch the overnight ferry for the mainland. There's a youth hostel in Hania, as well as lots of hotels and pensions. It's a delightful town to relax in while you prepare for your return to mainland Greece.

Be sure to visit the Agora, a huge covered food market in the center of town. It's a visual delight of color, texture, and movement, and the sensual

The covered market in Hania is a produce lover's paradise.

avalanche of smells, sounds, and tastes you'll find there will make the supermarkets back home seem incredibly dull. Walk through the old Venetian district behind the harbor, shop for sandals or a fisherman's hat in one of the shops, or climb the fortified hill west of the old city for a great view of the tiled roofs of the town.

The **ferry** from **Hania (Souda)** to **Piraeus** runs daily. Reserve a bunk or a room for the overnight trip, or simply claim a dark corner on the deck and snooze the hours away to your 7:00 a.m. arrival.

Piraeus to Thebes: 75 kilometers

Arrive in the ship-filled, pollution-hazed harbor of Piraeus, and begin your ride to Delphi, Patras, and a ferry trip to Italy. If you're cutting this tour short with a flight for home, the international airport at Athens isn't far away. To ride for Delphi, cycle along the edge of the **harbor** in a **counterclockwise** direction, and turn right on **Ag. Dimitriou.** Follow the busy street for about **2 km,** then veer left at a sign for **Perama.**

Stay on this road to a **Y** intersection and then angle right for **Athens** (*Athina*) and **Patras** (*Patra*). Veer left for **Patras** soon after. This road was in the midst of a major construction project when we cycled it, so some of these turns may change. Basically, you'll be riding **toward Elefsina** from Piraeus.

Traffic to Elefsina is heavy and annoying, and you'll have a steady climb as you cycle away from Piraeus. A gradual descent leads to **Skaramangas.** Join the **main road** for **Elefsina** there. Abandon the main route about **8 km** later, turning left at the **sign** for *Non-Toll Road — Elefsina*. Pedal into Elefsina, following signs for **Corinth** (*Korinthos*), then go right onto the road for **Thebes** (*Thive*). Climb gradually past Mandra, then ascend a punishing hill to **Agios Sotira.**

Coast down into a cultivated valley, then climb another steep ridge. Descend steeply to **Inoi,** then pedal gradually upward through a gentle valley that soon gives way to tougher hills. A seemingly endless climb (about 14 km) ends at a ridge above **Erithres.** Sail down a 10-percent grade into the city.

Throughout this exhausting day of riding, you'll be encouraged by the friendliness of the rural Greeks you encounter. One truck driver stopped at the bottom of a long hill to offer us and our bicycles a ride, then passed us again just as we struggled to the crest. His enthusiastic honks of congratulations cheered us almost as much as the sight of the downhill on the other side. The hills are merciless, but traffic is light, the road surface is good, and the Greek countryside is lovely.

Descend gradually after **Erithres,** then gain level riding as you pedal the final 13 km to **Thebes.** Follow signs for **Livadia** and **Delphi** as you wind your way through Thebes. If you're not camping, Thebes is the last good opportunity to find a room until Livadia, 46 km farther on.

Thebes has a place of honor in Greek history. At one time the city was the capital of all Greece. According to tradition, Thebes was the home of the tragic King Oedipus. You can visit the city's archaeological museum to learn more about the area.

Thebes to Ossios Loukas: 81 kilometers

Leave Thebes on the road for **Livadia** and **Delphi,** and enjoy easy riding across the flat Teneric Plain. Watch for the elusive peak of **Mount Parnassus** lurking in the clouds ahead. Livadia is a large, busy market town with lots of shops. Follow signs for **Delphi** as you cycle through the city, then climb gradually from the valley floor. There's a **300-meter tunnel** near **Tsoukalades.** It's straight and not too bad to ride through if traffic is light, but you can avoid it by turning off for Tsoukalades and taking the **old road** over the hill.

Continue a steady ascent with lovely mountain scenery for several more kilometers, then descend briefly to the turnoff for **Distomo** and **Ossios Loukas.** You'll have a couple of options here. We asked permission to stash our bags beside the auto shop at the junction, made the 24-km round trip to Ossios Loukas Monastery without our gear, then continued on for Delphi. Or you can cycle on to Distomo (3 km), get a room in town, then ride the final 9 km to the monastery. There are no lodgings available at Ossios Loukas itself.

Swing left for **Distomo** at the **junction,** and pedal into the compact town. Signs for **Ossios Loukas** will direct you to **Stiri.** Pedal on to a junction for Kiriaki and angle right for **Ossios Loukas.** Climb steadily through almond orchards, then enjoy a swift descent to the lonely monastery on its hill.

You won't regret the energy you spend to reach Ossios Loukas, a quiet group of buildings strikingly situated on a hillside above a wide, tree-dotted valley. The well-kept grounds, the surrounding almond trees, and the glittering mosaics in the monastery church combine to leave the visitor with a sense of the richness and timelessness of Greece.

Ossios Loukas to Delphi: 36 kilometers

Retrace the route to **Distomo** and continue to the **main road.** Go left to resume the climb to **Delphi.** A final 12 km of steep uphill on a winding, mountain-shadowed road leads to **Arachova.** The small city of Arachova, perched at the crest of the long climb to Delphi, is buried in shops and postcards, trinkets and tourists. It will always be linked in our minds to the persistent, blanket-toting shopkeeper who followed us down the road out of town calling, "No money — just look!" Despite the commercial overkill, Arachova is a beautiful spot with a fantastic view of the shimmering Gulf of Corinth.

As a cyclist, you'll prize Arachova even more, for it marks the end of your grueling ascent from Piraeus. Fly through a joyous 10 km of crazy **switchbacks** to arrive at the site of **Delphi,** where a wooded cleft in the side of Mount Parnassus holds the most sacred ruins of Greece. Just around the bend, the modern city offers scores of hotels, restaurants, and cafes, but in the quiet beauty of the wooded glen, when dawn turns the columns golden or sunset paints them pink, you can marvel at the sacred stones in solitude.

There are two campgrounds west of Delphi. The closest is 1½ km outside town. There's a youth hostel in the city, and you can visit the tourist office on the main street for help with finding a hotel room.

Delphi to Agios Nikolaos: 62 kilometers

Leave Delphi and coast down a winding road to the **olive groves** below, enjoying vistas of the Gulf of Corinth as you go. Turn left at a **small sign** for **Itea,** and pedal a quiet road through olive groves before joining the **main road** to cycle on toward Itea. On the **outskirts of Itea,** go right for **Nafpaktos** and **Galaxidi.** You'll have 17 km of gently rolling terrain as you hug the coastline to Galaxidi, an attractive seaside town with a pretty harbor. Continue on toward Eratini on the up-and-down road along the sea.

Swing down off the main road to cycle into **Eratini,** a built-up seaside town with lots of hotels and a long sandy beach. You can find a room in Eratini if you need one, or continue for 10 km along the coast to camp at Agios Nikolaos. Take the **beachside road** through Eratini and continue out of town to rejoin the **main road.** Cross a ridge before descending to **Agios Nikolaos.** Watch for a campground sign to the right as you approach the town.

Agios Nikolaos offers ferry connections to Egio on the Peloponnese Peninsula, and you can pedal on to Patras from there. We decided to stay on the north side of the Gulf instead, delaying our ferry ride until Antirrion.

Agios Nikolaos to Patras: 55 kilometers

From Agios Nikolaos, continue on toward **Nafpaktos.** The hills are gentle and the road surface is good. Light traffic and views of the sea and the ever-present olives make for pleasant riding until just **before Nafpaktos,** where you'll join **another road** and pick up heavier traffic. Explore the midsized town of Nafpaktos with its handsome Venetian castle and small medieval harbor. Continue on through the city and cycle the **9 km** to the **Antirrion turnoff.**

Veer left for Antirrion and the ferry, and pedal to the **ferry dock,** where there are frequent departures for **Rion,** just across the water. Arrive in Rion, and follow signs for the **new road** and **Patras** to pedal toward the city. There's an old road to Patras, as well, but it's narrow and has heavy traffic.

Cycle into Patras and head for the waterfront. The **ferry terminal** is on the north edge of the docking area, and there's an office of the GNTO nearby. Check on ferry connections to Ancona and Brindisi at either spot. There are dozens of hotels and pensions in Patras. If you want to camp, follow the harbor road northeast past the ferry terminal. You'll see campground signs within a few kilometers.

TOUR NO. 14

TOURING TUSCANY
Ancona to Genoa, Italy

Distance: 668 kilometers (414 miles)
Estimated time: 9 riding days
Best time to go: May, June, September, or early October
Terrain: Lots of challenging hills, with a few easy days
Connecting tours: Tours No. 11, 13, and 15

You'll pedal through the green heart of Italy on this tour through Umbria and Tuscany, and you'll get a chance to visit four of Italy's loveliest cities along the way. Assisi, Siena, Florence, and Pisa will dazzle you with art and architecture, and the vine- and olive-covered Tuscan hills and the cliff-lined Mediterranean Coast will thrill you with natural beauty.

Italian drivers have a world-wide reputation for speed, recklessness, and incessant honking. Although a brief ride we made between ferry ports in southern Italy supported that reputation, the northern drivers continually surprised us with their friendliness and courtesy. And Italy's reputed proliferation of tourist-preying thieves didn't materialize, either. Instead, we found easy-going, smiling people in the country; helpful, honest shopkeepers in the cities; and a magnificent blend of landscape and art that made our time in Italy a "masterpiece" of good experiences.

You'll love the Italian tradition of *Passeggiata,* the evening "parade." The strollers come out before supper, when the coolness of evening descends, and the city streets are filled until well after dark with talking, laughing crowds of neatly dressed Italians. Join the window shoppers to get a feel for Italian culture at its most gregarious.

Avoid the high-intensity (and high-temperature) months of July and August when you're scheduling your trip. Your days in Italy will be more pleasant, your quest for accommodations more successful, and your visits to churches and museums less crowded if you do.

CONNECTIONS. Ancona is a popular stop for ferries from Zadar, Split, and Dubrovnik in Yugoslavia, as well as Patras, Greece, so you'll have lots of options for hookups with our cycle tours in those countries. Ancona is also served by rail lines from cities throughout Italy and Northern Europe.

INFORMATION. Write to the Italian Government Travel Office, 630 Fifth Avenue, New York, New York 10111, and request specific information on

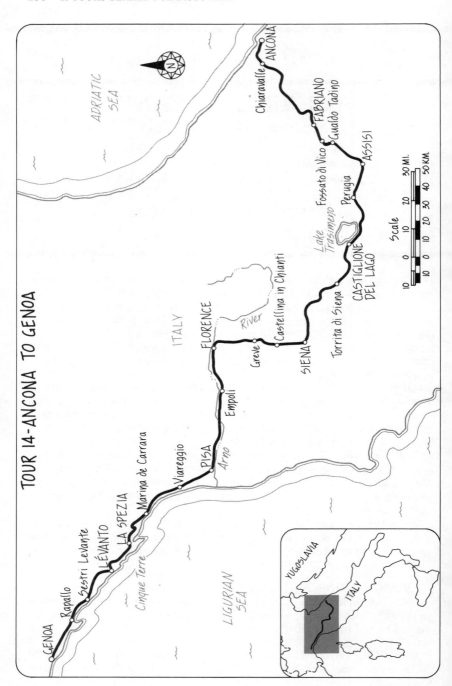

TOUR 14 - ANCONA TO GENOA

cycling, camping, and sightseeing. They'll provide a list of campsites and an overall map. Ask for street maps of the larger cities you plan to visit, too.

Michelin's *Green Guide Italy* is a good reference source for your trip—well worth its weight, even on the Tuscan hills. Other guidebook options include *Baedeker's Italy,* two *Blue Guides* and *Let's Go: Italy.*

MAPS. Pick up detailed maps for route finding once you arrive. The Auto Club of Italy, with offices in many of the larger cities, sells regional maps at 1:275,000 scale. There's also an excellent 15-map series at 1:200,000 scale published by the Touring Club Italiano. It's available in bookstores. Tourist offices are plentiful in Italy, and staff people usually speak English. You'll be able to get free literature, city maps, and accommodation information without difficulty.

ACCOMMODATIONS. Campgrounds in Italy are pleasant, convenient, and inexpensive. Most big cities have at least one site near the city center, and you can get campground listings from tourist offices. Freelance camping is acceptable, too, but always ask for permission first.

Inexpensive rooms can be found in a variety of establishments (called *albergo, pensione, soggiorno,* or *locanda*). According to law, prices must be posted on the door of every room, so double-check the price when you check the springs. You'll usually have to pay extra for a shower, and you'll invariably have to give up your passport for paperwork.

SUPPLIES. Italy is a hungry cyclist's dream. Few foods fill a growling stomach like pasta and pizza. And the huge meals that are an Italian tradition will seem just right after you've pedaled an 80-km day. Compared with other Southern European countries, Italy isn't cheap, however. Restaurant meals can set you back, so if you're on a tight budget, you may be doing lots of picnicking. But that's no hardship here.

Wonderful cheeses like Bel Paese and Gorgonzola, tasty lunchmeats, excellent produce, and lots of fresh-baked rolls (*panini*) — what more could a picnicker ask? And, if you grow tired of sandwiches, most supermarkets offer deli-counter pizza at affordable prices as well.

Italians are addicted to sweets, and you'll have an overwhelming assortment of cookies, pastries, and chocolates from which to choose. Again, prices can be surprisingly high, but a few bites will convince you that your *lire* were well spent.

Shopping hours in Italy vary between the city and the country. You can almost always find something open in big cities like Florence or Genoa, although you will find Sunday closures everywhere. In small towns, shops shut down between 1:00 and 3:00 p.m. while the Italians escape the heat and enjoy their main meal of the day. Most of Italy's museums and cathedrals adhere to the afternoon lockup, too, with Mondays the most common for all-day closures. (Remember that Italy is a very religious country. Short shorts or halter tops — even for a cyclist — are not appropriate attire in churches.)

Needless to say, cycling is big in Italy. Well-stocked bicycle shops abound in larger cities, and you'll be dazzled by the scope and variety of products. Of course, touring gear is buried by the avalanche of racing equipment, so you may have to hunt for specialized needs.

Ancona to Fabriano: 75 kilometers

Ancona is crowded, busy, and loud — a startling (but true-to-life) introduction to big-city Italy. But despite the traffic and industry, Ancona is an attractive town, climbing away from the sea on a steep hillside and ruled by a hilltop cathedral (*duomo*).

Leave the **ferry dock** and follow signs for Rimini and Pesaro as you pedal along the coast. If you need to buy maps in town, swing left onto **Corso Stamira,** and walk about seven blocks into the downtown core to reach the Auto Club of Italy (ACI). It's on the right, just past a park. You can buy detailed maps for your ride at the office. Ancona's tourist office is on the opposite side of the peninsula, on the road toward Portonovo.

Return to the **Rimini/Pesaro road** and leave Ancona, riding beside the sea and the train tracks. Keep **straight** when the main road angles left for Rimini and Pesaro. Follow signs toward **Falconara.** Join **Road 16** for **Rimini** soon after, cross the **Esino River,** and angle left onto **Road 76** for **Chiaravalle** and **Iesi.** Cycle through gentle terrain, paralleling the main road as you pass farms and scattered industrial districts.

Cross **under the A14 freeway** and ride through **Chiaravalle,** following signs for **Iesi.** Chiaravalle is a pleasant small town, a welcome contrast to the hubbub of Ancona. Traffic increases on the secondary road between Chiaravalle and Iesi, so you might want to opt for the wide shoulder of the main road and roomier pedaling. Swing left to reach the main road **after Chiaravalle,** following signs for **Rome** (*Roma*) and **Ancona,** then turning right for **Rome** when you reach the **wide thoroughfare.**

Road 76 parallels the main route for **20 km** beyond Iesi before the two roads **merge.** If you're pedaling this tour in the fall, you'll be treated to a lovely palette of autumn color as you ride — dark brown fields of freshly turned soil next to broad yellow swathes of corn stubble, and tightly trellised vines painting the hillsides with brilliant streaks of red and gold.

Begin a climb into hillier terrain as the two roads merge. There are a series of uncomfortably long but well-lit tunnels ahead as Road 76 dives into the hills. Avoid the tunnels and gain a winding route through a beautiful river gorge by turning left onto a **small paved road** at the **large gravel plant** just before the **first tunnel.** Play hopscotch with Road 76 and its tunnels to **Gattuccio,** then climb a **small hill** while the main route burrows through the mountain. Rejoin **Road 76** just beyond.

Follow signs for **Fabriano** along Road 76. Truck traffic increases and the road narrows for the final kilometers into the midsized city. Fabriano has a handsome central square, a 17th-century cathedral, and many medieval buildings. You'll be able to find a *pensione* in the city if you need a bed.

Fabriano to Assisi: 60 kilometers

Leave Fabriano on **Road 76** for **Rome** and begin a climb into the hills. The rugged terrain will challenge and reward you for the remainder of the day. Follow the narrow, winding route beside the river to **Cancelli** and pedal through a **tunnel.** Turn right for **Camodiegoli** just afterward, to avoid a second, longer tunnel. Cross an **overpass** and go left at the **T** to climb steeply up and over a long hill. You'll have lovely vistas of green hillsides sprinkled with oak and maple as you pedal up the carless secondary road.

Descend steeply to rejoin **Road 76,** then veer left for **Fossato di Vico** less than 1 km later. Cross the train tracks on a somewhat suspect **bridge** (we walked), and ride through Fossato di Vico before following signs for **Rome** onto **Road 3.** Continue on Road 3 toward **Gualdo Tadino,** and veer right for **Perugia** and **Assisi** onto **Road 318** on the edge of town. Ride **3 km,** then go left for **Assisi** as you begin a long climb away from the valley floor, passing through **Grello** and cycling on to Osteria di Morano.

Coast down a short hill, then climb a steep hill beyond Osteria, enjoying one beautiful vista after another. You'll have a stretch of level riding before **San Presto,** then descend steeply to the river below. Cross the **river** and swing around the hillside for your first glimpse of Assisi, an enchanting city perched on a mounded hill, its towers standing guard above its walls.

Assisi's campground is on a steep hill above the city core. To reach the **campground** (or the youth hostel next door), turn left as you enter the city and puff up the **via Santuario delle Carceri.** There are signs for the campground (2 km from the city center). Rooms in Assisi are scarce during high season, but things are quieter in spring and fall. Seek out the tourist office on the Piazza del Comune if you need help.

The medieval streets and picturesque alleys of Assisi are a treat to wander through. And Assisi's churches — particularly the magnificent St. Francis's Basilica — will take you several hours to explore. Marvel at the wealth of paintings in the basilica dedicated to the city's most famous son, St. Francis, and then pedal out into the surrounding countryside to sense the beauty that inspired him to worship.

Assisi to Castiglione del Lago: 80 kilometers

From St. Francis's Basilica, take the **via Frate Elia** down the hill and turn right to follow signs for **Perugia** to the **valley floor** beyond. Cycle west on **Road 147** through flat agricultural land, joining the **main road** toward Perugia **15 km** from Assisi's center. Cross the **Tevere River** and take the **first exit** off the main road for Perugia. Go left at the **T.**

The road **branches** soon after, with signs for Rome (*Roma*), Florence (*Firenze*), and Perugia. Continue **straight** for **Perugia,** pedaling cautiously in the thick traffic. Climb a long, steep hill into the city center. Perugia squats atop its mounded Umbrian hill like a grim dragon turned to stone. The city has an abundance of regal buildings, ornate facades, and massive palaces. Stop to admire the view out over the surrounding countryside from the small park across from St. Peter's Church.

Continue upward through the Porta San Pietro toward the Piazza 4 Novembre, Perugia's central square. The Great Fountain (Fontana Maggiore) in the impressive square is a masterpiece of Italian sculpture. Walk around and around it, deciphering the stories in the carved panels. Perugia's tourist office is at Corso Vannucci 96. Walk south from the Great Fountain past the Priors's Palace to gain the Corso Vannucci.

To leave the city, follow the **via dei Priori** west from the Priors's Palace to the **Oratory of San Bernardino,** a beautiful 15th-century church. Then take the **via A. Pascoli** down the hill, veering left at the **T.** Continue downhill and follow signs for **Roma** and **Firenze.** Go under the **train tracks** and keep to the left for **Rome,** then go right for **Florence** a short distance later.

Follow signs for **S. Sisto** to gain **Road 220** southwest from Perugia. Coast downhill, climb a short, steep hill, then descend into S. Sisto on a lightly trafficked secondary road. Stay on Road 220 for about **13 km** more. Then angle right for **Mugnano,** turning toward the shore of Lake Trasimeno, the largest lake in central Italy. Keep right in **Mugnano,** following signs for **Magione** and pedaling through acres of olive trees.

Ascend a gentle hill, then coast to an **intersection** with **Road 599.** Veer left for **Chiusi.** Pedal **8 km** along the flat, marshy lakeshore and angle right for **Castiglione del Lago.** Enjoy easy, quiet riding before joining the **main road** into Castiglione for the final 7½ km of the day. There are several campgrounds along the lake in this area, or you can look for a room in Castiglione, a pretty lakeside town with a 14th-century castle. The city tourist office is near the train station.

Castiglione del Lago to Siena: 80 kilometers

Leave Castiglione by pedaling west on **Road 454** for **Pozzuolo** and **Montepulciano.** Negotiate a series of small hills covered with vineyards and yellow-faced sunflowers, and enter a long valley dominated by the distant form of Montepulciano on its hilltop. Follow signs for **Montepulciano** and **Siena** past Pozzuolo and Acquavua to arrive at **Nottola.** From Nottola, you can make the 7-km trip to Montepulciano if you'd like a closer look at the lofty town. Otherwise, turn right for **Siena** in Nottola, and follow signs for Siena and **Sinalunga** through **Torrita di Siena.** Pedal through rolling hill country of vineyards and small towns. Ride through **Sinalunga** and join **Road 326,** veering left toward **Siena** and a final 38 km of busy main-road riding.

You'll have level going at the start, then a final stretch of roller-coaster hills as you approach Siena. Armaiolo is a particularly attractive town, with a lovely bell tower embellishing its medieval silhouette. Reach a junction just before Siena and savor the view of the city on its hill, with its many fine buildings standing out against the sky. Go **straight** at the **junction,** following signs marked *Siena Stazione.* (The route signed for *Siena Centro* does a huge loop around the town, adding several confusing kilometers to your ride.)

There's a well-marked campground near the train station if you want to camp during your stay, and there's a youth hostel in the city, as well. Climb the hill to the city center and head for the magnificent Piazza del Campo, using the tall tower of the Palazzo Pubblico as your guide. The tourist office is at Piazza del Campo 55, and you can get a city map and a list of hotels there.

Siena stands out among Italian cities. The fan-shaped Piazza del Campo is one of the most impressive plazas in Europe. The mesmerizing *duomo,* with its shocking striped exterior of multicolored marble and its exquisite interior of inlaid stone, will demand at least a couple of hours of your time. And the

A grandfather and grandson share a Sunday morning in Siena's Piazza del Campo.

The view of Florence from the Piazzale Michelangelo.

streets of the city, full of talking, laughing, strolling residents, will delight you with their variety and life.

Be sure to savor the culinary treasures Siena has to offer, too. Slices of moist white bread piled with chunks of fragrant Gorgonzola cheese, and a tasty after-dinner treat of nutty *panforte,* rich with candied fruit and honey, will make your stomach rumble with contentment.

Siena to Florence: 70 kilometers

Leave Siena on the **via di Camollia** and follow signs for **Florence** (Firenze) as you ride. After a few kilometers, reach a **junction** signed for Florence to both left and right. Veer right and follow signs for **Castellina in Chianti** onto **Road 222.** Stay on Road 222 for Florence throughout the day.

Climb through challenging hills, with vistas of steeply sloped vineyards and vibrant green fields. Short descents and brief level stretches break up the mostly uphill riding to Castellina, an attractive town of old houses ruled by a tower-topped fortress. Descend from Castellina, then climb a long hill past acres of vines. Pedal on to **Greve,** a midsized town with lots of stores, then ride through short rolling hills to Strada.

Follow signs for Florence down a long hill to **Grassina,** cross under the **A1 freeway,** and enter the outskirts of the city. You'll arrive in Florence on the south bank of the **Arno River,** then swing west along the shore to pedal toward the **city center.** The view of Florence's old core, dominated by the mighty *duomo* and the bell tower of the Palazzo Vecchio, is a fitting finale to a day of lovely Tuscan hills.

There are several bridges across the Arno into the heart of the city.

Florence's tourist office is at via Tornabuoni 15. Take the **Ponte Santa Trinita** across the river, and continue straight to reach the tourist office. You can get a city map and lodging information here. There are two campgrounds in Florence. Parco Comunale, on the olive-covered hillside east of the Piazzale Michelangelo, is closest to the city center and offers a wonderful view of the city across the Arno. There's also a campground next to the youth hostel, a few kilometers northeast of the city center.

Inexpensive rooms abound on the streets around the main train station and the *duomo,* but you'll have to convince some of the proprietors to let you haul your bicycle inside. Many of the rooms are up several flights of stairs.

Florence, city of Michelangelo and artistic capital of Tuscany, is a lovely town that is best appreciated during the off season, when tourist crowds begin to dwindle. You'll have a long list of "must-see" attractions here, with the magnificent cathedral, the Uffizi Gallery, and the Palazzo Vecchio near the top of the heap. Try to get out on the streets early to avoid the crowds. Dive into the museums and churches to savor Florence's art. Climb to the Piazzale Michelangelo or struggle up the campanile's 414 steps to get a panoramic view of the city. And stroll the jam-packed streets after dark to experience Florence's throbbing city life.

By the way, if you think a tour of Italy wouldn't be complete without a visit to Rome, Florence makes an excellent base for a train ride to the south. We left our bicycles and gear tucked away in a courtyard at our *pensione,* then made the four-hour trip to Rome for a few days of frenzied city sightseeing.

Florence to Pisa: 82 kilometers

Cross to the south side of the **Arno River** and cycle west onto **Road 67.** Follow **blue road signs** for **Pisa** as you draw away from Florence. The mostly flat, easy ride to Pisa follows the Arno River on Road 67 throughout the day. During your early kilometers on the winding secondary road, you'll pedal through lush green valleys of vines, olives, and oak, and small towns along the way provide interesting breaks in the scenery.

Pass through two short **tunnels** near **Capraia,** about 24 km from Florence. Just past **Empoli,** you can veer right for **Fucecchio** to cross the Arno if you'd like to abandon Road 67 for a **smaller thoroughfare.** Traffic is just as heavy on the north side of the river, however, and a long succession of towns overlooks the road. The final 30 km into Pisa are dull.

Enter Pisa either by crossing the **Arno River** into the old city (from Road 67) or by approaching from the east (on the secondary road). Head for the *duomo* on the northwest edge of the city center. You'll never forget your first look at Pisa's famous Leaning Tower beside the massive Pisa Cathedral. The bizarre tilt of this skinny white cylinder, set off against the perpendicular lines of the hulking church beside it, is a spectacular sight. And the overall picture created by lush green grass, the white wedding-cake cathedral, the dome-shaped baptistry, and the drunken tower produces a remarkable composition.

Venture inside the *duomo* and the baptistry, or climb to the balcony at the top of the Leaning Tower (if you dare), and absorb the visual splendor of Pisa's Piazza del Duomo. The city tourist office is just across the lawn from

Pisa's Leaning Tower is no slouch with sightseers.

the Leaning Tower. There are several inexpensive *pensioni* near the cathedral, and there's a large campground just outside the western city gate on Viale delle Cascine. It's within walking distance of the *duomo*.

Pisa to La Spezia: 85 kilometers

Leave Pisa by cycling west from the Piazza del Duomo onto **Viale delle Cascine.** Ride past the campground and continue on to an intersection with **Road 1.** Follow Road 1 for **14** busy **kilometers** toward **Genoa** (Genova) and **Viareggio.** Veer left for **Torre del Lago Puccini** to gain a smaller road, still with lots of traffic. Pedal on through level terrain to **Viareggio.**

In Viareggio, follow signs for the **center,** circling across the **train tracks** and working your way down to the beach and your first look at Italy's Mediterranean Coast. The solid succession of restaurants, hotels, shops, and campgrounds probably won't impress you. Follow the flat seaside road through a string of small resort cities to **Marina de Carrara.** Cycling this stretch during high season could be nerve wracking, despite the wide road.

Things lighten up a bit after Marina de Carrara. Cross the **Magra River,** then turn left for **Montemarcello, Ameglia,** and your introduction to the Italian Riviera. Ameglia is an attractive town of tall, fortlike houses. Labor up a long, steep hill to **Montemarcello,** passing through fragrant pine forests and terraced olive groves. There's a fine view from the top of the ridge.

Pedal through rolling terrain to a **junction** for **Lerici** and **Sarzana.** Turn left and descend steeply to **Lerici** and the sea. Lerici is a busy resort town with a castle-guarded harbor. Follow signs for **La Spezia** from here, climbing with **Road 331** along the sea. There are several campgrounds along this section, if you want to camp before La Spezia. Otherwise, follow the seaside Road 331 into the city and ride along the busy harbor. Look for a room in the city center.

La Spezia to Lévanto: 42 kilometers

Continue through La Spezia on the **harbor road,** veering left at the edge of town for **Portovénera** and **Riomaggiore.** Then right to ascend a **steep hill** signed for **Riomaggiore.** Enjoy stunning views of La Spezia and the sea before you dive into a well-lit tunnel of about ½ km. The vistas beyond the tunnel are more spectacular still, as you ride along a hillside high above the Mediterranean.

Gaze ahead to Italy's matchless Cinque Terre, the Five Lands. Five tiny fishing villages cling to this cliffy, curving section of coast, linked by the sea, by train tracks, and by a rocky cliffside footpath. Although a connecting road is scheduled for construction between the towns, the project will probably take several years.

Arrive at a **junction** signed for **Riomaggiore** and **Manarola.** If you feel like exploring (and working very hard), make the steep descent to Riomaggiore and take a look around the compact town. You can continue on to Manarola from Riomaggiore by pushing your bicycle along the path called the Via del Amore, but it's really not a hike for a bike. A better option is to stow your bicycle and gear in Riomaggiore and walk the trail, then return to the city by train.

You'll have spectacular views of the whole section by simply keeping to the high road and pedaling through. If you choose to see it this way, continue **straight** at the Manarola/Riomaggiore **junction,** ride through another **tunnel,** then go right for **Volastra** up an extremely steep hill. The incline will probably have you off and shoving before you reach the top.

Come to a **junction** signed for **Vernazza** and **Lévanto.** Go right for **Lévanto** onto a **dirt road** and wind through a high pine forest with wonderful views of the sea. The surface isn't too bad and you'll regain pavement after about 6 km. At a **T** signed for **Lévanto** and **La Spezia,** veer left for **Lévanto** and descend a steep hill to **another junction.** Turn right here to continue a long descent to the sea.

If you want to camp, there's a nice site in a hillside olive grove about **2 km above Lévanto.** Watch for the campground signs as you coast down the hill. Lévanto offers hotels and *pensioni.*

Lévanto to Genoa: 94 kilometers

From Lévanto, follow **blue road signs** for **Genoa** up a long, steep hill. As you climb, you'll have fantastic views of the cliffs and beaches below and of the jagged coastline stretching toward Genoa. Turn inland for the final leg of the 19-km ascent to the **Bracco Pass.** Reach the crest of the hill and continue on to **Road 1.** Go left for **Genoa** on Road 1.

Cycle a short level stretch, then fly down a precipitous descent to **Sestri Levante** and the heart of the Italian Riviera. Hotels, restaurants, villas, and non-stop traffic will accompany you for the remaining 56 km to Genoa. From Sestri Levante, the riding is pleasant to **Chiávari,** with only one tunnel to make your skin crawl. Climb steeply from Chiávari, then descend to **Zoagli,** sharing the road with Mercedes, Porsches, and a few Rolls Royces along the way.

Ascend again from Zoagli and swing left onto a **side road** around the ridge to avoid another **tunnel.** Speed downhill into **Rapallo** and follow **blue Genoa Road 1 signs** through town and up another steep hill to (guess what) another tunnel. Enjoy a final steep descent to **Recco** and the sea.

The 7 km between Recco and **Bogliasco** are rolling and winding — tough riding after a hard day. The terrain moderates after Bogliasco, and Genoa reaches out to draw you in with heavy traffic and solid development. At **Nervi,** the narrow coast road grows into a more comfortable four lanes. Follow signs for *Genova Centro* into the throbbing heart of the city.

Genoa is Italy's largest seaport. It's sprawling, loud, and dangerous, so ride with caution. If you're ending your tour here, you'll be heading for either the train station or the airport west of town. Since Tour No. 14 starts in Genoa and departs to the west, you can check the start of that tour for directions to the airport. To reach the Stazione Brignole, continue following signs for *Genova Centro* to Piazza Verdi, the Brignole train station, and a city tourist office.

TOUR NO. 15

ROLLING ALONG THE RIVIERAS
Genoa, Italy, to Barcelona, Spain

Distance:	1,119 kilometers (694 miles)
Estimated time:	17 riding days
Best time to go:	April, May, June, September, or October
Terrain:	Fairly easy throughout
Connecting tours:	Tours No. 14, 16, and 17

This tour follows the Mediterranean coastlines of Italy, France, and Spain. You'll have a brief respite from the heavily developed seaside areas when you swing inland for a look at the pastoral loveliness of Provence, avoiding the urban chaos of Marseilles along the way.

CONNECTIONS. You can reach Genoa and the start of this tour by plane or train, or you can cycle in via Tour No. 14 (Ancona to Genoa). Ancona's airport is west of the city, and the Brignole train station is in the center of town. As befits Italy's largest port, Genoa is also served by ferries — you can arrive by boat from either Corsica or Sardinia.

INFORMATION. For preparatory information on Italy, read the introduction to Tour No. 14. Look at Tour No. 2 for material on France, and skip ahead to Tour No. 17 to prepare for your ride in Spain.

ACCOMMODATIONS. One warning note. If you're cycling this tour late in the year, be aware that many hotels, pensions, and campgrounds along the Riviera are closed up tight in November, while management takes a holiday. You'll have to scramble to find rooms in some of the smaller Riviera towns.

MAPS. You'll need maps for three different countries on this tour. Read the map section in Tour No. 14 for help with Italy, and check the map information in Tour No. 2 for information on France. The *Firestone Mapa Turistico* series will cover your ride in Spain (see Tour No. 17 for more details).

SUPPLIES. For information on shopping hours and food purchases in Italy, France, and Spain, refer to Tours No. 14, 2, and 17, respectively.

Genoa to Finale Ligure: 71 kilometers

From the Brignole **train station,** head south on **Viale Brigata Bisagno.** Follow signs for **Pegli** and **Savona.** Take **Corso A. Saffi** to the right just before the harbor, and climb a small hill, cycling above the water. The **freeway** will be on your left. Descend and join **via Sopraelevata Gramsci** to continue beside the freeway, and stay with **blue signs for Savona.**

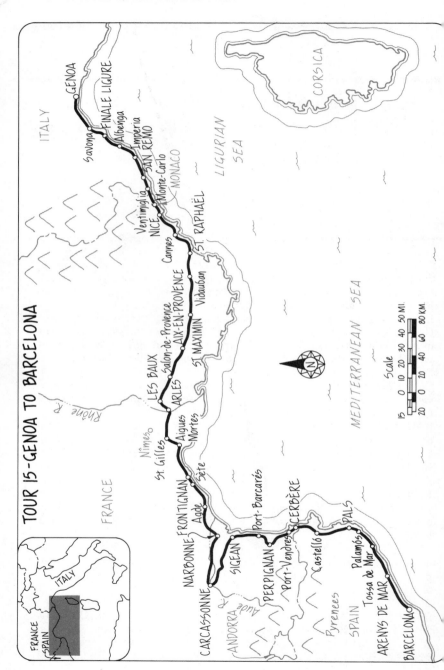

Continue following the blue road signs for **Pegli** and Savona as you pedal away from the city on **Road 1.** Pass the airport turnoff and cycle on to Pegli as the noise and pollution of Genoa begin to fade. Ascend a small hill at Arenzano and climb another just past Cogoleto. Traffic is not too bothersome along this section, and there are pleasant interludes of sea, cliffs, and olives between the built-up seaside towns.

Varazze has a long stretch of sand beside it. Pedal on toward **Savona** and pass through two short tunnels before the busy city. Stay along the sea as you ride through Savona, following signs for **Imperia.** Cycle on to **Noli,** an attractive fishing town, and come to a scenic stretch of curving road cut into the cliffs. Speed through several short tunnels along the level, winding route.

Enter **Finale Ligure** (actually a string of small villages) and choose from three campgrounds and several hotels and *pensioni.* The small downtown area beside the palm-lined beach at **Marina** makes a pleasant setting for an evening stroll.

Finale Ligure to San Remo: 74 kilometers

Begin your last full day of riding in Italy by pedaling away from Finale Ligure, continuing southwest on **Road 1** toward **Imperia.** You'll have lots of level riding and fewer built-up areas to block your views of the placid Mediterranean along the way. Swing left **off Road 1** to explore **Albenga,** a handsome town with a 13th-century cathedral and a fifth-century baptistry. Cross the **river** in Albenga and turn left to follow signs for **Imperia** on a quiet road beside the sea. **Rejoin Road 1** soon after.

You'll have a small hill at Cape Santa Croce and a fine view, as well. Descend to **Alássio,** a resort town sprawled beside the sea, then climb to Cape Mele and another impressive vista. Pedal on **past Cervo,** a unique village perched on a hill above the road, and endure a long, steady climb to Cape Berta just before **Imperia.** Follow signs for **San Remo** and **Ventimiglia** through Imperia. The city's old quarter, on a small promontory to the left of the road, will tempt you to stop and explore.

There are several campgrounds just beyond Imperia, if you decide to end your riding day. The road is level between Imperia and San Remo (26 km), running close to the sea and passing through small villages along the way. Ride past handsome olive groves, vineyards, and vibrant fields of flowers as you approach **San Remo,** capital of Italy's "Riviera of Flowers." Carnations, chrysanthemums, roses, and mimosa are grown along this temperate coastline and sold all over Europe.

The quiet beauty of old villages and flowers gives way to traffic and hotels as you enter the busy city of San Remo. Follow signs for **Ventimiglia** to pedal through the town and reach the year-round campground on the western edge. You'll be within walking distance of the city center (about 3 km) from the large, well-equipped site, or you can hop a bus into the city for a faster trip.

Explore San Remo's colorful, palm-lined promenade, and rub shoulders with furs and three-piece suits while you window-shop for pearls or count Mercedes. Then climb into the twisted streets of the old city, and join the locals in a vast outdoor market where the opulence and wealth of the Riviera seem very far away.

San Remo to Nice: 56 kilometers

Follow **blue road signs** for **Ventimiglia** as you leave San Remo **on Road 1.** Ospedaletti is an attractive resort town nearly buried in palms. Continue on to Ventimiglia, a hilltop city of tall, rectangular houses, and prepare to say *"Bonjour"* to France. Cross the **river** on the far side of Ventimiglia and follow signs for **France - SS1.** Turn right to ascend a **short hill,** then pedal through a long uphill **tunnel.** You can avoid the tunnel by swinging left after the river, then circling up and around the point to rejoin Road 1.

Reach a **junction** signed for the **French border** (left or straight). We went **left** to avoid a climb but endured a few **tunnels** along the way. Continue on to the border crossing. You'll be waved through by friendly guards more interested in your bicycle than your passport. **Menton,** just across the border, is a large Riviera resort with a pretty waterfront. **Keep to the left** to stay along the sea as you pedal through the town.

Follow signs for **Nice** to climb a steep hill away from Menton, and rejoin the **main road (now Road N7)** to ride toward **Monaco.** Look for signs for **Monte-Carlo's center,** and descend to the wealthy capital of Monaco. Watch for the unique license plates of the small principality on the cars that pass you as you ride. Signs in Monte-Carlo lead past high rises, hotels, and shops to the **Casino,** a classy-looking building set on a flower-filled avenue.

Swing left to get a closer look at the Casino and continue down to the waterfront to marvel at the money floating in the yacht-filled harbor. Continue pedaling along the sea on **Road N98** for **Nice.** Just beyond Cap d'Ail, we hit a road closure that resulted in a detour up a long, steep hill and back to **Road N7.** If you can stay on Road N98 for the ride into Nice, you'll avoid the hill and enjoy a much pleasanter ride. But it may stay closed to accommodate the mansion owners on this scenic stretch of coast.

Road N7 ascends a long hill to **Eze,** a magnificently situated town set on a rocky pinnacle. There are lovely views to recompense you for the climb if you have to ride this way. Beyond Eze, sail down several kilometers of smooth road with one long tunnel, then make a final steep descent into **Nice.**

Head for the old city (Vieille Ville) to search for a room in Nice. It's a fascinating enclave within the modern city, and there are lots of inexpensive hotels to choose from along its streets. Road N7 leads to **Place Barel.** From Place Barel, cycle along **rue Barla** to **Avenue Saint Jean Baptiste.** Go left and continue on to **Place Masséna.** There's a city tourist office to the right, near the Municipal Casino. Veer left onto **Boulevard Jean Jaurés** and dive left again to enter the tangled streets of the old town.

There are two youth hostels in Nice, but neither one is centrally located. Get a room instead, and stay close to the street life that gives the city its appeal. Nice is a wonderful city for walking. After you've exhausted the alleyways of the Vieille Ville, head for the Promenade des Anglais along the sea and join the strollers there. Modern Nice has attractions of its own, with shops, movie theaters, and restaurants, but it has little of the charm of the somewhat seedy old town.

Nice to St. Raphaël: 77 kilometers

Leave Nice by cycling west along the **Promenade des Anglais,** following signs for **Cannes.** Pass the Nice airport and continue on the busy **Road N98** for about **2 km** before veering left for **Villeneuve-Loubet-Plage.** Follow the road along the sea to **Antibes,** a midsized Riviera city with a pleasant old core. You can add some scenic riding to your day by cycling the small road around the Cap d'Antibes and rejoining Road N98 beyond.

Otherwise, follow signs for **Cannes** onto **Road N7** as you pass through Antibes, and abandon N7 about **8 km** later, angling left for **Palm Beach.** Cycle around a small promontory and enter Cannes along a lovely waterfront road. Pass a tree-filled city park where men bowl in the afternoon sun, and continue on through the city, following the seaside **Road N98** to la **Napoule-Plage.**

Climb a long hill just beyond **Théoule-sur-Mer,** then descend to ride along the Corniche de l'Esterel, a strikingly scenic route that winds beside the sea from Cannes to **St. Raphaël.** You'll have views of the inland peaks of the Massif de l'Esterel, the Mediterranean, the red cliffs, and the scattered mansions tucked among them as you ride.

There are several campgrounds between **Agay** and **St. Raphaël,** including some deluxe, Riviera-priced sites near the city. St. Raphaël is a pretty resort town with a harbor full of expensive boats and a tidy downtown core. Take a final look at the opulence of Riviera life in St. Raphaël. Pastoral, peaceful Provence is ahead.

St. Raphaël to St. Maximin: 90 kilometers

Ride through St. Raphaël on **Road N98,** and follow signs for **Aix.** Turn inland with N98, then cycle through **Fréjus,** an ancient Roman town with the remains of the oldest amphitheater in France. Veer left for **Aix** and **Road N7** just before the **train tracks,** then turn right at the **T** to pass under the **tracks** and N7. Go left onto N7 for **Aix.**

Cycle along the comfortably wide shoulder of the uncomfortably busy N7 for the 24 km to **Vidauban.** Take a brief break from the traffic on the way by pedaling through **le Muy** when the main road makes a loop around the handsome town. Pass through **Vidauban** and turn right for le **Thoronet,** leaving the traffic and N7 behind. Ride a winding route on **Road D84** beside the Argens River, passing by fields of vines and deep forests on the quiet road.

Leave the river to climb to **le Thoronet,** and cycle **through town,** continuing uphill to a **turn** toward **Carcès.** Go right to **regain D84,** then descend to cross the **Argens River** and join **Road D562** toward **Carcès.** Cycle the 7 rolling kilometers into Carcès and follow signs for **Brignoles,** continuing on **D562.** Pedal gradually uphill for the 12 km to le **Val.** You'll fall in love with rural France as you cycle quiet roads past olive groves and vines, exchanging *bonjours* with smiling field workers along the way.

Just past the center of **le Val,** turn right on **Road D28** for **Bras,** and climb gently beside the Ribeirotte River. Ascend steeply through a scraggly forest of aspen and oak. Reach the ridgetop, keep right, and descend into the small town of **Bras.** Follow signs for **St. Maximin** in Bras, and stay on **D28** for the final 10 km to that city. The road is level most of the way.

St. Maximin is a midsized town with a good selection of shops and a handful of inexpensive rooms. Visit the Gothic church or explore the narrow streets of the city core, and nibble on a crispy *baguette* from a local *boulangerie.*

St. Maximin to Aix-en-Provence: 38 kilometers

Follow signs for **Aix** out of St. Maximin and pedal steeply uphill on **N7** for about 4 km. From the crest, you'll have mostly downhill and level riding the rest of the way to Aix-en-Provence. Traffic is fairly heavy on N7, but you'll make good time through the easy terrain. Views of the rocky white mountains to the north increase the pleasantness of the ride.

Stay on N7 and follow the course of the **Arc River** into a scenic canyon, then continue on into **Aix.** Look for signs for the **center** (*centre*) as you climb a gradual hill on **Cours Gambetta** to enter the city. Continue straight, walking your bicycle through a bustling pedestrian area on rue d'Italie. Proceed to Place Forbin, where **Cours Mirabeau** angles left toward the beautiful Fontaine de la Rotonde.

Cours Mirabeau is Aix-en-Provence's lovely main boulevard. Lined with cafes and dotted with fountains, it leads to the main tourist office on **Place Général de Gaulle** (on the left across from the fountain). Get a city map, literature on the city, and accommodation information at the tourist office. There's a youth hostel in Aix, and there are lots of hotels in the streets around Cours Mirabeau.

Spend your afternoon strolling beneath the plane trees, browsing in the city's many bookstores, or sitting at a streetside cafe, and watching people watching people.

Aix-en-Provence to Les Baux: 67 kilometers

From the Aix tourist office, take **Avenue Bonaparte** to **Boulevard de la République,** and continue on past a large **supermarket,** then veer left at the next intersection onto **Road D10.** Cycle under the **train tracks** and over the **freeway,** then go straight on **Road D17** for **Eguilles.** Climb steadily to Eguilles on the quiet secondary road. Veer left onto **Road N543** at **Eguilles,** then continue straight onto **D17** for **Salon-de-Provence** and **Pélissanne.**

Descend gently to Pélissanne, an attractive small town, and swing left onto **N572** toward Salon. At the far edge of Pélissanne, go right to **regain D17** for **Salon.** Pedal the 5 km to Salon's center, entering on a long boulevard lined with plane trees. Come to a **T** by the fountain and Town Hall. Go left to get a look at the city castle, built between the 10th and the 15th centuries.

Return past the fountain (wrong way on a one-way) and turn right by the **large church.** Continue on this street to a junction with **Road N538.** Veer right toward **Avignon,** then go left a **short distance** later to gain **D17** for

Eyguières. You'll have short ups and downs for the 9 km to Eyguières, another pretty Provençal town approached by a long, tree-lined boulevard. In Eyguières, swing left onto **Road N569,** then go right onto **D17.** Intersections aren't well marked.

Pedal away from the city on D17 toward **les Baux,** climbing gently, then continuing on level terrain. The lush fields of vines give way to dry, rocky olive groves as you continue northwest toward **Arles.** Descend a short hill to the **D5 junction,** and go right toward **Mouriés** and **les Baux.** There's a campground at **Maussane,** and it makes a good base for cycling to les Baux and St. Rémy (uphill) without your bags.

If you need a room, you can pedal the 9½ km from Maussane to **St. Rémy** on **D5,** then backtrack to visit les Baux on the following day. St. Rémy has several Roman remains, including a triumphal arch and a mausoleum, but you'll have a stiff climb to reach the town. Don't pass up a visit to les Baux. It's an amazingly situated village, perched on a stern outcropping of stone and guarded by the walls of a medieval castle.

To reach ancient les Baux, turn onto **D5** for St. Rémy at **Maussane.** Ride gradually uphill for **2½ km,** then turn left for **les Baux.** Pedal steadily uphill through shimmering olive groves with the stone city on the ridge luring you on. Pass through the modern tourist village below to arrive at the long-dead city, and enjoy a spectacular view from the top.

Les Baux to Arles: 20 kilometers

Continue around the **hill** from les Baux, following signs for **D17** and **Arles** as you descend past olive groves. Go right on **D17** to pedal the final 13 km into Arles. Ride through **Fontvieille** and continue on to Montmajour Abbey with the 12th-century Church of Notre Dame. The abbey's massive walls command a hill beside the road.

Turn left onto **Road N570** and follow signs for Arles's *Centre* into town. There are several inexpensive hotels in the midsized city, and you'll have a host of sights to induce you to an afternoon of wandering. Begin at the tourist office on the **Boulevard des Lices.** To reach the office, head for the Roman Arena as you pedal into town, and continue south past the Roman Theater to the pretty Jardin d'Eté. The tourist office is just beyond the garden.

If you're planning to do some heavy-duty sightseeing in Arles, invest in a *billet global,* an overall ticket for the arena, the theater, and several other attractions. It will save you a fistful of *francs.* Don't miss Arles Cathedral with its elaborate carved portal depicting the Last Judgment, and take a melancholy walk along the Alyscamps, a quiet lane whispering with golden-leaved trees and lined with empty Christian tombs. Vincent Van Gogh painted the spot when he lived in Arles.

From Arles, you'll have the option of hooking onto Tour No. 16, Nîmes to Sens, if you'd like to head north along the Rhône River through Lyon and on into Burgundy. Nîmes is 30 km northwest of Arles via the busy N113, or you can follow this tour to **St. Gilles** and pedal 19 km on the quieter **Road D42** to arrive at **Nîmes.**

Arles to Frontignan: 92 kilometers

As you ride away from Arles, you'll be entering an area of Provence known as the Camargue. It's a marshy plain created by the Rhône River, and it holds rice fields, vineyards, and a 33,000-acre reserve for migratory birds. If you're lucky, you might spot a flock of pink flamingos on your ride.

From Arles's **tourist office**, go left on the **Boulevard des Lices** to **rue Gambetta**. Swing right on rue Gambetta to reach the **bridge** across the Rhône River. Follow signs for **Nîmes** under the **train tracks**, then angle left and follow signs for **St. Gilles** onto **Road N572**. Pedal 16 busy kilometers on N572 to St. Gilles, a midsized town with a wonderful Romanesque church. The three carved doorways on the front of the church are outstanding (if timeworn) examples of Romanesque sculpture.

Reverse your route into St. Gilles, pedaling back out on **N572** and following signs for **Marseille**, but veer right onto **Road D179** for **Aigues Mortes** just after crossing the **Rhône Canal**. Pedal through a pancake-flat agricultural delta of vineyards and rice fields on a delightfully deserted zigzagging road, staying with signs for **Aigues Mortes** along the way.

Gain **Road D58** for the final 11 km into the walled city of Aigues Mortes. St. Louis sailed from this port on a crusade to the Holy Land in 1248. Climb to the top of the wall for a view of the city and the sea, or walk the entire circuit if you have the time. Leave Aigues Mortes south on **Road D979** for **le-Grau-du-Roi**. Cross the **bridge** in the old port city, and stay beside the sea to gain **Road D255** for **la Grande-Motte**, a bizarre resort settlement filled with modernistic buildings, immaculate parks, and tidy tennis courts.

Go left for **Carnon-Plage** in la Grande-Motte, then turn right onto **Road D59** to ride between the sea and the main coast road. Traffic is heavy in this area, as the massive city of Montpellier isn't far away. Ride through **Carnon-Plage** and keep to the left for **Palavas** on **D59**. Watch for flamingos in the lake to the right of the road. Reach a junction with **Road D986** and go right for **Montpellier** and **Villeneuve**.

Pedal **3 km** and veer left for **Villeneuve** onto **Road D185**. Ride through Villeneuve and follow signs for **Mireval**. Angle right to join **Road N112** after Mireval and pedal on toward **Frontignan**. There's a small year-round campground (Camping DOC, on the left side of N112) 3 km before Frontignan. If you're looking for a room, try Frontignan or continue on to Sète.

Frontignan to Narbonne: 85 kilometers

Stay on the busy **N112** through Frontignan, and pedal the 7 km to **Sète**, a large port in the French region of Roussillon. Sète is a main port for trade with North Africa. Follow signs for the *Centre* and Béziers as you ride through Sète. Cross a **canal** and go left for **Béziers**, staying beside the sea. Reach an **intersection** on the far end of town, and veer left for **Bèziers** and **Agde.**

Pedal a flat, boring 20 km of seaside road to Agde. Go straight at the **intersection** just before town. With its forbidding black cathedral and narrow streets, Agde makes a great lunch stop—if you haven't already fallen prey to the sandy Mediterranean beaches on the route in. Follow signs for

The eroded Romanesque stone carvings on St. Gilles's church.

Bèziers through Agde, crossing the Hérault River and continuing on **N112** with a marked increase in traffic.

Pass a **turnoff** for Portiragnes, descend a **short hill,** and veer left off N112 at the bottom. Then go right onto **Road D37** and ride to **Villeneuve.** Leave Villeneuve south on **D37** toward **Sérignan,** and swing right to cross the **Orb River** into Sérignan 5 km later. Follow signs for **Vendres** through the city, and ride on **D37** through Vendres and on to **Lespignan.** Vendres, Lespignan, and Fleury are all delightful small towns.

Go left onto **Road D14** for **Fleury** in Lespignan, and cross under the **A9 freeway** and over the **Aude River.** In Fleury, follow signs for **Salles d'Aude** and ride on **Road D31** to **Coursan.** Join **Road N113** for the final 7 km to **Narbonne.** If it's late in the day, Courson has an inexpensive (albeit primitive) municipal campground. It's near the city soccer field.

Enter Narbonne on N113 and head for the Cathedral of St. Just. The cathedral is on the left, just before the Canal de la Robine. Narbonne's tourist office is on **Place Salengro,** north of the cathedral. You'll find an outstanding selection of English-language literature on the city, and you can get information on Narbonne's hotels and pensions from the office staff.

Narbonne's cathedral is an architectural freak, but it's a magnificent one. The church was begun on a grand scale in 1272, but it was never completed. As a result, the lofty Gothic choir has been left without a nave. Explore the lovely interior, exchange winks with the staring gargoyles in the cloister, then continue on to the Archbishop's Palace right next door. You'll be delighted by the sights this southern wine town has to offer. Use the tourist office map to direct your wandering.

Narbonne to Carcassonne: 58 kilometers

The ride to the walled city of Carcassonne is essentially a **two-day detour** from Narbonne, but if you have the time, it's worth the trip for the scenic pastoral cycling it provides and for the undeniable charm of Carcassonne. If you're beating a hot trail to Barcelona, however, you can easily cut out the ride to Carcassonne without leaving the tour route for long.

Leave **Narbonne** on N113, following signs for **Carcassonne.** The road is very busy, with heavy truck traffic. Pedal the unpleasant N113 west for the 12 km to **Villedaigne.** Breathe a sigh of relief as you dive right for **Homps** onto the quiet **Road D11.** Follow D11 past endless rows of vines, cycling through mild hills and silent countryside.

At the junction 8 km later, turn right onto **Road D611,** then go left for **Escales** soon after. Ride on the small road through the handsome village of Escales and keep right, continuing onto **Road D127** for **Castelnau, Roquecourbe,** and **Puichéric.** In Puichéric, veer left onto **Road D610** toward **Carcassonne.** Cross the **Midi** and the **Aude Rivers** at **Trèbes,** then rejoin **N113** for the final hectic kilometers into **Carcassonne.** You'll see the turreted walls of the old town (la Cité) on a hill above the road.

You can turn off N113 to climb the hill to la Cité, but if you're looking for a cheap room, continue on to the modern town on the banks of the Aude River and do your looking there instead. There are a few hotels within the walls of la Cité, but you'll pay for the atmosphere. There's a youth hostel on top, too.

There's a sign for Carcassonne's campground just before N113 crosses the Aude to enter the modern town. Plan to spend several hours exploring the cobblestone streets of la Cité, and be sure to visit the beautiful Cathedral of St. Nazaire with its impressive collection of stained glass. A walk along the golden-hued walls of la Cité at dawn, with a view of the snow-capped peaks of the Pyrenees beckoning from Spain, will make your visit a memorable one.

Carcassonne to Sigean: 68 kilometers

Make your way out of Carcassonne on **N113** toward **Narbonne.** Cycle past the turnoff for the **A61 freeway** and veer right **1 km** later onto **Road D3** for **Lagrasse.** Cycle roller-coaster terrain, climbing to **Monze** and **Pradelles-en-Val,** then veer left onto **Road D114** for **Camplong.** In **Montlaur,** a lovely town of stone, keep right for **Camplong,** and pedal gently downhill through a small river gorge.

Climb briefly before Camplong, then continue on past endless fields of vines, following signs to **Fabrezan.** Turn right onto **Road D611** toward **Thézan** and swing left **9 km** later, staying on D611 for Thézan. Pedal through Thézan and ride through rolling terrain to **Ripaud,** then go left onto **D611A** toward **Perpignan.** Ride along the Berre River and pass through **Portel-des-Corbières.** Cross over the **A9 freeway** as you approach **Sigean.**

From Sigean on, there are lots of opportunities for camping along the coast. If you're looking for a room, begin your search in Sigean.

Sigean to Perpignan: 50 kilometers

Leave Sigean by pedaling **south** on the busy **Road N9** for **Perpignan.** Climb two hills, then turn off N9 **11 km** outside of Sigean onto **Road D627** for **les Barcarés.** Climb a short hill, then descend to ride beside the *Etang de Leucate* and the sea. Pass a series of resort villages, complete with boat-filled harbors, tacky modern buildings, and scores of campgrounds.

Angle left to gain **Road D90** beside the sea when **D627** becomes the four-lane **D83** in **Port-Barcarés** (road signs say les Barcarés). Run the gauntlet of "campground alley" before angling inland on **D90** to reach **St. Laurent.** After the ramshackle tourist settlements on the coast, you'll appreciate the timeworn beauty of St. Laurent, a quiet stone town squatting beside its church. On the far side of town, veer left for **Torreilles** and cross the **Agly River** and a small canal, then turn right onto **Road D31** for **Perpignan.**

Follow D31 to the outskirts of Perpignan, and arrive at the **Pont Joffre** and a main road running left across the **Têt River** into the heart of the large city. There are **signs** for the **tourist office** (Syndicat d'Initiative) as you pedal in. Pick up a free city map and a list of accommodation options at the tourist office. Perpignan has good points and bad, with some rundown quarters and lots of "down-and-outers." Be sure to see the Tour du Castillet, a handsome tower on the northern edge of the old town; the Place de la Loge, an attractive square flanked by fine buildings; and the Gothic Cathedral of St. Jean, with glimmering stained glass and a poignant carved crucifix from 1307.

Perpignan to Cerbère: 53 kilometers

From Perpignan's **Place de la Resistance,** go east on **Boulevard Wilson,** and angle right onto **Boulevard Jean Bourrat.** Go right again on **Boulevard Anatole France,** then angle left on **Avenue Guynemer.** Follow Avenue Guynemer to the edge of town, and continue straight on **Chemin de Pou de Las Couloubres.** Pedal through quiet vineyards to **Saleilles** and gain **Road D22** for **Alenya.**

In Alenya, swing right onto **Road D11** for **Elne.** You'll turn left for **St. Cyprien** just before Elne, but it's worth the extra kilometers to continue into town for a look at Elne's hilltop cathedral. The cloister is a wonderful example of Romanesque stone carving.

Cycle **Road D40** toward **St. Cyprien** and turn right into **Latour** after about 1½ km. Ride through Latour, swinging right on the **edge of town** to pedal east toward **Road D81.** Go right on D81 for **Argelès-s-Mer.** Continue past Argelès and go right for **Collioure,** following signs to **Road N114.**

Veer left onto N114 for **Collioure** and exchange flat riding for a series of vine-sprinkled coastal hills.

Climb steeply for a short distance, then descend into Collioure, a beautiful harbor town ruled by a stout church and a sprinkling of hilltop forts. From Collioure, stay on **N114** for the **20** rolling **kilometers** to **Cerbère.** Summer traffic could be heavy along this section, but cars were a rarity on the December day we pedaled the route. Descend to the seaside towns of **Port-Vendres** and **Banyuls,** climbing into vine-covered hills in between.

End your day in Cerbère and celebrate your final night in France. The small town offers a handful of pensions, a campground (south of town on N114), a few well-stocked *patisseries,* and a grocery store where you can assemble a farewell feast.

Cerbère to Pals: 82 kilometers

Climb a **long hill** away from Cerbère to the crest of Cape Cerbère and an exciting look at the snakelike Spanish coast stretching to the south. Pass the **border station** with a friendly nod to the card-playing guards and descend to **Portbou,** your first Spanish city. Continue south on **Road C252,** climbing and descending to Colera, then climbing once more before the descent to **Llançà,** a midsized town with several exchange offices.

In Llançà, follow signs for **Figueres,** and angle inland along the **Balleta River.** Enjoy level riding for the rest of the day. Turn left for **Vilajuiga** after **9 km,** then cycle through quiet farmland to **Palau Saverdera.** Veer right for **Castelló.** Castelló's church has a fine carved portal and black-and-white marble stairs.

From Castelló, follow signs toward **Figueres** across the **Llobregat River,** then veer left for **Sant Pere Pescador.** Continue on toward **Vilademat** and **La Escala.** At Vilademat, go right, then turn left to take **Road C252** toward **La Tallada** and **Palafrugell.** Pedal the 9 km to **Verges** and turn left for **Torroella,** an attractive town with a fortified church and 13th-century walls.

From Torroella, continue south across the **Ter River,** following signs for **Pals** and **Palafrugell.** Pals is a medieval city perched on a ridge above the road. If you're looking for a room, Pals or Palafrugell are good places to begin. Campgrounds are abundant in this area, as well.

Pals to Arenys de Mar: 98 kilometers

From Pals, continue on to **Palafrugell,** then follow signs for Palamós onto the busy **Road C255.** Stay on the main coast road (**C253**) past **Palamós,** following signs for **Sant Feliú** along the way. In Sant Feliú, a busy resort town, stay beside the sea to ride for **Tossa de Mar.** Enjoy a hilly but exquisite ride along the cliffside route, with views of the sparkling sea and sand-rimmed, curving bays. Climb steeply from Sant Feliú and pedal up-and-down terrain for the 34 km to **Lloret de Mar.**

Tossa offers a good midway break. It's a popular resort town with a walled fishermen's quarter. Continue on to **Lloret** and follow signs for **Barcelona** to gain **Road N11** and a marked increase in traffic. Riding is easier (but more nerve wracking) from here, with scattered hills and lots of level going.

You'll have dozens of campgrounds to choose from as you pedal south past the condominium-crammed towns of **Pineda** and **Calella. Arenys de Mar** is a bit less brash than its neighbors, and its attractive streets climb away from a large pleasure-boat harbor and the sea. Hunt for a room in the city if you need a bed.

Arenys de Mar to Barcelona: 40 kilometers

You'll need courage and vigilance for your final day of riding into Barcelona. If you have an opportunity, pick up a detailed street map of Barcelona before you take on the town. Your day will go more smoothly if you do. Barcelona will reach out to embrace you with traffic and noise long before you're ready to be introduced. Console yourself with thoughts of the charms that Barcelona offers, and try to endure the curses that cycling in for a visit brings.

Continue south on **N11** to Mataró. The road splits just past the town, with the **A19 freeway** angling inland. Follow the **white Barcelona road signs** straight to stay on the **coastal road.** Unfortunately, most of the traffic will do the same. From **El Masnou,** you'll have non-stop city to pedal through.

Reach a **Y** and a second opportunity to join the freeway (to the right). Continue straight, looking for **Barcelona signs** along the way. Go under the **freeway,** over the **Congost River,** then pedal on to the wide **Guipúscoa Boulevard.** Continue to **Avenue de la Meridiana** and go left to pedal to the **Plaza de les Glories Catalanes.** Here, you'll gain the **Gran Via de les Corts Catalanes.** Continue on it into the heart of the city.

The Barcelona tourist office is at Gran Via de les Corts Catalanes 658, and the competent staff at the office will load you down with English-language pamphlets and supply you with information on accommodations. You can pick up literature on other cities in Spain at the office, as well. There's a youth hostel in Barcelona, and there are scores of affordable *hostals, residencias,* and *fondas.* The closest campground is 6 km out of town.

If you're ending your cycling with a plane or a train in Barcelona, you can get advice at the tourist office on making arrangements. Bicycles are transported on separate baggage trains in Spain, so if you're heading north for France or south for the start of Tour No. 17, you'll need to send your bicycle two or three days in advance.

Barcelona is a delightful city — a wonderful introduction to Spain. The city's Catalan inhabitants are proud, independent and creative, and Barcelona reflects the spirit of its people. Spend a day exploring the twisted streets of the Gothic Quarter (Barri Gotic) and visiting Barcelona's cathedral; lose your heart to the flower-strewn expanse of Las Ramblas, one of the most famous streets in Europe; or dive into the noise and activity of the modern city, with its fantastic Gaudi buildings, its straight-arrow boulevards, and its busy stores and theaters.

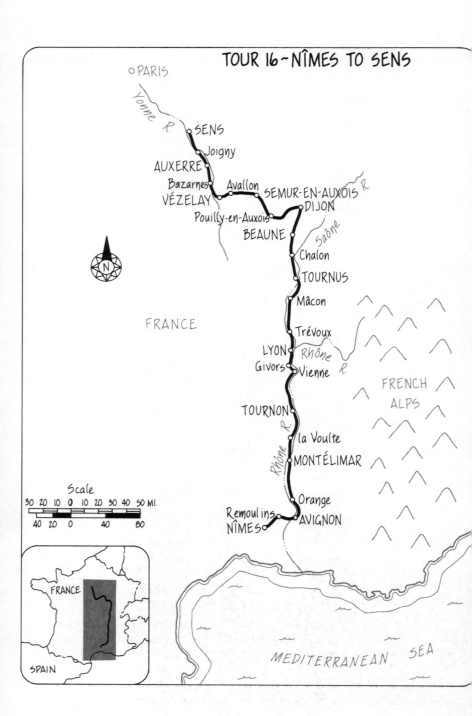

TOUR 16–NÎMES TO SENS

○ PARIS

Yonne R.

○ SENS

○ Joigny

AUXERRE ○

Bazarnes ○ Avallon ○ SEMUR-EN-AUXOIS

VÉZELAY ○ ○ ○ DIJON

Pouilly-en-Auxois ○ ○ BEAUNE

Saône

○ Chalon

○ TOURNUS

○ Mâcon

○ Trévoux

Rhône R.

LYON ○

Givors ○ ○ Vienne

TOURNON ○

○ la Voulte

Rhône R.

○ MONTÉLIMAR

FRANCE

FRENCH ALPS

○ Orange

Remoulins ○ ○ AVIGNON

NÎMES ○

Scale

30 20 10 0 10 20 30 40 50 MI.

40 20 0 40 80

FRANCE

SPAIN

MEDITERRANEAN SEA

210

TOUR NO. 16

ALL IN GOOD TASTE
Nîmes to Sens, France

Distance:	758 kilometers (471 miles)
Estimated time:	11 riding days
Best time to go:	April, May, June, or September
Terrain:	Lots of level cycling, some moderate hills
Connecting tours:	Tours No. 2 and 15

You'll get a chance to sample some of France's finest culinary treasures, and you'll pedal through some of the most famous winemaking areas in the country on this tour from Nîmes to Sens. Continue north from Sens by reversing Tour No. 2, and you'll add the captivating Champagne district to your ride through Burgundy and Provence. Big cities along the route have much to offer, and visits to some of the loveliest churches in France will mesmerize you with stunning stained glass and cunning stonework.

CONNECTIONS. Nîmes is easily accessible by train from Paris, and you can make rail connections from other cities in France, Spain, and Italy as well. There's also an airport south of the city, if you prefer to fly in. You can cycle into Nîmes by linking this tour with Tour No. 15 (check the "Les Baux to Arles" entry for details). We hopped a train to Nîmes from Madrid, Spain (end of Tour No. 18), to begin our ride north toward Sens.

INFORMATION. Michelin doesn't provide an English translation of its Burgundy or Rhône Valley *Green Guides*. However, there is an English-language *Green Guide* for Provence. *Baedeker's France, Let's Go: France,* or the *Blue Guides* for France are other guidebook options. Check the introductory section of Tour No. 2 for information on French tourist offices.

MAPS. As mentioned in Tour No. 2, Michelin maps blanket the country thoroughly, and they're inexpensive and easy to find.

ACCOMMODATIONS. Refer to the accommodation section in Tour No. 2, and check at tourist offices along your route for camping and accommodation lists.

SUPPLIES. Be sure to review the shopping suggestions in Tour No. 2 as well. You're not going to want to be caught without a meal in this domain of delicious foods. *Bon appetit!*

Nîmes to Avignon: 49 kilometers

The first-century Roman Arena in Nîmes is an impressive monument to the city's prominence in the Roman world. And its busy streets, glittering shop windows, and brightly lighted movie theaters give testimony to its modern-day prominence, as well.

You'll probably arrive in Nîmes at the main train station or via Arles and Tour No. 15. There are lots of inexpensive hotels around the train station, but the area is a bit seedy. Make your way across the city to the tourist information office at 6 rue Auguste to get help with lodgings and literature on the sights in town. Be sure to visit the Roman Arena and the cathedral, and take a walk up the hill to the Tour Magne for an impressive view of the sprawling city. The extensive gardens around the tower make a great spot for a picnic lunch.

From the main **train station,** go north on the road paralleling the train tracks, following **blue road signs** for **Avignon.** Cross **under the tracks** and go left at the **T** onto **Road N86** for Avignon. Keep to the left when the road **branches** (a right turn puts you on the freeway) and continue along the flat N86, enduring steady traffic and a narrow shoulder much of the way to Remoulins.

Just **before Remoulins,** take the left turn marked for the **Pont du Gard,** and cycle the quiet 3 km on **Road D981** to this impressive Roman aqueduct. The massive bridge makes a spectacular picnic spot, and you can wheel your bicycle out onto the ancient stones of the span to find your seat. There are campgrounds on both sides of the Pont du Gard if you're in need of a tent spot.

Backtrack to the **main road** and pass through **Remoulins,** following signs for **Avignon** on **Road N100.** Cross under the freeway and climb a long, steep hill before regaining easy cycling. Ride through rolling fields of vines and fruit trees before descending to cross the **Rhône River** and enter Avignon.

The road branches after the **bridge** across the Rhône. Angle left for **Centre.** The walls encircling the oldest part of town will be on your left. Breach Avignon's defenses by turning left in front of the **train station** onto **Cours Jean Jaurés.** The tourist office is on the right a few blocks farther on, at 41 Cours Jean Jaurés.

There are lots of inexpensive accommodations in Avignon, including a convenient municipal campground. If you visit in July, be prepared to face the hordes that come for the Festival d'Avignon — a cultural and touristic melée. Visit the Papal Palace (Palais des Papes), where the roaming and Rome-less popes settled in for 100 years. The palace is a handsome structure, and it totally overwhelms the church beside it. Avignon's old core has many fine buildings, lots of tempting shop windows, and the self-satisfied look of a popular tourist town.

Avignon to Montélimar: 81 kilometers

Retrace your route from Avignon's center on the **Cours Jean Jaurés** and turn left just outside the **city walls** onto **Boulevard Saint Roch.** Ride beside the wall and veer right on the **Route de Lyon,** following signs for **Valence.** Turn left toward Valence onto **Road N7,** and cross over the **train tracks** and **Road D225.**

Continue toward Valence and **Orange** through **Sorgues,** then abandon the busy main road to turn left onto **Road D17** for **Châteauneuf-du-Pape** and quieter riding. Enjoy the view as you approach this vine-surrounded hillside town dominated by the ruin of a stout castle. Châteauneuf-du-Pape was the summer residence of the Avignon popes, and the small town is world famous for its wine. You can stop for a tour of the popes' wine cellar if you have the time.

Continue straight **through the first intersection** when you reach the edge of the city, turn left toward **Orange** at the **next junction,** then take the right soon afterwards marked for **Orange** and the château. Climb a moderate hill through rock-strewn fields of sturdy vines, and exchange greetings with the friendly field workers as you go. Cross under the **Lyon freeway** and cycle the last few kilometers to **Orange.**

Go left at the **T** when you reach Orange, and follow signs for **Théatre Antique** as you pedal into town. Begin your Orange sightseeing at the first-century Roman theater. It's one of the best-preserved in the world. Continue on the road past the theater and turn right toward Orange's other outstanding Roman monument, a beautiful triumphal arch set on a grassy island circled by plane trees. Admire the 2,000-year-old stone arch while modern machines whiz by on the road beside you.

Cycle past the **arch,** cross the **Aigues River,** and turn right for **Sérignan.** Go left on **Road D11** after crossing under the train tracks, and follow signs toward **Bollène.** Climb a slight hill and keep left toward Bollène at the **Y.** Descend and go left onto **Road D994** at the junction marked for **Bollène** and **Valence.** Veer right for **St. Paul** soon after.

Follow signs for St. Paul onto **Road D26,** a busy road with a comfortable shoulder, and continue straight for about **14 km.** Then angle left for **Donzère.** Cross Road N7, cruise into Donzère and turn right for **Montélimar.** Go left for **Châteauneuf-du-Rhône** on the edge of Donzère. Climb a moderate hill on **Road D144** before descending steeply once again.

Châteauneuf-du-Rhône is a haunting town, set into a hillside where the skeleton of a gutted castle looks out toward the industrial haze of the Rhône Valley. There's a small municipal campground in town that's open mid-June to mid-September. Follow signs for **Montélimar** out of town and onto **Road D73,** and continue into the outskirts of the large industrial city, famed as the nougat capital of France.

Try to resist the nougat posters and watch for *Centre* signs instead as you pedal into the city. There's a pleasant riverside campground in the heart of town (on the right as you cross the bridge). Room options are also available.

Montélimar to Tournon: 66 kilometers

From the **bridge** by the campground, continue north through the next **intersection,** then angle left at the following **Y.** Go past the turnoff for the train station, and veer left for the **Aerodrome.** Stay left as the road branches again, pass under the **train tracks,** and gain **rue Rochemaure.** Cycle along this quiet road, following signs for **Rochemaure** as you cross **Road N7,** the Rhône, and the Rhône Canal.

At Rochemaure, an attractive town with a set of ridgetop ruins, link up with **Road N86** and head north along the Rhône toward **Lyon.** There are roads on both sides of the flat Rhône Valley, but we chose the east side, hoping for fewer cars along the route. As it was, the traffic was heavy enough to be irritating, but the interesting towns along the way, the flat riverside riding, and the endless vistas of vines made the pedaling pleasant.

Watch for the handsome Romanesque church in Cruas, the hilltop château at la Voulte, and the majestic fortified château at Châteaubourg that gazes out toward the Rhône over acres of fruit trees. There are a campground and a handful of inexpensive hotels in **Tournon,** a small Rhône city. Venture out to stroll the old core, where a stout fortified château commands a massive chunk of rock, and visit the quiet church below the château. It has a velvet-dark interior colored by stained glass.

Tournon to Lyon: 97 kilometers

Vines and orchards line the easy ride **north** from Tournon along the Rhône. Continue on **N86** along the **west bank** of the river. The road is level, with a good surface, moderate traffic, and no shoulder most of the way. At **Andance,** the road branches. Keep to the right toward **Lyon,** staying on the west side of the river. Pass through **Serrières,** a city with an attractive church, then continue on for **Condrieu.** You can share *baguette* crumbs from your lunch with the hungry swans at a waterfront park in Condrieu.

You may be tempted to cross the river at **Vienne,** a midsized town that boasts several handsome churches. Or you can enjoy the view from across the river while cycling a paved waterside bike path. It's marked with small **blue bike path signs** from the main road. The path turns into a small road along the Rhône. Cross **under the freeway** on the road. Then go left to pass under the **train tracks** and regain N86 for **Lyon.**

At **Givors,** a sprawling industrial city with little appeal, cross the **Gier River,** go over the **freeway,** and take the first right. Follow signs for **Grigny.** You'll leave the main road for the rest of the ride to Lyon. Follow signs for **Vernaison,** crossing under the train tracks, then over the train tracks, and then turning right on **Road D15** for **Vernaison** and **Lyon.**

Short rolling hills and a narrow road with steady traffic will keep you occupied for a few kilometers, but you'll catch glimpses of Lyon's skyscraper-studded profile as you pedal on. Cross a main road and continue straight into **Pierre-Bénite,** paralleling the freeway until an intersection with **N86.** **Cross N86** and follow the **west bank** of the **Saône River** into France's third-largest city.

The riverside route leads straight into the Vieille Ville, where the Cathedral of St. Jean snuggles at the foot of the hill of Fourvière, over-looked by the basilica of Notre Dame de la Fourvière. Don't skip a climb to the top of the hill. On a clear day, you can see all the way to Mont Blanc and the snow-capped French Alps.

There's a deluxe campground in Lyon, as well as a youth hostel and countless hotels. For information on the city and the area, visit the large tourist office at **Place Bellecour** on the east side of the Saône. From the old town, cross the Saône on **Pont Bonaparte** and continue straight to reach Place Bellecour.

There are a host of museums, churches, and interesting buildings in Lyon.

The view from a hotel room on Tournus's main square.

Be sure to ask at the tourist office for the brochure that details a walking tour of the old town. The Cathedral of St. Jean, with its lovely stained-glass windows and its subtle blend of somber half-darkness and luminous soaring pillars, makes a memorable stop along the way.

Lyon to Tournus: 110 kilometers

Leave Lyon by continuing **north** along the **west bank** of the Saône. Reach an intersection with **N7**, but continue straight to stay on the quieter **Road D51** along the river. At **Villevert**, turn right to cross the Saône for **Neuville-sur-Saône**, then veer left onto **Road D433** toward **Trévoux**. The terrain is flat or gently rolling for most of the day.

Trévoux is an attractive riverside town with a large Romanesque church perched on a bluff above the water. Traffic is lighter after the city. Continue on **Road D933** for **Chalon** and **St. Didier-sur-Chalaronne.** Churches give way to a long string of mammoth châteaux beyond Beauregard. Pass through **St. Didier,** continuing on D933, then turn left onto **D51** for **Cormoranche** just after a **sharp curve** leads into a gradual hill.

In **Cormoranche,** angle right toward **Grièges.** Then continue on D51, staying to the left for **St. Laurent** and **Mâcon.** Reach a junction in **St. Laurent** and go right, then take the **first left** (unsigned) to gain **Road D68A** toward **Replonges.** Mâcon is just across the Saône from St. Laurer⸱ It offers hotel rooms and a pretty waterfront, if you're looking for a place ⸱ end the day.

Turn left onto **Road D933** at **Replonges** and pass through gently rolling terrain to **Pont-de-Vaux.** Explore this bustling town with attractive old buildings and a busy main street. There's a small municipal campground nearby. Stay on D933 through Pont-de-Vaux and pedal on through Arbigny and **Sermoyer.** Then angle left onto **Road D476** for a tree-lined ride to **Préty.**

Reach Préty and turn right at the **junction** marked for **Tournus.** Follow signs for Tournus into **Lacrost.** Ride through Lacrost and keep right at the **Y** to enter **Tournus** on a **secondary road.** There's a campground on the east bank of the Saône, or you can cross the bridge into town to look for a room. The Tournus tourist office is at **Place Carnot** on rue du Centre. It's to the left as you ride into the city. The office has English-language literature on the town and its ninth-century St. Philibert Abbey. The abbey church has a complex interior with stout round columns of pinkish stone and incredibly complicated vaulting. It's worth a visit.

Tournus to Beaune: 55 kilometers

If you'd like to trade a few extra kilometers of riding for lighter traffic, **backtrack** from Tournus to **Lacrost** and go left on **Road D44** through **l'Abergement.** Then turn left onto **D933** toward **Chalon.** We endured heavy traffic and shoulderless riding by choosing **Road N6** instead, and we wished we hadn't. **Sennecey** is one of the few bright spots on the N6 route. It's an attractive town with a walled monastery complex.

Enter the growing industrial city of **Chalon,** and reach a junction with **Road N75** (the other route joins here from across the Saône). Continue hugging the west bank of the river and turn **left** at the **next intersection** to dive into the city proper. You may want to stop to investigate the large, twin-towered church or the photography museum in Chalon. We simply battled through the heavy traffic and yearned for the city limits.

Pedal through town, following signs for the **airport.** Cross a set of **train tracks** as the city begins to fade. Veer right onto **Road D19** for **Demigny** just past some large **sports fields.** Enjoy the lightly traveled route through the Forêt de Gergy and pedal toward Demigny. Re-enter rolling, open countryside after Demigny, and continue on **Road D18** for the final 10½ km to **Beaune.**

Beaune's tourist office is across from the Hôtel-Dieu in the heart of the old walled city. You can pick up information on accommodations or on visiting the numerous local wineries specializing in the famed Burgundys of the Beaune hills. Don't miss a visit to the colorful 15th-century Hôtel-Dieu with its fantastic tiled roof and an unforgettable painting of the Last Judgment by Roger van der Weyden. A visit to the Collegiate Church of Notre Dame and a walk around the old town are also rewarding.

There's a campground north of town on the road to Dijon (open March through October), or get a list of hotels from the tourist office. Prices are high for rooms and restaurant meals in this popular tourist town, but there are a few "one-star" hotels outside the city center that are affordable.

Beaune to Dijon: 39 kilometers

It's a short, easy ride to **Dijon** from Beaune — barely enough pedaling to help you work up an appetite for one of the gastronomic capitals of France. You can follow **Road N74** the entire way, putting up with lots of cars as you pass through sprawling vineyards and steal glimpses of regal-looking country homes set back from the road. Or, if you have extra time and favorable weather, you can try out some of the secondary roads that parallel the main road, and take a more meandering route to Dijon.

Our weather was cold and grey, so we pedaled doggedly north through rolling hills to Dijon, planning our sightseeing while we watched dozens of gloved and jacketed field workers trimming and burning the winter-bare vines. Enter Dijon on **N74,** following signs for *Centre Ville.* A **Y** intersection leads left for the **tourist office** and right for the center. Go left, then angle right to cross under the **train tracks** toward *Centre Ville* once more.

Reach a busy intersection at Place Darcy with a large stone arch (Porte Guillaume) on the right. Dijon's tourist office is to the left, in the building with the Air France sign. Be sure to ask for their walking tour of the city. Dijon has a campground (2 km west of town on Avenue Albert 1er), and there's a youth hostel in the city, too.

Walk your bicycle through the Place Darcy and past the Porte Guillaume onto the busy main street of Dijon, the rue de la Liberté. This street leads to the impressive Place de la Liberation and the Palace of the Dukes of Burgundy, which houses an outstanding museum. You won't find a church facade to match the one on the Church of Notre Dame, and the Cathedral of St. Bénigne is worth a visit, too.

Spend a long afternoon tracing the route of the walking tour and investigating the Palace of the Dukes of Burgundy, then plan a proper Burgundian feast to quiet your hunger pangs. A restaurant meal of *boeuf bourgignon* or a cookstove supper of hot sausages and Dijon mustard (*moutarde*) will make your stomach murmur with delight.

Dijon to Semur-en-Auxois: 90 kilometers

Leave Dijon on **Road N5** west, following signs for **Paris.** At **Plombières,** continue straight onto **Road D10** toward **Velars,** forsaking the freeway-

The rounded towers and spire-topped church of Semur-en-Auxois.

bound N5 and heavy traffic. Turn left to cross the **canal** in Velars, then go right onto **Road D905**. Cross under the **freeway** just before **Pont-de-Pany,** following signs toward **Sombernon.** Then turn left onto **Road D33** toward **Pont-d'Ouche.**

Parallel the Canal de Bourgogne along a scenic valley for about 20 km, then veer right at Pont-d'Ouche onto **Road D18** for **Pouilly-en-Auxois.** The canal turns here as well, and the smooth, quiet roads and pastoral scenery produce wonderful cycling. A lovely hilltop château with rounded towers dominates the valley at Châteauneuf. Pass within a few kilometers of the château as you follow **D18** into **Vandenesse.** Then go left under the **freeway** and turn right for **Pouilly.**

From Pouilly, ride through rolling hills along **Road D970** toward **Semur-en-Auxois.** There's a 13th-century church with a lofty choir at **St. Thibault.** Go left for a short distance on **Road D70,** then turn right to **regain D970,** and pedal the final 14 km to Semur-en-Auxois.

Semur-en-Auxois is a walled city perched on a bluff above a meandering river. Its picturesque skyline is studded with towers, walls, and a tall Gothic church. Follow signs for **Avallon** and **Centre** through the cobblestone streets of town. The Church of Notre Dame is a beautiful twin-towered sanctuary covered with cavorting stone creatures and made awesome by a narrow, soaring nave.

There are a handful of hotels in Semur, or you can continue another 15 km to the tiny village of **Toutry,** where a creekside campground awaits. Save a photograph for your backward glance at Semur when you leave. The best view of towers and church is from the Avallon road.

Semur-en-Auxois to Vézelay: 53 kilometers

Leave Semur on **Road D954** toward **Avallon,** climbing a steep hill away from town. The route from Semur follows gently rolling terrain to Pouligny, then cycling is easy again. A walled and moated château at **Epoisses** will invite you to explore. Pass **Toutry** and its municipal campground, and follow **Road D11** across the creek and up the hill toward **Avallon.**

Veer right toward **Guillon** just before the **freeway** overpass. From Guillon, continue straight on the quiet **Road D50** for **Avallon,** climbing a short hill and gaining the busy **Road N6** for the final 5 km into town. Admire the carved portals of Avallon's church and get a close-up look at its clock tower by turning left off N6 at the sign for **Centre** and **Vézelay** via Vallée du Cousin. Ride through the old clock tower and arrive at the church. Avallon's tourist office is nearby.

To resume your ride to Vézelay, continue on the road past the church and descend a **steep hill.** Go left just before the bottom at a sign for **Vézelay,** and follow the winding and beautiful Vallée du Cousin to **Pontaubert.** In Pontaubert, turn left onto **Road D957** for **Vézelay.** The road climbs gradually at first, then more steeply to crest before Fontette. Watch for Vézelay's striking church commanding a distant summit.

Descend quickly to St. Père (there's a campground here), then climb steeply for the final 2 km to Vézelay and its Basilique de la Madeleine. There are a handful of hotels in the ridgetop city. Buy a guidebook at the Basilique and spend a couple of hours wandering among the carved columns and deciphering the stories in the stone. The tympanum carved above the inner portal is a magnificent example of Romanesque art.

Vézelay to Auxerre: 54 kilometers

From Vézelay, descend on **Road D951** toward **Clamecy.** Turn right at the bottom of the hill onto **Road D36** for **Châtel-Censoir** and **Asnières.** Climb a long, steady hill, then descend to Asnières. Traffic is light and the scenery is lovely as you pedal **Road D100** to Châtel-Censoir. From Châtel-Censoir, follow signs for Auxerre. Cross the **Yonne River** to **la Gravelle,** a pretty riverside town.

Continue on **D100** and leave the Yonne at **Bazarnes** to climb a long, gradual hill toward Auxerre, then descend to **N6** and turn left. Follow N6 to **Bellombre** and continue straight for **Vaux** onto **Road D163** (don't recross the Yonne). Enter Auxerre along the west bank of the Yonne. The massive bulk of its hilltop cathedral will draw you on. There's a well-marked campground on the left as you approach the city.

Keep right at the **first main junction** in Auxerre, and follow the **west riverbank** to the tourist office, just below the Cathedral of St. Etienne. On its perch above the city and the Yonne, the cathedral is an impressive Gothic blend of flying buttresses and flamboyant design. The facade is beautiful, and the interior is a wonderful weave of soaring pillars and glowing glass.

Wander the streets of Auxerre and stop to visit its many churches. Pick up a custard (*flan*) or an ice-cream sundae (*coupe glacée*), and savor the flavor of life in France.

Auxerre to Sens: 64 kilometers

Leave Auxerre, following signs for **Joigny** and **Sens** on **N6.** Climb briefly away from town, then enjoy flat, easy riding. The road has moderate traffic. Follow the Yonne toward Joigny and veer left onto **Road D955** just before crossing over the **train tracks** on the southern edge of Joigny. Ride about **2 km** and turn right on **Road D582** at a sign marked *VERS C. D943.* Cycle on the small road to reach **Road D943** and go left. Ride a short distance, then veer right for **St. Julien** and **Villeneuve.**

Pedal through St. Julien and continue through level terrain to Villeneuve, an attractive small town with a handsome church. At Villeneuve, cross the train tracks and go straight for **Rousson.** Begin following signs for **Sens,** staying on **Road D72** for the final 17 km of the day.

Approach Sens and follow signs for the **Centre.** Cross the **Yonne River** into town and look for tourist information signs to lead you to the tourist office a few blocks from the cathedral. Refer to the entry for Sens in Tour No. 2 to get more information on the city and its sights. From Sens, you can join Tour No. 2 and cycle west toward Fontainebleau and Paris, or reverse the tour route and pedal north into Champagne and on to Brussels.

TOUR NO. 17

COASTING THE SOL
Málaga, Spain, to Lisbon, Portugal

Distance: 864 kilometers (536 miles)
Estimated time: 11 riding days
Best time to go: April, May, June, September, October, or November
Terrain: A blend of easy pedaling and horrendous hills
Connecting tours: Tours No. 15 and 18

Spain is a vast, diverse, and rugged land, and the Spaniards are friendly, easy-going hosts. Spain's culture, history, and spectacular natural beauty combine to make the country an excellent place to explore by bicycle. Be cautious on the busy coastal roads — more because of the speeding Northern European tourists than the local drivers. And use common sense about your money and belongings in big tourist cities like Barcelona, Málaga, Seville, and Madrid. Be careful, enthusiastic, and appreciative, and you'll discover a treasure-filled land of art, architecture, and religious heritage that will make your visit special.

Work on your language skills while you ride. The Spaniards won't ridicule your fumbling. Instead, they'll greet even your weakest efforts with warmth and appreciation. If you have time, read a book on Spain before you go, and gain some understanding of this country that once ruled much of the New World. James Michener's *Iberia* is an excellent choice.

CONNECTIONS. You can reach Málaga and the start of this tour by pedaling from Barcelona and the end of Tour No. 15, riding through Valencia and Almería along the way (this is the route we took). Or you can travel to Málaga by plane or train from Madrid (end of Tour No. 18). Málaga also has ferry connections with Melilla, Ceuta, and Tangiers in Africa.

INFORMATION. Write ahead to the Spanish National Tourist Office, 665 Fifth Avenue, New York, New York 10022, and ask for information on specific cities, city maps, campground information, and so forth.

An overall guidebook is also nice to have. *Baedeker's Spain,* the *Blue Guide Spain,* Michelin's *Green Guide Spain* and *Let's Go: Spain, Portugal, and Morocco* are all good options. Once in Spain, look for *Turismo* offices. In Barcelona, Madrid, and Seville, you can stock up on beautifully illustrated English-language pamphlets for the whole country.

For preparatory information on cycling in Portugal, skip ahead to the introduction for Tour No. 18.

MAPS. For route finding on this tour, you can use Michelin's 1:400,000

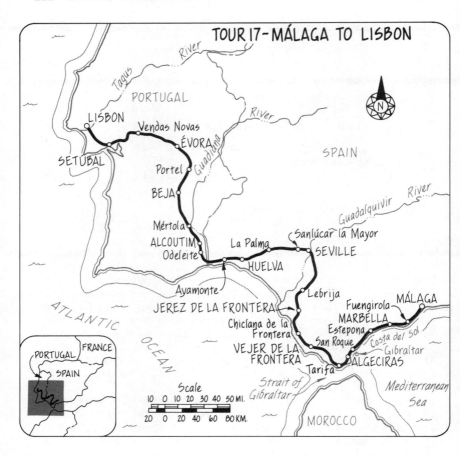

series for Spain (Nos. 446 and 447) and its 1:500,000 map (No. 37) for Portugal. A good option for the *Costa del Sol* is the *Firestone Mapa Turistico* at a scale of 1:200,000. It indicates sights of interest, campgrounds, and hotels.

ACCOMMODATIONS. Campgrounds in Spain are plentiful along the coast and near large cities. They're generally clean and inexpensive. Tourist offices supply the *Mapa de Campings,* a pamphlet that lists campgrounds all over Spain by area and by rating. The Spanish rating system has little to do with the price of camping; however, it can have a bearing on the quality of the facilities. Freelance camping is acceptable as long as you stay away from populated areas. Always ask for permission.

Rooms in Spain are delightfully affordable and Spanish hosts are usually good natured about finding a spot for a road-weary bicycle. Look for *fondas, pensiones, hostal-residencias,* and hotels. Check out rooms in advance and

The intricate design of a Spanish street.

look for the prices listed on the doors. Breakfast may or may not be included, and showers usually cost extra.

If you want to splurge occasionally, the Spanish government maintains a network of *paradors* in castles, palaces, and historic buildings that make for special one-night stops. Ask for a list from the Spanish National Tourist Office. You may need reservations.

SUPPLIES. Eating well in Spain is another inexpensive treat. Specialties in restaurants include the delicious rice and seafood dish called *paëlla* and a huge assortment of seafoods such as squid (*calamares*) and cod (*vizcaina*).

Picnic materials abound as well, with a host of regional cheeses, lots of tasty lunchmeats, and incredibly inexpensive tins of tuna and sardines. Spanish beer (*cerveza*) is excellent and a bottle of red wine (*vino tinto*) accompanies almost every Spanish meal. Don't leave Spain without sampling a breakfast snack of *churros* — a deep-fried treat that will line your stomach walls with lead — along with a cup of delicious Spanish coffee.

Stores are generally open Monday through Friday from 9:00 a.m. to 8:00 p.m., with an afternoon shutdown between 1:30 and 5:00 p.m. You can shop on Saturday morning for the weekend, but most Spanish skopkeepers lock up Saturday afternoon and all day Sunday.

The Spaniards are serious about cycling, so there are scores of good bicycle shops in the country. Of course, "cycling" means racing here, so you won't find specialized touring gear. You will find helpful, interested bike shop owners, however.

Málaga to Marbella: 56 kilometers

Málaga is the somewhat glitzy capital of the Coast of Sun — the *Costa del Sol*. Try not to be too put off by this modern, tourist-infested city. It really is a slice of Europe. Málaga is the annual vacation destination of thousands of sun-seeking northerners.

The city is big and brash. Take time to appreciate its finer points — the 16th-century cathedral, the Moorish palace, and the colorful downtown promenade (Paseo del Parque) — then begin your pedaling toward Portugal. Málaga's tourist office is at Marques de Larios 5, near the cathedral. There are scores of inexpensive rooms in the city, and there's a youth hostel, as well.

Leave Málaga by cycling **west** along the **harborside road** to the Plaza de Queipo de Llano. Follow signs for **Torremolinos** onto **Road N340.** The cycling is nasty at first, as traffic is heavy around Málaga. Unfortunately, the main coast road is also the only coast road. Bear with the speeding trucks and flying cars as you pedal the 13 km to Torremolinos, a wasteland of high-rise apartments and condominiums. Follow signs for **Fuengirola** from there.

Cycle through small, rolling hills as traffic begins to lessen and development thins. **Fuengirola** is another bizarre Costa del Sol city. Swing left off **N340** to cycle through **town.** English signs hang from almost every shop, and elderly tourists stroll the shop-lined streets. Rejoin **N340** and follow signs for **Marbella** to pedal the final 27 km of the day.

Pass one luxury development after another. There are scores of deluxe hotels and a handful of campgrounds along the way. The large campground just past **Elviria** is open all year. In Marbella, a Spanish town with tourism in its blood, explore the narrow, flower-hung streets of the eastern quarter to get a glimpse of an older and more desirable Spain. There are lots of *hostals* and *fondas* in Marbella, and there's a youth hostel, too. The tourist office is at Avenida Miguel Cano 1, and you can get a map and accommodation list there.

Marbella to Algeciras: 77 kilometers

Leave Marbella on **N340,** cycling west toward **Estepona.** Enjoy mostly flat, easy riding on four-lane road for the 28 km to Estepona. Traffic travels fast along this stretch, so hug the shoulder and ride cautiously. From Estepona on, you'll see a change for the better in riding conditions — lighter traffic and fewer tourist developments are good omens of pleasant cycling to come. As you leave Estepona and cycle along the Mediterranean shoreline, begin scanning the coast ahead for the mighty bulge of **Gibraltar** rising out of the sea.

At **San Roque Torre Guadiaro,** leave flat riding and the concentrated tourism of the Costa del Sol behind, and **climb steadily** for about **10 km** on N340. Rolling green hillsides dotted with cork trees and wandering cattle, vistas of the shimmering sea, and views of Gibraltar and the dark mountains of North Africa make the ride a pleasant one. Just beyond the **pass,** a turnoff for **La Linea** will take you down to the sea and the Rock of Gibraltar. Or you can continue on the **main road,** descending to **San Roque,** and ride to La Linea from there.

When we cycled this tour, the British and Spanish forces had not yet reopened the border at Gibraltar. Currently, the crossing from Spain to the British-held outpost is open. Unless you really want to say you've been there, settle for the view of Gibraltar from afar. The view is really the best thing about the famous Rock.

Continue on through increasing congestion to the sprawling port of **Algeciras.** From the harbor, you'll get one of your finest views of Gibraltar. Algeciras has frequent **ferry** connections with Ceuta and Tangier in **North Africa.** It also has a disproportionately large itinerant population, so be especially careful with your gear in the city.

There are lots of cheap accommodations in the old town around the harbor, and there's a campground near the city, as well. Check at the tourist office near the harbor for more information.

Algeciras to Vejer de la Frontera: 72 kilometers

Climb away from Algeciras on **N340** toward **Tarifa** and **Cádiz.** Ascend steadily for about 9 km, riding through quiet grazing land dotted with cork and enjoying views of Africa across the Strait of Gibraltar. Descend steeply and climb again to a second pass, then coast downhill to Tarifa, the most southerly point of Spain. From the small port city, Africa is less than 15 km away, separated from Europe only by the narrow Strait.

Cruise down past the whitewashed houses of Tarifa's old core, entering through a fine medieval gateway. The castle of Guzmán the Good rules the town, and Atlantic waves lap Tarifa's sandy beaches.

From Tarifa, turn northwest on **N340,** paralleling the coast for a flat **10 km** and passing several campgrounds on the way. Turn inland to climb gradually toward **Vejer de la Frontera.** Enter a long, broad valley, and watch for the majestic black bulls who share their pastures with gangly storks.

Cycle through gently rolling hills to Vejer, a striking white city flowing down a steep hillside. A Moorish castle rules the heights. To reach Vejer, climb 2½ **km** away from **N340** on a **winding road.** There are several accommodation options in the city.

Vejer de la Frontera to Jerez de la Frontera: 70 kilometers

From Vejer, continue on **N340** toward **Cádiz.** As you draw near the Atlantic once again, the terrain flattens and signs of development increase.

Pedal the 29 km to **Chiclana de la Frontera,** a pretty fishing town, and continue on **N340** for Cádiz. Reach an intersection with **Road N IV** and go right toward **Puerto Real** and **Seville** (Sevilla).

Cycle through salt flats for about 10 km. From Puerto Real, continue straight for **Seville** and **El Puerto,** staying on **N IV** and pedaling toward Jerez de la Frontera. Road N IV has heavy traffic for the 14 km to **Jerez de la Frontera.**

Jerez de la Frontera, the sherry capital of Spain, has a booming sherry and brandy industry, and the vast fields of vines and countless advertisements that surround the city give evidence of the trade. Enter Jerez on N IV and continue into the **city center.** Pass the Alcázar, the city's Moorish fortress, and enter the busy heart of town. There are several *hostals* and *residencias* near **Plaza Reyes Católicos.**

You can sign up for a tour at one of the wine cellars (*bodegas*) in Jerez, but don't neglect the city's other attractions. There are several fine churches in Jerez, and the narrow streets of the old town are wonderful to explore.

Jerez de la Frontera to Seville: 100 kilometers

Plan to get an early start for this day of cycling. It's a long one, but the terrain is easy and the spirited city of Seville awaits. Treat yourself to several kilometers of quiet country riding by staying off the main road to Seville (N IV) and taking the **secondary road (CA 601)** for **Trebujena** instead. Unfortunately, it's hard to find from Jerez's center. **Retrace your route** out of town, and turn right onto the **N IV bypass road** that circles west of Jerez's center. Pass a turnoff for Sanlúcar, and watch for a **turn signed for Trebujena.** Ask a local, if you can't find the turn.

Cycle through rolling farm and grazing land for the 23 km to Trebujena. This city has a permanent place in our hearts as one of the friendliest towns in Europe. When we rode through Trebujena during a steady Andalusian downpour, soaked to the skin and thoroughly miserable, everyone in town cheered us on from the shelter of cafes, houses, and garages, and their encouragement warmed our soggy spirits for the remainder of the day.

The terrain grows more level after **Trebujena.** Veer right onto **Road C441** toward **Seville** and **Lebrija,** and ride through flat, marshy countryside. Pass Lebrija and continue on to cross the **A4 freeway** and reach **Las Cabezas.** Follow signs for Seville and pedal **14 km** on the quiet **C441** before rejoining **N IV** for the final 39 km of the day.

There's a wide shoulder on the busy road, so the ride isn't too unpleasant. You'll have tidy fields of olives to cheer you along the way. Despite its position as Spain's fourth-largest city, Seville isn't really a headache to cycle into. N IV widens to four lanes at **Dos Hermanas,** 17 km from the city. Continue into Seville, following signs for the *Centro.*

Enter Seville on **Paseo de las Delicias,** the street bordering the large Parque de Maria Luisa. Angle right onto **Avenida de Roma** just past the **San Telmo Palace.** Follow Avenida de Roma to the Plaza Calvo Sotelo. Seville's tourist office is a short distance farther on at Avenida de la Constitución 21B. Pick up information on lodgings and sightseeing at the tourist office. The staff is competent and helpful.

Seville's cathedral is the hub of a lovely city.

Seville has a youth hostel and a few inconveniently located campgrounds. You should be able to find an affordable room without difficulty, however. Stow your bicycle and gear and begin your love affair with a beautiful city. Start at Seville's cathedral, a fantastic structure of soaring stone that will mesmerize you for hours. Climb to the top of the cathedral's *Giralda,* a Moorish minaret transformed into a Christian church tower. The view from the top is magnificent.

Seville has too many treasures to list here, so be sure to pick up some English-language literature and plan to invest a couple of days in the city. Since this tour turns west for Portugal from Seville, you might want to consider a one-day detour by train or bus to visit Córdoba, the Muslim-influenced city to the east. It's a two-hour ride by train, buses are slightly slower and more expensive. A visit to Córdoba's unique cathedral/mosque makes the trip worthwhile.

Seville to Huelva: 96 kilometers

From Seville's **cathedral,** follow signs for **Huelva** to gain the **Paseo de Cristobal Colon** along the banks of the Guadalquivir River. Cycle north along the river and turn left just before the **train station** to cross the

Guadalquivir, following signs for Huelva. The road turns into freeway after it crosses a second bridge. Take the exit marked for **Road N431** and **Castilleja,** and climb a steady hill away from Seville.

Ride through Castilleja and **Espartinas,** cycling roller coaster terrain. Descend swiftly after **Sanlúcar la Mayor.** You'll see olives, vines, citrus orchards, cork, and eucalyptus as you pedal the lightly trafficked N431 toward **La Palma.** Swing left **off the main road** to pass through La Palma, and look for the stork nests on top of the city church. **Rejoin N431** outside of town.

Climb a short hill at **Niebla,** a small walled city, and continue through level countryside to **San Juan del Puerto.** Follow signs for **Huelva** and pedal into the midsized port city. In 1492, Christopher Columbus sailed for the New World from the Huelva estuary, and he returned in 1493, to change the face of Spain forever.

You can find cheap accommodations in the streets around Huelva's **train station.** There's a campground several kilometers beyond the city. It's noted in the next section.

Huelva to Alcoutim (Junction): 90 kilometers

From Huelva, follow signs for **Punta Umbria** and **Ayamonte.** Cross a long **bridge** on **Road H414** over the estuary, and take the route signed for **Ayamonte** and **Portugal** to join N431 heading west. There's a campground on the road to Punta Umbria, about 10 km from Huelva. Go left on **N431** and pedal through rolling terrain for the 36 km to **Ayamonte** and the Spanish/Portuguese border.

In Ayamonte, an attractive seaside town, follow signs for **Portugal** to reach the **ferry** across the **Guadiana River.** Crossings are frequent, short, and inexpensive. Arrive at the small border town of **Vila Real** and pass through a businesslike customs post before diving into town. There's a tourist office next to the customs building. Stop to pick up literature for your ride. By the way, you'll need to set your watch back an hour with the border crossing, as Portugal is an hour off of Spanish time.

Filled to the brim with the tourist trappings of the Costa del Sol, we decided to pass up a ride west along Portugal's famed Algarve Coast, riding north instead to search for more serene inland riding. As a result, we enjoyed two days of incredibly tough hills, uncomfortably rough roads, and some of the loveliest scenery and most uncluttered countryside we found in all of Europe.

If you don't have camping equipment, you may want to look for a room in Vila Real and ride for Mértola (72 km) the following day. Lodging options are few and far between once you leave the coast. If you're camping, carry an evening meal and plenty of liquids.

From Vila Real, follow signs for **Lisbon** (Lisboa) and **Castro Marim** out of town. Turn right for Castro Marim and Lisbon onto **Road 122** and cycle past Castro Marim's brightly painted houses and hilltop fort before winding into the Portuguese countryside on a roughly paved road. You'll have grueling uphills and bone-rattling downhills as you ride through a gorgeous blend of farmland and cork forests.

Watch women doing their laundry in streams beside whitewashed villages and wave to the men plowing vast fields behind straining teams of oxen, and you'll feel as though you're pedaling back in time. Battle the hills past small towns like **Azinhal** and **Odeleite,** and let your legs dictate the day's distance. We pulled off the road a few kilometers before the Alcoutim junction, pitched our tent while the stars glimmered overhead, and fell asleep feeling hill weary, road rattled, and deeply in love with Portugal.

Alcoutim (Junction) to Beja: 82 kilometers

The terrain is brutal for the 35 km to Mértola. It's an almost constant series of ups and downs, and the rough road surface makes even the downhills a challenge. The vibrant green countryside and the smiles of black-garbed women in the fields will ease your suffering while you ride. Mértola is a stunning fortresslike city crowning a rounded hill, and pink, blossom-laden trees color the slope below it.

Life will come to a stop in the small town as you pedal through, but the staring locals will offer friendly smiles in return for yours. Stay on **Road 122** for **Beja** as you leave Mértola. Climb a long hill to the **Alentejo Plateau.** The hills flatten out as you enter a gently rolling landscape of green fields dotted with cork and olive, carob and eucalyptus.

Pedal into **Beja,** an attractive city with a busy agricultural trade. The 13th-century castle on the northern edge of town is worth exploring, as is the nearby former Convent of the Conception. And the old streets around the castle, lined with tile-fronted buildings and overhung with wrought-iron balconies, are a treat to wander through.

There are several *pensões* in the city, and there's a municipal campground southwest of town.

Beja to Évora: 78 kilometers

From Beja's **castle** (look for signs for *Castel*), angle to the left, following signs for **Lisbon** and **Évora.** Coast downhill to the Alentejo Plain. Stay with signs for Évora, cycling north on **Road 18.** Enjoy easy riding through flat wheatlands for the 23 km to **Vidigueira,** an attractive whitewashed town. Stay on Road 18 toward **Évora** and climb into rolling hills covered with cork trees. Portugal is the world's leading producer of cork, and you'll see why as you pedal past endless rows of trees.

Pass **Portel,** a small, castle-shadowed town, and continue north through rolling hills. Then cruise through a long descent to **Monte de Trigo.** Traffic is light and the road surface is good along the way. The terrain softens after Monte de Trigo, and you'll cycle through a wide, wheat- and cork-covered plain.

A molar-loosening **4-km of rough cobblestone** road begins just before the intersection with **Road 256.** Rattle through to the **junction,** then gain gloriously smooth pavement, swinging left to sail the final 16 km into **Évora.** Enter Évora and follow signs for the **city center.** The tourist office is in the central square, Praça do Giraldo. You can get a map of town and accommodation information there.

Portuguese schoolchildren claim a corner for a rope-jumping game in Évora.

Évora offers a youth hostel, a campground, and several inexpensive *pensões*. The city dates back to Roman times, and one of its chief treasures is the second-century Temple of Diana, a beautiful collection of standing marble columns that looks like it should be in Greece. The 12th-century cathedral (*Sé*) is also a treat, with carved choir stalls and an interesting treasury. And don't miss the Ossuary Chapel of the Church of San Francisco. This "chapel of bones" is a sight you won't soon forget.

After your day of sightseeing, join the Portuguese for their evening "parade," and explore the balcony-shadowed alleyways, the lovely tiled houses, and the flower-brightened corners that make Évora a special town.

Évora to Setúbal: 103 kilometers

Leave Évora on **Road 114** toward **Lisbon** (Lisboa). The road surface is excellent and the terrain is gently rolling to Montemor-o-Novo, a fortress-guarded town on a hill. Traffic increases at **Vendas Novas,** and the hills flatten out to become dry pasturelands dotted with cork. Continue west toward Pegões-Cruz and Setúbal.

In **Pegões-Cruz,** swing left onto **Road 10** for **Lisbon** and **Setúbal,** and pedal a short stretch of narrow, rough road. You'll rue the passing of pastoral Portugal as you draw near Lisbon. Traffic increases, cars travel faster, and cities grow more industrial throughout the day. In **Marateca,** swing right with **Road 10** for Setúbal, and pedal 21 km into the sprawling port city.

The **A2 freeway** to Lisbon starts in Setúbal. Stay left and follow the

Setúbal signs to cycle **Road 10** into the city. Trace a labyrinthine route through the heart of town, watching for **white signs for Lisbon.** You'll stay on **Road 10** as it climbs away from Setúbal when you leave.

There are lots of accommodation options in Setúbal, including a municipal campground. The tourist office is in the old town on Largo do Corpo Santo, across from the Church of Santa Maria. While you're in Setúbal, be sure to pick up a street map of Lisbon in preparation for your upcoming visit.

Setúbal to Lisbon: 40 kilometers

Leave Setúbal on **Road 10** for **Lisbon** and climb a long, steep hill with moderate traffic. Descend through rolling coastal hills and pedal on to **Coina.** Traffic increases from here, and you'll ride past a long succession of factories and congestion as you follow **white road signs** for **Lisbon** on **Road 10.**

Reach **Corroios** and follow signs for **Cacilhas** (Lisbon signs go to the freeway). Pedal on to reach the **ferry** that will carry you across the **Tagus** (Tajo) **River** to Lisbon's harbor. You'll see the massive freeway bridge to Lisbon on your left and the overwhelming sprawl of the city across the water as you pedal into Cacilhas. Ferries run throughout the day.

You'll be deposited in the heart of Lisbon at either the Praça Duque de Terceira or the Praça do Comércio in the busy harbor district. From the **Praça do Comércio** (to the right along the harbor from the Praça Duque de Terceira), head straight into the city on **Rua Agusta.** Continue through the Praça Dom Pedro IV (*Rossio*) with its statue of King Pedro IV, and reach the **Praça dos Restauradores.** Lisbon's municipal tourist office is on the righthand side of the square on Rua Jardim do Regedor (next to the grocery store).

You'll be able to get lots of English-language literature at the tourist office, and the staff can help you with accommodations, too. There are hundreds of cheap *pensões* in Lisbon, and there are a youth hostel and a campground. Try the streets on either side of the wide **Avenida da Liberdade** as a starting place in your hunt for a bed. Be sure to take good care of your bicycle and gear in this immense city.

If you're ending your cycling here instead of continuing on with Tour No. 18 to Madrid, you'll probably be heading for Lisbon's airport in the northern quarter of the city. Trains to northern Portugal and Spain leave from Santa Apolónia Station, east of the Praça do Comércio along the harbor road.

You'll have lots to see in Lisbon, and you'll have plenty of opportunities to stretch your legs if you like to walk. Climb through the narrow streets of the Alfama, the oldest part of the city, and enjoy the tile-fronted houses, the streetside fish markets, and the flower-filled balconies that make the district famous. Visit the hilltop Castle of St. George above the Alfama and claim a vista of the Tagus River and the city sprawled beside its harbor. Or stroll along the grand Avenida da Liberdade, a mile-long avenue lined with theaters, cinemas, hotels, and travel agencies, and eat a picnic lunch in Edward VII Park, where you'll have a fine view of the mighty maritime city sloping down to the water.

Storks rule the tower-studded skyline of Cáceres.

TOUR NO. 18

CORKS, STORKS, AND CONQUISTADORES
Lisbon, Portugal, to Madrid, Spain

Distance:	799 kilometers (495 miles)
Estimated time:	10 riding days
Best time to go:	April, May, June, September, or October
Terrain:	Lots of rolling hills
Connecting tours:	Tour No. 17

Portugal is exhilaratingly beautiful and painfully poor. You'll see a good cross-section of the country if you pedal both tours listed here (Nos. 17 and 18), and you'll surely wonder how the pristine loveliness of the Portuguese countryside can exist beside the big-city madness of Lisbon. Portugal's fantastic monasteries, colorful villages, and enchanting countryside more than make up for its poor road surfaces and bitter hills. And the Portuguese people, with their warmth, enthusiasm, and ready smiles, will win a special place in your heart.

Portugal has strong cultural ties with Spain, but it has maintained its national identity despite an enormous disadvantage in size and population. Respect the qualities that make Portugal unique. Practice your *"bom dia"* (good day) as you pedal, and remember that this 20th-century country where women still do their laundry in streams and men still plow with oxen once led the world in the discovery of new lands.

CONNECTIONS. You can ride into Lisbon by cycling Tour No. 17 (Málaga to Lisbon). Otherwise, reach the start of this tour by flying into Lisbon's international airport or utilizing the city's excellent train connections with northern Portugal and Spain.

INFORMATION. Write to the Portuguese National Tourist Office, 548 Fifth Avenue, New York, New York 10036, for information on the country. Ask for a map of Lisbon while you're at it.

Guidebook options include Michelin's *Green Guide Portugal, Baedeker's Portugal,* and *Let's Go: Spain, Portugal, and Morocco.* Local tourist offices (*Turismo*) are stocked with English-language literature (Portugal is a favorite vacation spot for British tourists), and they'll provide area maps and information on camping and hotels.

MAPS. To find your way around once you arrive, you can turn to Michelin's 1:500,000 map (No. 37) covering all of Portugal. The Automobile Club of Portugal (ACP) also offers a 1:550,000 map of the country, with a 1:250,000

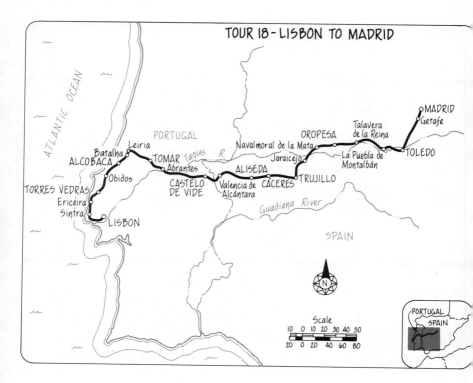

TOUR 18 - LISBON TO MADRID

cutout of the Lisbon area. It lists *pousadas* (hotels) and shows campgrounds and sights of interest.

ACCOMMODATIONS. Camping is cheap in Portugal, but you won't find many sites away from the coast or main tourist towns. Freelance camping is permitted, but you *must* obtain the landowner's permission.

You'll be able to afford an occasional splurge on accommodations in Portugal. Rooms are inexpensive, with a *pensão* being one of the cheapest ways to go. The government-run *pousadas* (hotels) have nicer facilities — and a higher price tag. There are about 30 of them in the country, and you'll need to make reservations in advance.

SUPPLIES. The cost of living in Portugal is incredibly low, so treat yourself to some delicious restaurant meals during your stay. Try the seafood specialties that dominate Portuguese cuisine. Dishes with cod (*bacalhau*) are especially good. Portuguese pastries are tasty, too, and there are local specialties for every region you'll ride through. Try the small, round sheep and goat cheeses for lunch. Piled on heavy Portuguese potato bread (*broa*), they make a filling picnic.

Portugal is world famous for its port wine, but this is definitely not a drink designed to keep you light on your pedals or your feet, so try something lighter if you still have some cycling to do.

Shops in Portugal are usually closed from 12:30 or 1:00 p.m. to 3:00 p.m., but they stay open until 6:00 or 7:00 in the evening. Most shops are closed Saturday afternoons and Sundays. Museums and other tourist attractions are generally closed Mondays.

Plan to carry spare cables, spokes, tubes, and patches for your ride in Portugal, as bicycle shops are scarce and quality touring gear is scarcer still. And make it a habit to check your nuts and bolts at the end of every rattling riding day. (You might want to check your fillings, too!)

Lisbon to Torres Vedras: 85 kilometers

From Lisbon's **Praça do Comércio,** cycle **west** along the harbor on **Avenida Das Naus,** pass through Praça Duque de Terceira, and continue on to **Avenida 24 de Julho.** Follow signs toward **Cascais** and **Estoril.** Pass Lisbon's beautiful Hieronymite Monastery and the Belém Tower as you leave the city. If you didn't visit the monastery during your stay in Lisbon, be sure to stop for a look inside. The cloister is one of the finest in Europe.

Continue along the coast on **Road 6,** passing through small resort towns and gently undulating hills. In **Estoril,** swing right for **Sintra** and **climb steeply** inland. Stay with signs for Sintra, joining **Road 9,** then climb more gently toward the city. Sintra was the summer home of Portugal's kings for 600 years, and the city boasts a royal palace (open for tours) and an attractive old town.

If you have time, you can also visit the lofty Moors' Castle commanding a hilltop 3 km outside the city, or explore the Pena Palace, another hilltop attraction. Sintra's tourist office is at Praça da Republica 19. From Sintra, you can also make the 40-km round-trip journey to Cabo da Roca, the westernmost point in continental Europe. Buses run from Sintra to the cape.

Follow signs for **Ericeira,** pedaling away from Sintra and entering an area of green rolling hills, fresh ocean breezes, and intensively cultivated farmland. You'll have a gradual climb as you leave Sintra, then level riding on nicely surfaced road. Stay with signs for Ericeira on **Road 247.** Pass through **Carvoeira,** and follow the coast road along the bluffs.

Endure a series of short but steep ascents and descents. There's a large campground beyond **Ericeira** (open summers only) if you want to camp on the ocean. From Ericeira, follow signs for **Torres Vedras,** staying on **Road 247** through **Ribamar** and **Barril,** then turning inland to gain mostly level riding for the rest of the day.

You'll see many signs of Portugal's poverty in this farming region — women planting seed by hand, men breaking mounds of soil with hoes, and wrinkle-faced grandmothers pushing wheelbarrows along the road.

Torres Vedras is a pleasant midsized town, overlooked by a Moorish castle and made colorful by the characteristic tile-fronted buildings that enliven Portuguese towns. There are a couple of small *pensões* in the city, if you need a room.

Torres Vedras to Alcobaca: 67 kilometers

From Torres Vedras, follow the winding **Road 8 north** toward **Bombarral.** Light traffic, gently rolling terrain, and a rough road surface will mark your first 24 km as you cycle through eucalyptus forests and quiet vineyards. The road improves after Bombarral. Continue on for **Caldas da Rainha** and **Obidos.** Watch for stout windmills on the hillsides as you ride.

Swing left **off the main road** to visit **Obidos,** an enchanting city surrounded by well-kept walls. Spend an hour wandering the narrow streets stacked with brightly painted houses, and peek into the countless shops where plates, sweaters, and cotton tablecloths tumble out the doors. From Obidos, **rejoin Road 8** and follow signs for **Caldas da Rainha.** Ride through rolling hills toward the busy city. You'll pick up more traffic 2 km before town when Road 115 joins Road 8.

Follow **signs for Leiria** as you wind through Caldas. Caldas has handsome buildings and interesting streets. There's a campground there, if you decide to stay and explore. Leave Caldas on **Road 8** for **Leiria** and ride with steady traffic for the 25 km to **Alcobaca.** The terrain is rolling for the first 11 km.

Climb a long, steep hill to gain a ridge, then descend and follow a winding river valley into Alcobaca. The massive form of the 12th-century Santa Maria Monastery dominates the city. Alcobaca's tourist office is just across the square from the church. Get recommendations on rooms there. Two campgrounds also serve the city.

Spend an hour exploring the monastery complex at Alcobaca. Begin with the vast church, where soaring pillars mesmerize you. Marvel at the intricately carved tombs of Dom Pedro and Inês de Castro, then continue on to the beautiful Cloister of Silence, where hundreds of Cistercian monks once prayed. Alcobaca's streets are a delight, as well. If you can escape the city without investing in at least one hand-painted souvenir, you have more will power than we do!

Alcobaca to Tomar: 76 kilometers

You'll have two more monastery complexes to visit today, and you'll have an optional side trip to one of Portugal's most revered religious shrines, as well. Begin by leaving Alcobaca on **Road 8** for **Leiria** and **Batalha.** Climb a long, steady hill with heavy traffic and a narrow shoulder. Gain a long ridge and enjoy level riding to a junction with **Road 1,** where you'll pick up more traffic and a wider shoulder.

Continue straight and sail down an invigorating descent to **Batalha,** with the magnificent bulk of the Gothic monastery church towering over the valley floor below. The luminous walls of elaborately decorated stone and the pinnacles and buttresses that sprout from every side of Batalha's church combine to make a majestic building. Walk to the rear of the church to explore the Unfinished Chapels. The decoration is overwhelming, made more powerful by the play of light and shadow through the open roof. The inside of Batalha's church holds treasures of its own, and the magnificent Royal Cloister is a poem in stone, rich in rhythm and rhyme.

From Batalha, endure up-and-down riding and steady traffic to **Leiria,** a large city ruled by a squat, square-towered castle. Take the **first exit off Road 1** for **Leiria** and climb a short hill to a **T.** Turn right, then go left as you follow **blue-and-white signs** for *Sanctuario Fátima.* Descend a short hill and continue straight toward **Tomar.** Follow Tomar signs up a **hill** and turn right (east) onto **Road 113.**

You'll have a roller-coaster ride on the roughly surfaced road to Tomar, but the light traffic and vine-covered hillsides are a welcome change from the congestion of Road 1. If you have time, consider making the short side trip to **Fátima,** a world-famous pilgrimage site where a large basilica has been built in honor of Our Lady of Fátima. To reach the site, turn right on **Road 357** at **Q ta da Sardinha,** 15 km past Leiria. You'll add 12 km to the day's ride by cycling to Fátima. Rejoin **Road 113** via **Road 356.**

Continue on toward Tomar, passing through rustling eucalyptus groves and green valleys where women beat their laundry in the streams. Descend into **Tomar,** a small town on the **Nabão River.** It huddles beneath the 12th-century walls of its fortified Convent of Christ. There's a campground in the park on the river as you enter Tomar.

Tomar's tourist office is near the **train station** on the southern edge of the city, and there are several inexpensive *pensões* in town. Climb the hill above the main square (Praça Republica) to reach the Convent of Christ. Stroll the parklike grounds to the beautifully decorated church, and go inside to see the Templars's Rotunda, an octagonal sanctuary styled after Jerusalem's Holy Sepulchre. Don't miss the elaborate Manueline window, immortalized by thousands of Portuguese tourist posters.

Tomar to Castelo de Vide: 107 kilometers

Follow signs for **Lisbon south** on **Road 110** as you leave Tomar, and enjoy flat, easy cycling for about 6 km. Pass the turnoff for **Abrantes** and **Castelo de Bode,** and climb a hill before veering left for **S. ta Cita** and **Abrantes.** Pedal up a steady hill to a eucalyptus-covered ridge, then descend to the **Tagus** (Tejo) **River** to join **Road 3** for **Abrantes.** Traffic increases as you cycle beside the river through farmland dotted with olives.

Climb steadily from the river valley to Abrantes, a bustling city perched on a ridge above the Tagus. There's a fine view of the valley from the city's ruined fortress, and the 15th-century church has a lovely tile-covered interior. Descend steeply from Abrantes, following signs for **Portalegre** and **Castelo Branco.**

Cross to the **south bank** of the Tagus and go left onto **Road 118** toward **Castelo Branco.** You'll have up-and-down riding for the 15 km to **Alvega.** Then make the long, steep climb to Gavião. **Gavião** is the last town of any size until Castelo de Vide, 55 km farther on. If you're not camping, you should keep that in mind.

Climb through **Gavião** and angle right for **Portalegre** and **Castelo Branco.** Descend a short **hill** and veer left toward **Castelo Branco** and **Portalegre** at the **Y.** Climb again to reach a flat plateau and enjoy excellent road surfaces and easy pedaling for the next 20 km.

Stay right on the lightly trafficked **Road 118** toward Portalegre, and climb a short, steep hill into **Tolosa.** Continue on through Gáfete and Alpalhão past endless acres of cork. Road surfaces deteriorate in the towns, then improve again outside them. In **Alpalhão,** go left toward **Castelo Branco,** then turn right for **Castelo de Vide** and gain **Road 246** toward Spain.

Pedal through gently rolling farmland and climb a long, steady hill to Castelo de Vide, a pretty town flowing down a hillside ruled by a 12th-century castle. Look for a room in the city, then go for an evening stroll in the picturesque streets of the Jewish Quarter and anticipate your entry into Spain.

Castelo de Vide to Aliseda: 96 kilometers

Rejoin **Road 246** toward **Spain** and continue climbing for a short distance. Reach the ridgetop and enjoy level or downhill riding to the **junction** for **Marvão,** a tiny town clinging to a hilltop north of the road. Decide for yourself whether the punishing 7-km climb to the amazingly situated city is worth the fantastic view from the top. If you're looking for a splurge, Marvão is a great place to do it. There's a fine *pensão* across from the city tourist office that provides stunning views of the surrounding countryside from its moderately priced rooms. (You may need reservations.) We celebrated our 10,000th European mile in the city.

Continue east on **Road 246** toward **Spain** (Espanha), and climb gradually to the border. You'll note a marked improvement in road surface as you coast past customs and pedal gradually downhill (now on **Road N521**) to **Valencia de Alcántara.** Follow signs for **Cáceres** throughout the remainder of the day. From Valencia de Alcántara, you'll have mostly level riding with scattered hills as you enter a vast plateau of grassland, cork, and olive.

Pass through the small towns of **Salorino, Herreruela,** and **Aliseda.** Accommodation options are few along this lonely stretch of road. If you don't have a tent, Valencia de Alcántara is your last sure bet for a room until Cáceres, 93 km farther on. You can ask in the smaller towns and hope a hospitable local will take you in. **Aliseda** has a few small grocery stores, friendly townfolk, and a pleasant olive grove just past town that makes a great spot to camp.

Aliseda to Cáceres: 30 kilometers

From Aliseda, descend gradually to the Salor River, then climb gently toward **Cáceres.** The countryside is quiet, and you might spot a few long-bodied storks wading in the streams you cycle past. Enter the suburbs of Cáceres and join increasing traffic as you swing right onto **Road N630** and pedal into the city's busy core. Go past the turnoff for Madrid and Trujillo, then veer left at the **roundabout** in the **Plaza de América** onto the tree-lined **Avenue de España.**

Cáceres is rich in architecture and history, and you'll see mansions, medieval walls, and towers that give evidence of the city's illustrious past.

Spanish schoolgirls pose at a street market in Cáceres.

One of the most entertaining things about Cáceres is its popularity with storks. The city's rooftops and towers are dotted with the nests of these ungainly creatures, and you'll hear their clacking calls as you explore the streets below.

From the Avenue de España, angle right onto **San Antón** and then onto **San Pedro** as you head into the oldest part of town. The tourist office is just outside the Star Arch (Arco de la Estrella) in the old city walls. There are lots of inexpensive accommodations in the streets outside the Star Arch, and a walk through the walled quarter is particularly nice at night.

Cáceres to Trujillo: 49 kilometers

Return to the **Avenue de España** and retrace your route to the **junction** for **Trujillo** and **Madrid** to gain **N521 east.** The wide road has an excellent surface and heavy traffic. Turn back for a look at Cáceres's tower-studded profile as you enter a rolling plain of farmland and twisted cork. Stay on N521 for the entire ride to **Trujillo,** with gentle hills most of the way.

You'll spot Trujillo's striking silhouette ahead, its castle walls and towers following the crest of a low hill down into the city. Trujillo claims an important place in Spanish history as the "cradle of the conquistadores." The most famous of its sons is Francisco Pizarro, conqueror of Peru. The buildings that resulted from this glorious period of Trujillo's past are clustered around the Plaza Mayor. Veer left **off N521,** following signs for *Centro Ciudad,* and climb into the hillside city to reach the plaza.

A handsome equestrian statue of Pizarro rules the square, and a circular amphitheater of stairs and palaces surrounds it. Look for the spike-topped Alfiler Tower, where Trujillo's storks hold court, and climb the hill to the castle for a view of the city and the surrounding countryside.

Trujillo's tourist office is on the **Plaza Mayor.** Ask for help with your accommodations search there. Then devote an afternoon to exploring the city's twisted streets, wishing for all the world you had stayed awake in freshman social studies.

Trujillo to Oropesa: 106 kilometers

Return to the main road from Trujillo's center, turn left, then angle left on **Road E4** toward **Madrid** soon after. Stay on E4 the rest of the day. There's an excellent shoulder but steady traffic. Follow signs for Madrid. The terrain is fairly level from Trujillo, with descents and climbs as you cross the Tozo and Almonte Rivers.

Cycle through **Jaraicejo,** a small town with a big church, and coast downhill to cross the **Arroyo de la Vid.** Then climb a **long hill** (about 5 km) to reach a pass above the Tagus Valley. Enjoy the view before diving into a long, winding descent. The kilometers will fly by rapidly. Cross the **Tagus River** and climb a short, steep hill before gaining level riding again.

Climb gently to **Navalmoral de la Mata,** a midsized town with several hotels and inns, and continue east on **E4** to enter vast grasslands sprinkled with cork. Traffic increases after Navalmoral. **La Calzada de Oropesa,** 22 km beyond Navalmoral, has a large church inhabited by skinny storks, and **Lagartera** is famous for its embroidery craft. Swing off the main road to enter Lagartera, and watch for the townswomen busily working at their windows.

Continue on to **Oropesa,** an attractive town overshadowed by two large churches and a 14th-century castle (now a *parador*). There are a handful of rooms available here, or you can try to get permission to pitch your tent in a secluded spot in one of the surrounding fields.

Oropesa to Toledo: 113 kilometers

From Oropesa, continue **east on E4** toward **Madrid.** Pedal through level countryside to **Talavera de la Reina,** a large town that thrives on the ceramic tile industry. Wind through the city core, following **E4** for **Madrid,** and enjoy the colorful ceramics shops that line the road. Stop on the far edge of town to explore the Prado Virgin Hermitage in a park to the right of the road. The interior of the church is almost completely covered in tilework dating from the 14th to the 20th centuries.

Cross the **Alberche River** and angle right soon after, forsaking the traffic on E4 for a quiet **Road C502** toward **El Carpio de Tajo.** The first 10 km are flat, but hills increase as the road follows the winding course of the Tagus River toward Toledo. Stay on C502 with hilltop castles, olive groves, and vines to make your riding pleasant. **Pass El Carpio de Tajo** and cross a **creek.** Then climb a long, steady hill before descending to the **turnoff** for **La Puebla de Montalbán.**

Continue straight on C502 and climb another hill, then coast down to cross the **Tagus River** and follow its southern bank toward **Toledo.** Stop to admire the famous silhouette of Toledo springing from the valley floor, with pinnacles and turrets and church towers piercing the Castilian sky. Toledo's castle and cathedral rule a ridgeline over the tumbled city of brown stone.

There's a year-round campground on the left side of the road, 3 km from the city center, and there are two seasonal campgrounds closer in. Continue on **C502** and follow signs for the **center** to **recross the Tagus** and climb into town. Toledo's tourist office is just outside the **Bisagra Gate** (Puerta de Bisagra). Get a map of the city and help with accommodations here. There are scores of inexpensive rooms tucked in among Toledo's mazelike streets, and you shouldn't have any trouble finding a spot to call your own.

You'll quickly fall in love with this exquisite city of architecture, art, and history. Toledo's cathedral is overwhelming, a glowing white monument of soaring stone, and the treasures within its walls will occupy you for hours. Return to the city streets and join the strolling masses in the Plaza del Zocodover, or walk down to the banks of the Tagus to view the city from below. There are several churches in Toledo that deserve a look, and be sure to check out the Santa Cruz Museum as a warmup for your visit to the Prado in Madrid. If you're a fan of El Greco, Toledo will be a special treat.

Toledo to Madrid: 70 kilometers

Despite the fact that it's Spain's largest city and has a population of more than 3 million, Madrid is surprisingly easy to cycle into, and it's a wonderful city to visit. Pick up a detailed Madrid street map in Toledo before you leave. It'll help make your arrival in the Spanish capital go more smoothly.

Leave **Toledo** via the **Bisagra Gate** and join **Road N401** for **Madrid.** We pedaled this main road the entire way, finding the steady traffic endurable and the wide shoulder and smooth surface an aid to quick kilometers. However, there are several options for secondary routes if you feel like dawdling along the way. You can swing east along the Tagus to visit the Royal Palace at Aranjuez, if you're looking for ideas.

Road N401 climbs a long, gradual hill away from Toledo before entering rolling hill country dotted with farms and small towns. Truck traffic increases as you draw closer to Madrid, and the road gains extra lanes after **Getafe.** Pass a **large park** on the left as you enter Madrid. Continue on the **main road,** angling right and crossing the **Manzanares River** before climbing a **hill** deeper into the city.

Arrive at a **busy intersection** and turn right, then swing left on **Paseo de las Delicias** to climb a gentle hill. Reach the **Atocha Train Station,** and veer left on **Calle de Atocha.** This long boulevard leads into the heart of the city and to the majestic Plaza Mayor and Madrid's municipal tourist office. There are a host of affordable rooms in the city, as well as two youth hostels. Finding lodgings should be easy.

Get a map and English-language literature at the tourist office, and plan to spend a couple of days wearing the rubber off your shoes as you explore Madrid's streets. City life revolves around the Plaza Mayor and the Puerta del Sol, but you'll want to venture west to the Royal Palace (Palacio Real) and east to Retiro Park and the Prado Museum. Madrid's Prado Museum has one of the richest collections of paintings in the world, and it will take you hours to cover the place at anything short of a gallop.

If you're taking a train from Madrid to France or beyond, take your bicycle to Chamartin Station, north of the city center. Pedal the long boulevard that runs north from the Prado to get there. You'll have to send your bicycle a few days in advance, and it's important to remove all baggage, computer wiring, lights, and so forth for safe transport. There's a central train information office at Alcalá 44 where you can check on times and prices. Madrid's international airport is about 14 km northeast of the city at Barajas, if you're catching a plane for home from Spain.

SUBJECT INDEX

bicycle, buying   17-18
   equipment   19-21
   transporting   22-23

camping
   gear   24-25
   permits   13-14
clothing   23
conditioning   17

hostels   14

information sources   28
   Austria   135
   Belgium   56, 109
   Denmark   87-89
   England   36
   France   56, 211
   Germany, West   97-98
   Greece   161-63
   Holland   72
   Italy   185-87
   Luxembourg   109
   Portugal   233
   Spain   221
   Sweden   77-78
   Yugoslavia   146
insurance   14

mail pickup   17
maps   16
   Austria   135-36
   Belgium   56, 109-10
   Denmark   89
   England   36
   France   56
   Germany, West   98
   Greece   163, 175-77
   Holland   72
   Italy   187
   Luxembourg   110
   Portugal   233-34
   Spain   221-22
   Sweden   78
   Yugoslavia   146-47
money   21

passports   13
plane tickets   22

road signs   29-30

safety   26-28
security   21-22, 26

visas   13

GEOGRAPHICAL INDEX

Aachen   110-11
Aerø   94
Aerøskøbing   94
Agios Nikolaos   178, 184
Aix-en-Provence   202
Alcobaca   236
Alcoutim   229
Algeciras   225
Aliseda   238
Ambleside   48

Ameboda   83
Amsterdam   75-76
Ancona   188
Angers   69
Arenys de Mar   209
Areopoli   167
Arles   203
Arundel Castle   39-40
Assisi   189
Athens   173

Augsburg 132
Austria 135-39, 140-44
Auxerre 220
Avebury Circle 43
Avignon 212

Bacharach 122
Bad Mergentheim 127
Bad Pyrmont 104
Bad Wimpfen 126
Bagenkop 95
Bar 159
Barcelona 209
Barnard Castle 51
Baška 152
Bastogne 113
Batalha 236
Bateman's 38-39
Bath 42
Beaugency 65
Beaune 217
Beilstein 119
Beja 229
Belgium 58-59, 112-13
Bernkastel-Kues 119
Bingen 122
Blois 67
Bodiam Castle 38
Bois d'Arcy 64
Borgholm 81-82
Braunau 139
Bridgnorth 45
Brighton 39
Brussels 58
Budva 159
Buscot Manor 43

Cáceres 238-39
Canterbury 37
Carcassonne 206
Carlisle 50
Castelo de Vide 238
Castiglione del Lago 190
Celle 102
Cerbère 208
Chambord 66-67
Chartres 65
Châteaudun 65
Chaumont 67

Chedworth Roman Villa 44
Chenonceaux 67
Chinon 68
Cochem 119-20
Copenhagen 86, 89-91
Corinth 172
Cotswolds 44
Courcay 68
Crete 175-82

Delft 74
Delphi 183-84
Denmark 84-95
Dijon 217
Dinant 59
Dinkelsbühl 130
Donauwörth 131
Dubrovnik 158-59
Durham 51
Dürnstein 143

Echternach 115
Egeskov Castle 93
England 35-53
Épernay 61
Evora 229-30

Fabriano 188
Finale Ligure 199
Florence 192-93
Fontainebleau 63
Fountains Abbey 53
France 55-69, 200-208, 211-20
Fredensborg 84
Frederiksborg Castle 85
Frontignan 204

Genoa 196
Germany, West 97-108, 110-11, 115-33, 139-40
Gibraltar 225
Gortys 179
Gotland 80-81
Grankullavik 81
Grasmere 49
Greece 161-84
Grein 142
Gundelsheim 126

Haarlem 75
Hadrian's Wall   50
Hämelschenburg Castle   104
Hania 180-82
Hässleholm 83
Heidelberg 123-25
Helsingborg 84
Helsingør 84
Hexham 50-51
Hildesheim 102-103
Hillerød 84-85
Holland 71-76
Housesteads Fort   50
Hückeswagen 106-107
Huelva 228
Hvar 156-57

Ijsselmeer, the   76
Iraklion 177
Ironbridge 45-46
Italy 185-200

Jerez de la Frontera   226

Kalamata 166
Kalmar 82
Kato Almiri   172
Keswick 49
Kiel 99
Kineta 173
Kiparissia 165
Knutsford 46
Koblenz 120
Köln 108, 110
Koper 148-49
Korčula City   157
Korsør 92
Kotor 159
Kourouta 164
Krems 143
Krk 152
Kronborg Castle   84

La Spezia 195
Lacock 43
Lake District   48-49
Lancaster 47-48
Laon 60
Lauenburg 100

Leiden 74
Leifrange 113
Leigh 47
les Baux 203
Lévanto 196
Lewes 39
Lieser 118
Linz 141
Lisbon 231, 235
Lübeck 99-100
Lüneburg 101
Luxembourg 109-10, 113-15
Luxembourg City   113-14
Lyngby 86
Lyon 214-15

Madrid 242
Málaga 224
Malia 177
Mani Peninsula   167-69
Marbella 224
Marstal 94-95
Methoni 165
Mires 179
Mirtos 178
Möhne 105
Monaco 200
Montélimar 213
Mošćenička Draga   151
Mosel River   117-20
Munich 132-33
Mycenae 170-71

Nafplion 170-71
Namur 59
Nantwich 46
Narbonne 205-206
Nice 200
Nîmes 211-12
Nyborg 92
Nynäshamn 80

Odense 92-93
Öland 81
Olympia 164
Orange 213
Oropesa 240
Ossios Loukas   183

Paderborn   105
Pag   153-54
Pals   208
Paris   64
Passau   140
Patras   163-64, 184
Perpignan   207
Perugia   188-90
Petworth House   40
Piraeus   182
Piran   150
Pisa   193-95
Poreč   150
Portugal   228-38
Pula   151

Rab   153
Rambouillet   64
Reims   60-61
Rethymnon   180
Rhine River   120-22
Rijeka   152
Ripon   53
Rocroi   60
Roskilde   91
Rothenburg   129
Rotterdam   72-74
Rudkøbing   95

St. Florian Abbey   141
St. Goar   121-22
St. Maximin   202
St. Raphaël   201
Salisbury   40-42
Salzburg   136
San Remo   199-200
Saumur   69
Saxnas   82
Sawrey   49
Schöntal   127
Scotney Castle   38
Semur-en-Auxois   219
Sens   62-63, 220
Setúbal   231
Seville   226-27

Sibenik   155-56
Siena   190-92
Sigean   207
Spain   208-209, 221-28, 238-42
Sparta   169
Split   156
Stockholm   79
Ston   158
Stratford-upon-Avon   44-45
Svendborg   94
Sweden   77-84

Tarifa   225
Tatton Park   46
Tauber River   127-30
Thebes   182-83
Toledo   241
Tomar   237
Torres Vedras   235
Tournon   214
Tournus   216
Tours   67-68
Traben-Trarbach   119
Trier   115
Tripolis   170
Trogir   156
Troyes   62
Trujillo   240

Vejer de la Frontera   225
Versailles   64
Vézelay   220
Vielsalm   112
Vienna   144
Visby   80
Volendam   76

Winchester   40
Windermere, Lake   48

York   53
Yugoslavia   145-60

Zadar   154

About the authors:

Karen and Terry Whitehill were active in the outdoors but not highly experienced cycle tourists when they embarked on the European adventure that sparked this guidebook. In planning their year-long trip, the authors found that the book they needed — this one — didn't exist. So they set out to create it, taking careful notes on their 11,000-mile tour through 14 countries, finding their way through 13 different languages.

When not out exploring the world, the Whitehills live in Portland, Oregon. Karen holds a bachelor's degree in English from Portland State University and a master's in journalism from the University of Oregon. She's published a number of freelance articles in newspapers and magazines. Terry, an engineer, honed his routefinding and outdooring skills during years of family and Boy Scout backpacking trips and backwoods scrambles. In 1986, the Whitehills began a year-long, 4,215-mile journey by foot and boat from Paris to Jerusalem, following an ancient pilgrimage route.

Other books from The Mountaineers include:

Miles from Nowhere, Barbara Savage. Delightful narrative of a two-year, 25,000-mile, round-the-world bicycle adventure.

Bicycling the Pacific Coast, Tom Kirkendall and Vicky Spring. Detailed guidebook with maps and photos to the 1,947-mile route from Canada to Mexico.

Freewheeling: Bicycling the Open Road, Gary Ferguson. Practical solutions for long-distance touring; a how-to written with both humor and experience.

Bicycling the Backroads Around Puget Sound, Erin and Bill Woods. *Bicycling the Backroads of Northwest Washington,* Erin and Bill Woods. *Bicycling the Backroads of Northwest Oregon,* Philip Jones. Fully detailed guidebooks for cycling routes away from city congestion. Maps, mileage logs.

Walking Switzerland — The Swiss Way, Marcia and Philip Lieberman. Routes for hikers staying in Alpine centers or traveling by public transport. Maps, photos.

100 Hikes in the Alps, Harvey Edwards and Ira Spring. Selects the best Alpine hikes from seven countries. Maps, photos.

Greece on Foot, Marc Dubin. Detailed guide for exploring backcountry Greece: mainland, peninsula, islands. Maps, photos.

Write for illustrated catalog of more than 100 outdoor titles:
The Mountaineers
306 2nd Ave W., Seattle WA 98119